Second Thoughts:

Presidential Regrets with their Supreme Court Nominations

By

William T. Harper

Second Thoughts   William T. Harper

Published by:

Organization Management, Inc.
4752 Tiffany Park Circle
Bryan, Texas 77802
harpersferry_2000@yahoo.com

Copyright © by the Author, 2011

All rights reserved. No part of this book may be reproduced, stored in a retrieval system, or transmitted in any form or by any means – electronic, mechanical, recording or otherwise – without prior written consent of the Author, except that brief passages may be quoted for reviews.

ISBN-13: 9781466273542 (Organization Management, Inc)
ISBN-10: 1466273542

Harper, William T.,
    Eleven Days in Hell: The 1974 Carrasco Prison Siege at Huntsville, Texas, University of North Texas Press, 2004

    An Eye for an Eye: In Defense of the Death Penalty, 2005

    We Three: Fred, the Ferry Boat, and Me, Amazon Kindle, 2009

    The Rivers of Life – and Death, M.E.T. Publishing, 2010

    Second Thoughts: Presidential Regrets with their Supreme Court Nominations, O.M.I., 2011

Keywords:
1. U. S. Supreme Court–History, 1789-1975.
2. U. S. Presidents–Washington-Nixon.
3. Notable U. S. Supreme Court Justices–History (John Jay, John Marshall, Oliver Wendell Holmes, William O. Douglas, etc).
4. Political and social views, 1776-1975
5. Notable Supreme Court cases–*Marbury v. Madison, Dred Scott v. Sandford, Plessy v. Ferguson, U. S. v. Susan B. Anthony, U. S. v. Nixon.*

Second Thoughts   William T. Harper

Table of Contents

Chapter I	Second Thoughts Might Arise	4
Chapter II	As It Was in the Beginning	11
Chapter III	Washington's Struggles to Seat a Court	14
Chapter IV	A Bumpy Ride for the Adams' Court	28
Chapter V	The Court Comes of Age	33
Chapter VI	Politics Rears Its Ugly Head	37
Chapter VII	If at First You Don't Succeed, Mr. Madison	44
Chapter VIII	President Monroe's Only Candidate	55
Chapter IX	King Andy's Reign - Deceit and Petticoats	58
Chapter X	Van Buren's Problems with a "Mediocre" Justice	67
Chapter XI	Tyler Bats a Sickly 1-for-9	72
Chapter XII	Polk: "Ill-trained, Poorly Informed"	76
Chapter XIII	Fillmore – Lots of "Advice" but little "Consent"	79
Chapter XIV	James Buchanan – the Great Procrastinator	83
Chapter XV	Lincoln's Schemers and Scoundrels	86
Chapter XVI	Frustration for the First President Johnson	98
Chapter XVII	Grant's New Battlefield	101
Chapter XVIII	"Thanks, but No Thanks," President Hayes	116
Chapter XIX	President Arthur Is Also Snubbed	122
Chapter XX	Cleveland-Harrison and *Plessy v. Ferguson* Decision	125
Chapter XXI	President Cleveland Learns "Senatorial Courtesy"	131
Chapter XXII	McKinley Man – "Unfit, Slow and Incompetent"	137
Chapter XXIII	T. R. Prefers a Banana Split	143
Chapter XXIV	Taft Tries to Empty the "Old Fools" Home	149
Chapter XXV	Wilson's Man – "Selfish, Prejudiced, and Bigoted"	153
Chapter XXVI	Harding (Thankfully) Has a Second Thought	157
Chapter XXVII	Coolidge Finds What He Doesn't Want To	160
Chapter XXVIII	Hoover Wasn't Careful What He Asked For	164
Chapter XXIX	FDR – KKK, Liars, Internment – and More	172
Chapter XXX	"Give 'em Hell, Harry" Really Did	190
Chapter XXXI	"The Biggest Damn Fool Thing" Ike Ever Did	198
Chapter XXXII	LBJ Didn't Always Get His Way	206
Chapter XXXIII	How Many More Reasons Did Nixon Need?	213
Epilogue	We End This Journal Here	220
About the Author		225
Index		226
Notes		238

Chapter I
Second Thoughts Might Arise...

When a Supreme Court Justice:

Is having illicit sex in his judicial chambers...
Is thrown into debtor's prison – twice...
Is involved in the shocking "Petticoat Affair..."
Is recipient of a lifetime membership in the Ku Klux Klan...
Is saying the president who nominated him should die...
Is found to be lying about his military service...
Is calling his President "a crippled son-of-a-bitch"...
Is guilty of absolute and provable miscarriage of justice...
Is voting to enhance his President's chances of impeachment...
Is deemed "partially deranged" by a colleague...

...a President might have second thoughts about a Justice's qualifications for service on the Highest Court in the Land.

Also, when a president later says of his nominee(s) that:

He's "a dumb son-of-a-bitch..."
His nomination was the "biggest damn fool thing I ever did..."
He has "less backbone than a banana" and...
His own four Supreme Court nominees – along with the
    other five members – are "bastards"...

...you know the president is having regrets about some of those nominations.

Second Thoughts tells these stories and others about the "nine scorpions in a bottle," as Justice Oliver Wendell Holmes called his brethren. Those woes and others herein are part of President Truman's effort to "find out what make Justices of the Supreme Court tick."

* * *

You are President of the United States. One of your myriad of responsibilities is to nominate members for the Nation's Supreme Court and have the Senate confirm them. Sometimes you hit what some term a home run, as President John Adams did when he named John Marshall as

Second Thoughts — William T. Harper

Chief Justice. And sometimes, you hit a foul ball, as did President Harry S. Truman felt he did when he called one of his appointees "a dumb son-of-a-bitch." Across the spectrum of 220-plus years and 161 "official" nominations to the United States Supreme Court, astoundingly, more than twenty-two percent of them failed to make it through the process. Some of our presidents surely – as Mr. Truman did – had to rue their choices.

Among the more prominent reasons for failure to nominate have been:

(1) Opposition to the nominating president, not necessarily the nominee;

(2) The nominee's involvement with one or more contentious issues of public policy or, simply, opposition to the nominee's perceived jurisprudential or sociopolitical philosophy (i.e., politics);

(3) Opposition to the record of the incumbent Court, which, rightly or wrongly, the nominee presumably supported;

(4) Senatorial courtesy (closely linked to the consultative nominating process);

(5) A nominee's perceived political unreliability on the part of the party in power;

(6) The evident lack of qualification or limited ability of the nominee;

(7) Concerted, sustained opposition by interest or pressure groups; and

(8) Fear that the nominee would dramatically alter the Court's jurisprudential lineup.[1]

Throughout the history of this Nation, the selection and elevation of candidates to sit as members of the United States Supreme Court has ranged from the unanimous "advice and consent" on the part of the Senate to the outright hostility of a 9-24 negative vote. The same vacillations were often in the public's eyes and those of other beholders, such as the contemporary media. Yet, despite that wide range of approval/disapproval, many times – far too many times – once a candidate had been nominated, weathered the process, and finally took the oath of office to join his/her learned brothers and sisters on the bench, the president who appointed them has often – far too many times – sat back and pondered some second thoughts.

A classic case of revised thinking is that of President Dwight D. Eisenhower's nomination of California Governor Earl Warren as Chief Justice of the Supreme Court in 1953. What the president thought he was getting was a moderate conservative to lead the Court. What the president got was a man some labeled an unabashed ultra liberal who used the Court to effect social programs in historic decisions regarding civil rights, voting, legislative apportionment, criminal procedures, privacy rights, and school prayer. This was an anathema to the former five-star General of the Armies. President Eisenhower, with second thoughts, ruefully admitted as much when he said his nomination of Earl Warren as Chief Justice of the Supreme Court "was the biggest damn fool thing I ever did."

"Ike" was not alone in his woeful thinking….

President Richard M. Nixon must have had similar thoughts on July 24, 1974 when the Supreme Court handed down its fateful decision in the case of *United States v. Nixon*. On that day, the Court – including three of Nixon's four Supreme Court nominees – Lewis Powell, Harry Blackmun, and Chief Justice Warren Burger – voted 8-0 against the President's claim of "executive privilege" authorizing him to keep the Watergate tapes to himself (the fourth Justice, William Rehnquist, recused himself from the deliberations). That ruling made almost certain that impeachment proceedings would be launched in the House of Representatives and, if warranted, tried in the U. S. Senate.

The 37th President of the United States must have had not only second thoughts, but also third, and even fourth such thoughts as he read the devastatingly unfavorable decision. He may have already been suffering from remorse three years earlier when on July 1, 1971, in one of his self-incriminating taped telephone conversations with Federal Bureau of Investigation Director J. Edgar Hoover, he referred collectively to the Court as "…those clowns we got on there, I'll tell you; I hope I outlive the bastards."[2]

In a similar though not as personally traumatic instance fourteen years after the Nixon impeachment possibility, President Ronald W. Reagan sent Anthony M. Kennedy's nomination as an Associate Justice up to Capitol Hill. The Senate speedily confirmed the nomination in a 93-0 vote on February 18, 1988. Justice Kennedy, who had been called "more conservative than [even the ultra-right-wing] Robert Bork when President Reagan nominated him, [ended up…] voting to reaffirm abortion rights." This issue, plus many other liberal rulings that followed, kicked sand in the President's face on a matter Reagan was deeply opposed to, philosophically, morally, and legislatively.[3]

Likewise and as might be expected, "the Man from Missouri" named Truman was one to put his thoughts on almost any subject very succinctly. In another case when the Court ruled against him, he lamented, "I don't see how a Court made up of so-called 'Liberals' could do what that Court did to me." The former County Judge from Independence, Missouri had even stronger words for one of them, Tom C. Clark; that "dumb SOB" mentioned above.

Presidents Dwight D. Eisenhower, Harry S. Truman, and Richard M. Nixon were not the first to regret some of their Supreme

Second Thoughts William T. Harper

Court nominations. There were nominees and even members of the Court who spent time in debtors prison, were indicted for murder, were locked up in an insane asylum, and more. These and other factors caused many U. S. presidents to look back on some of them and say to themselves if not to others: "If I had it to do all over again, I would have done it differently...." Both the Roosevelt presidents, Theodore and Franklin, had problems – the former with an Associate Justice with "the backbone of a banana" and the latter with another Associate Justice – a member of the Ku Klux Klan. Surely none of the Chief Executives would be exempt from questioning their judgment in Supreme Court nominations. It all started with the first president, George Washington.

* * *

The Constitution said absolutely nothing about the makeup of the Third Estate – the United States Supreme Court. Article III, Section 1 of the Constitution – defines the Supreme Court in a mere 68 words:

> "The judicial Power of the United States, shall be vested in one Supreme Court, and in such inferior Courts as the Congress may from time to time to ordain and establish. The Judges, both of the supreme and inferior Courts, shall hold their Offices during good Behavior, and shall, at stated Times, receive for their Services a Compensation which shall not be diminished during their Continuance in Office."

Nowhere in the United States Constitution, adopted by the Constitutional Convention in Philadelphia on September 17, 1787, did the Framers define the size of the Court, how its members would be chosen, its jurisdiction, nor even its basic duties. The only reference even to a Chief Justice comes in Article II, Section 3 that says "The Senate shall have the sole power to try all impeachments...[and] when the President of the United States is tried, the Chief Justice shall preside." The mere establishment of a federal judiciary was in itself the subject of intense debate in Philadelphia's State House (later named Independence Hall). The reason: A Supreme Court was feared by some as a potential instrument for executive tyranny – the very thing that brought about the bloody American Revolutionary War a dozen years earlier.

Two years after the Constitution was signed, the United States Judiciary Act of 1789 was adopted on September 24 by the first session of the first United States Congress. The Act organized the Supreme Court, the federal circuit courts, the federal district courts, and it established the Office of the Attorney General. The fledgling Nation was divided into six

Circuit Courts, each to be covered by one of the six Supreme Court justices. It also reserved the President's right to nominate justices for appointment to the United States Supreme Court *with* the advice and consent of the Senate.

February 1, 1790 was supposed to be the opening day for the first session of the new Supreme Court. Transportation problems, which would become almost an overpowering problem for the new Court's members as well as much of the new Nation's citizenry, caused a postponement until February 2. When the Court was unveiled in the Nation's then-capital of New York City, six justices shared the bench. One justice, John Jay, appointed by President Washington as the Chief Justice, held additional administrative duties related both to the Supreme Court and to the entire federal court system. The other five were Associate Justices.

At its creation, the Judicial Branch was, by design, the weakest and most timid of all three government branches, holding back from strongly upholding and/or deciding controversial issues. At the same time, the Founders believed that an independent judiciary was critical to the success of democracy. To that end, they directed that federal judges be appointed for life; and that they can be removed from office only if impeached and convicted by Congress of "Treason, Bribery, or other high Crimes and Misdemeanors."

The Court was given exclusive jurisdiction over all civil suits between a state and the United States and in cases between two states. All Supreme Court Justices in the beginning were required by Congress to "ride circuit," attending 27 Circuit Courts and two sessions of the Supreme Court a year. This difficult duty meant logging thousands of miles annually. Those early Legislators thought circuit-riding to be a good thing because it kept the Justices in touch with the people and, maybe even more importantly, out of the Nation's Capitol where a sitting president might influence them unduly. The circuit-riding practice didn't end until 1891.

As President Washington quickly discovered when he tried to entice some of the heavy-hitters in early American history to join the Country's first Supreme Court, he was not saved from disappointment and embarrassment and, obviously, from some second thoughts. John Jay, after having been elected governor of New York in 1795, abruptly resigned as the Court's first Chief Justice – an unpleasant, even if unintended, rebuke to the President. Washington then tried to induce his former Secretary of the Treasury, Alexander Hamilton, to accept the Chief Justiceship. Hamilton flat-out rebuffed his leader. The harried President next offered the position to Patrick Henry, the famous "Give me Liberty or give me Death" Virginia patriot. He also declined.[4] Washington's sense of lament, this sadness, this inconvenience – as well

Second Thoughts   William T. Harper

as anger, frustration, and disappointment — were among the feelings that many of the first President's successors would share, as are seen in these pages.

* * *

Personal refusals notwithstanding, then came the advice and consent process. As Timothy R. Johnson and Jason Matthew Roberts, political science professors at the University of Minnesota, wrote about in more modern times...

> "Since President Reagan's public defense of Robert Bork (and arguably since Richard Nixon's nominations of Clement Haynesworth and G. Harrold Carswell), the Supreme Court confirmation process has become one of the most contentious aspects of American politics. It represents a seismic, and often public, struggle between the president and the U. S. Senate over the ideological makeup of the nation's highest court. This political wrangling is fueled by the fact that both the President and the Senate believe their institution plays the key role in determining the next Supreme Court justice. While President Nixon believed the Senate should always acquiesce to the President's choices, then Senate Judiciary Committee Chair Patrick J. Leahy (D-VT) pointed out that the Senate's role '...is to advise and consent. Not to advise and rubber-stamp'."[5]

Furthermore, it must be said about many of both the praises and condemnations of various Supreme Court justices and their decisions discussed herein, that they were made based on the mores of the times. For instance, the "separate but equal" doctrine is generally conceded as the "will of the people" following the American Civil War. Conversely, that is absolutely not the case in this, the Twenty-first Century. However, it can only be assumed — if one is to believe campaign rhetoric — both Presidents Grover Cleveland and Benjamin Harrison, as examples of the will of the minority of the American people in the Nineteenth Century, were against oppression of the freedmen and were therefore regretful when their Supreme Court appointees voted for "separate but equal" facilities in the *Plessy v. Ferguson* decision.

Likewise, the Father of Our Country also had to have had some *Second Thoughts* about some of his other choices for the Supreme Court. He surely regretted some of his decisions and some of his decision-making processes. He — and his successors right on down to President Nixon (for this book's coverage) — no doubt more than once looked back

Second Thoughts William T. Harper

and wondered about their choices. Obviously, reflecting on more than two centuries of American history, historians often have only hindsight to deal with. And hindsight, as everyone knows, is 20/20.

* * *

Chapter II
As It Was in the Beginning....

These are the words that began it all:

> To: THE ASSOCIATE JUSTICES
> OF THE SUPREME COURT
> New York
> September 30, 1789
>
> Sir: I experience peculiar pleasure in giving you notice of your appointment to the Office of an Associate Judge in the Supreme Court of the United States.
> Considering the Judicial System as the chief Pillar upon which our national Government must rest, I have thought it my duty to nominate, for the high Offices in that department, such men as I conceived would give dignity and luster to our National Character; and I flatter myself that the love which you bear to our Country, and a desire to promote general happiness, will lead you to a ready acceptance of the enclosed Commission, which is accompanied with such Laws as have passed relative to your Office. I have the honor....[6]

With these words and just a few more, George Washington, the newly-elected first President of the United States, invited John Blair from Virginia, William Cushing from Massachusetts, Robert Harrison from Maryland, John Rutledge from South Carolina, and James Wilson from Pennsylvania to become the initial Associate Justices for the Supreme Court of the United States. John Jay from New York already had accepted the President's invitation to serve as the Court's first Chief Justice.[a]

---

[a] Because of sometimes primitive reporting methods, research shows considerable differences and conflicting definitions in various dates of appointment, final Senate "advice and consent" or other disposition of nominations, judicial oath taken, etc. For instance, some texts unequivocally say William Cushing was the first associate justice appointed by George Washington. Another source reports James Wilson's term started on October 5, 1789 and Cushing's on February 2, 1790. The official United States Senate history of Supreme Court nominations

Second Thoughts — William T. Harper

Starting with President Washington's first Supreme Court appointee, John Jay on September 24, 1789, and running through President Barack Obama nominee Elana Kagen, confirmed as an Associate Justice on August 5, 2010, presidents have – according to the official U. S. Senate website – submitted 160 nominations for Chief and Associate justices of the Court. Of this total, 124 were confirmed (including three Associate Justices who were re-confirmed as Chief Justice). Thirty-six nominees did not get the "advice and consent" of the Senate or otherwise withdrew their nominations, sometimes under intense fire. Seven of those thirty-six followed Robert Harrison's 1789 lead and simply refused the President's honor and declined his "peculiar pleasure."[7]

Unlike President Washington who appointed eleven Supreme Court justices, four presidents have no legacy of Supreme Court nominations (and therefore, perhaps, no related second thoughts). William Henry Harrison, the ninth president, caught pneumonia while delivering his inauguration speech and died in office one month after being sworn in on March 4, 1841. Zachary ("Old Rough and Ready") Taylor got sick at a Fourth of July celebration in 1850 and the twelfth president died of gastroenteritis after only sixteen months in office. Andrew Johnson, serving out the forty-seven months remaining in assassinated-President Abraham Lincoln's second term, was in a constant war with the Senate. It even tried him for impeachment in 1868. His only nomination was never even formally considered. James Earl Carter was the only U. S. President to serve a full term in office without an opportunity to nominate a Supreme Court justice.

In golf, it's called a "mulligan." In chess, if you don't take your fingers off the piece, you can have a second thought, take back the move and make another. In baseball, if you hit an uncaught foul ball, you get to swing again. In football, if an ill wind blows the ball off the kicking tee, you get to re-kick. In politics, only second thoughts let you to dream about a do-over. Presidents Truman, Eisenhower, Nixon, both Roosevelts, and many others – even going all the way back to George Washington – must have looked back on some of their Supreme Court nominations with regret. Some were major as with Eisenhower/Warren and Truman/Clark. Some were minor, ala Washington/Harrison. Perhaps each President mused "what if," or bemoaned "if only," or pondered longingly to themselves their *Second Thoughts*....

---

shows that all six of the original justices were nominated on September 24, 1789 and all were confirmed two days later. But, due to travel limitations, the date on which they took their Oath of Office varies. For purposes of this reading, all dates concerning nomination and disposition thereof will be taken from two official United States websites: www.supremecourtus.gov/about/members.pdf and www.senate.gov/pagelayout/reference/nominations/Nominations.htm.

Second Thoughts — William T. Harper

There's an old saw among *The Brethren* (as famed author Bob Woodward labeled the members of the United States Supreme Court in his 1979 book). It goes like this:

> Being appointed to the Supreme Court is like being invited to spend the night on Cleopatra's barge – anticipation would quickly give way to anxiety/insecurity and eventually end in disappointment because one's imagination always exceeds reality in such matters.

* * *

Chapter III
Washington's Struggles to Seat a Court
(Term in Office: 1789-1797)

George Washington nominated more Justices to the Supreme Court than any other president.

That was quite natural in his role as this country's first president, charged with the initial selection of all six candidates *en bloc* for the first United States Supreme Court.

President George Washington's Nominees (in reverse order)					
Name	Replacing	Nominated	Vote	Result	and Date
Oliver Ellsworth[21]	Jay	Mar 3, 1796	21-1	C	Mar 4, 1796
Samuel Chase	Blair	Jan 26, 1796	V	C	Jan 27, 1796
William Cushing[22]	Jay	Jan 26, 1796		D	Jan 27, 1796
John Rutledge[23]	Jay	Dec 10, 1795	10-14	R	Dec 15, 1795
William Paterson	Johnson	Mar 4, 1793	V	C	Mar 4, 1793
William Paterson	Johnson	Feb 27, 1793		W	Feb 28, 1793
Thomas Johnson	Rutledge	Nov 1, 1791	V	C	Nov 7, 1791
James Iredell	Harrison	Feb 8, 1790	V	C	Feb 10, 1790
John Blair	New Seat	Sep 24, 1789	V	C	Sep 26, 1789
James Wilson	New Seat	Sep 24, 1789	V	C	Sep 26, 1789
Robert Harrison	New Seat	Sep 24, 1789		D	Sep 26, 1789
William Cushing	New Seat	Sep 24, 1789	V	C	Sep 26, 1789
John Rutledge	New Seat	Sep 24, 1789	V	C	Sep 26, 1789
John Jay[24]	New Seat	Sep 24, 1789	V	C	Sep 26, 1789

C=Confirmed D=Declined R=Rejected W=Withdrawn V=Voice vote
21. Nominated to Chief Justice.

22. Sitting justice nominated to Chief Justice, but declined and continued to serve as Associate Justice.

23. In June 1795, President Washington offered him a temporary commission as Chief Justice (Senate was in recess). The Senate re-convened and rejected the nomination.

24. Nominated to Chief justice.
Source: http://www.senate.gov/pagelayout/reference/nominations/Nominations.htm

Along with Robert Harrison who refused to serve, two of his other original candidates likewise caused the Sage of Mount Vernon to have some second thoughts. First, John Rutledge, noted above as one of the original five Associate Justices to serve on Chief Justice John Jay's Court, brought another problem for the President via his recess appointment by Washington and the subsequent refusal of the Senate to consent thereto. Then, after serving as Chief Justice for five years, Jay resigned from the Court on June 29, 1795, to become Governor of New York, thereby giving Washington additional regrets.

With Jay moving from the nation's capital to New York's then-state capital in Kingston, President Washington once again had to find a new Chief Justice. At the time of Jay's resignation, a philosophical battle erupted over the order of succession to the post of Chief Justice. Arguments emerged: Should the new Chief Justice of the United States be the best candidate available anywhere or should he emerge from the already seated Associate Justices? In the latter case, some advocated the process should duplicate the seniority rules in the Senate where committee chairmanships were based solely on length of service in that august body no matter what the senior senator's competence or incompetence? Or, asked others, should the nomination go simply to the best and the brightest?

This time the President selected former Associate Justice John Rutledge – a decision based largely on personal friendship. Without waiting, Washington put him immediately in Jay's chair via a recess appointment. Rutledge took the oath of office on August 12, 1795. There was just one problem with that move. According to the original wording of the United States Constitution, Article II, Section 2, the President "shall have Power, by and with the Advice and Consent of the Senate, to…[appoint] Judges of the supreme Court.…" These few words form a steel I-Beam that upholds the Nation's balance of power via its checks and balances between the Executive and Legislative Branches of government. Imagine the chaos should just one Branch have the sole power to appoint the members of the Judicial Branch. Upon reconvening four months later, the Senate, in its Constitutionally-mandated "Advice and Consent" role, abruptly rejected Washington's choice via an embarrassing 10-14 vote. Thirteen of the sixteen members of the President's own Federalist Party voted to deny him the Chief Justice of his choice.[b]

The shocking rejection came about primarily because of Rutledge's outspoken opposition to the Jay Treaty – a highly controversial agreement the former Chief Justice concluded with the United States and Great Britain in 1794-5. For a time, it averted another war with the

---

[b] In an effort to "un-confuse" things, references made herein to the Federalist Party would be akin to those of today's Republican Party; those to the Democratic-Republican Party would be like those of today's Democratic Party.

Mother Country. But Jay's Treaty became a political football in 1795. The Treaty was the result of increased tensions between the two countries following the end of the Revolutionary War and which ultimately led to the War of 1812. Despite the 1783 Treaty of Paris which officially ended America's Revolutionary War with Britain, the English were not adhering in good faith to parts of that Treaty. For instance, they continued to occupy military posts in the American west, and they pursued fur trading in the Great Lakes region. They also interfered with shipping traffic in the Caribbean Sea, searching American ships for contraband and impressing American seamen into the service of the Crown.

President Washington sent Jay to London in the spring of 1794, trying to negotiate a solution to these problems. The agreement Jay returned with in the summer of 1795 satisfied few. Although President Washington was disappointed with the Treaty's provisions, he felt it was the best hope to avert another war with Great Britain. He submitted it to the Senate for approval and it passed by a 20-10 vote, exactly the two-thirds required for approval. That didn't placate the U. S. House of Representatives and it sought annulment of the Treaty. President Washington, in turn, tactfully reminded those House members that the Constitutional Convention had very deliberately assigned power of treaty-making to the President and the Senate.

Shortly after receiving Washington's interim appointment as Chief Justice, Rutledge, vehemently and with far less discretion than the President showed, attacked the controversial Treaty and the U. S. Senate for approving what he believed to be an excessively pro-British pact. He reportedly said in the speech "that he had rather the President should die than sign that puerile instrument" – and that he "preferred *war* to an adoption of it."[8] Rutledge seemed blind to the fact the President supported – and the Senate recently consented to, though narrowly – that difficult Treaty.

Rutledge and the House of Representatives were not alone in their opposition to the Treaty. It was excoriated at the time and seen by some as a failure of George Washington's foreign policy. Future President Thomas Jefferson was enraged. John Jay became a hated individual. Later, Jay said he "could travel at night from Philadelphia to Boston mainly by the light of his own burning effigies." Rutledge became part of the escalating criticism while sitting as Chief Justice of the high court.[9]

Another factor damaging Rutledge's unsuccessful bid to retain the Chief Justice post came after Rutledge's wife died in 1792. He simply fell to pieces and spent time in an insane asylum.[10] Even before that, Rutledge embarrassed his mentor when he resigned his Supreme Court Associate Justice position to accept the chief justiceship of the South Carolina Court of Common Pleas. He left the federal bench, apparently miffed at not being confirmed as successor to John Jay as Chief Justice.

Also, exhausted by the duties of riding his federal circuit and his boredom caused by the Court's inactivity, he failed to attend many of its meetings.

Surely, Rutledge's obvious disdain for the honor bestowed upon him by President Washington appointing him as one of the first Associate Justices must have caused the American Cincinnatus (the citizen who takes on the burdens of office as a civil duty) to have second thoughts. Likewise, in this strange affair, there is correspondence that makes a reader wonder why the first president picked Rutledge at all. For instance, with all its implied florid pomp and circumstance (and an overabundance of commas – which may have been *de rigueur* for those times), Associate Justice Rutledge later immodestly and unabashedly promoted himself as Chief Justice John Jay's replacement. Witness the following letter to President Washington:

> June 12, 1795
> Charleston
> Dear Sir/
>
> Finding that Mr. Jay is elected Governor of New York, & presuming that he will accept the Office, I take the liberty of intimating to you, <u>privately</u>, that, if he shall, I have no Objection to take the place which he holds, if you think me fit as any other person, & have not made Choice of one to succeed him: in either of which Cases, I could not expect, nor would I wish for, it.
>
> Several of my Friends were displeased at my accepting the Office of an Associate Judge, (altho' the senior,) of the Supreme Court, of the United States, convincing, (as I thought, very justly,) that my Pretentions to the Office of Chief-Justice were, at least, equal to Mr. Jay's, in point of Law-Knowledge, with the Additional Weight, of much longer Experience, & much greater Practice – I was not, however, so partial, to myself, as, not to think, that you had very sufficient Reasons, for preferring it to him to any other, tho', I, certainly, would not have taken the Commission, but, for your, very friendly & polite, Letter, which accompanied it....
> y^r sincerely affectionate, obliged, & obed^t Servt
> J. Rutledge[11]

In addition to his braggadocio, Rutledge's embarrassing comment wherein he considered himself the "senior" Associate Justice renews the controversy emanating from the precipitous learning curve the new government and its governors were going through. As mentioned above, all six of those nominated for Chief Justice Jay's court were so *named* on September 24, 1789 and likewise *confirmed* by the Senate on

September 26, 1789. That list even included Robert Harrison of Maryland who subsequently said thanks-but-no-thanks as he dismissed the President's offer to serve. Washington substituted James Iredell on February 8, 1790 and he was confirmed two days later. (Harrison's reluctance to serve in the early days of the Republic and the Court was symptomatic of two broad feelings. For many, serving in a national government violated their belief in states' rights. For others, they perceived the Judicial Branch of government to be too weak to have any influence over the new nation's affairs.)

Admittedly, the first justices are listed in the U. S. Senate Supreme Court nominations document in the order of Chief Justice Jay, Rutledge, William Cushing, Harrison, James Wilson, and John Blair. But, Rutledge's grandiose claim to fame as the "senior" judge is belied by the fact that Wilson *took his oath of office* on October 5, 1789. Cushing was sworn in on February 2, 1790, and it wasn't until February 15, 1790 that the self-proclaimed "first" actually became the *fourth* judge sworn onto the Supreme Court.

Even more strangely during Rutledge's campaign for the chief justice position, an incident happened about three weeks after his June 12, 1795 letter above to President Washington who then issued the following statement:

> July 1, 1795
> To all who shall see these Presents – Greeting.
> Whereas the office of the Chief Justice of the Supreme Court of the United States is at present vacant – Know Ye, That reposing special Trust and Confidence in the Wisdom, Uprightness, and Learning of John Rutledge of South Carolina, I do appoint him Chief Justice of the Supreme Court of the United States, and do authorize and empower him to execute and fulfil [sic] the duties of that office according to the Constitution and Laws of said United States…until the end of the next Session of the Senate of the United States and no longer….[12]

Having acceded to Rutledge's self-promoting entreaty, Washington made the above interim appointment and he followed up on December 10, 1795 with the formal appointment seeking the Senate's "advice and consent." That legislative body gave its "advice" but not its "consent" when it made its wishes known five days later. In a stinging rejection of the President's most recent nomination as Chief Justice of the Supreme Court, the Senate tersely said:

> [December 15:] Agreeable to the order of the day, the Senate took into consideration the message of the President of the United States of the 10th instant, and the nominations therein contained, of
> John Rutledge Esqr and others to offices therein mentioned, and [the Senate]. Resolved, that they advise and consent to the appointments respectively, agreeable to the nominations; *except to that of John Rutledge* [emphasis added]....[13]

The vote to reject wasn't that close. At the time of the December 15, 1795 Senate vote on Rutledge, there were fifteen states in the Union with thirty senators. Vermont and Kentucky had by then joined the original thirteen states. Technically speaking, Washington needed the "Aye" votes of thirteen of the twenty-four senators – a simple majority – who actually voted on his nomination of Rutledge for Chief Justice. He got only ten. "Why?" one might ask, would George Washington presume that John Rutledge stood the slightest chance of being accepted by the Senate when he (Washington) must have known the Senate's recently-developed animosity, brought on by the Jay Treaty controversy, put the Rutledge's nomination as chief justice in extreme jeopardy?

* * *

Another of Mr. Washington's original choices for the Supreme Court, James Wilson, one of only six men to sign both the Declaration and the Constitution, seemed to fit perfectly into the President's mold of what a judge on the highest court in the land should be. Even though Washington's vision for the "law of the land" was inspired by his belief in Divine Law, he thought highly of the erudite Wilson, known extensively as "one of the most learned and profound legal scholars of his generation."[14] He was the first Professor of Law at what would later become the University of Pennsylvania. President Washington, Vice President John Adams, Secretary of State Jefferson and a "galaxy of other republican worthies," attended his lectures.[15] Even today, when historians and other scholars identify the most influential delegates at the Constitutional Convention, James Wilson is always among the names usually listed, second only to James Madison. "The breadth of his achievements was matched by few of his contemporaries."[16]

With all these virtues, Wilson had one monumentally overriding flaw. More than 200 years later, Gerald J. St. John, writing for the Philadelphia Bar Association, described James Wilson's downfall:

Second Thoughts — William T. Harper

"...a reclusive old man was found dead in his room at Horniblow's Tavern, in the tiny tidewater town of Edenton, North Carolina. He was gaunt. His clothes were ill-fitting and stained. He was a man on the run, a fugitive trying to elude a swarm of creditors. Twice he had been jailed, most recently on the complaint of Pierce Butler, the influential senator from South Carolina. He needed a place to hide, but where? Who could he trust? ...He looked much older than his fifty-six years. But this man was no derelict. He was an associate justice of the Supreme Court of the United States; he was a Philadelphia lawyer; he signed the Declaration of Independence; and he was a key figure in making the Constitution of the United States. He was James Wilson, a 'founding father.'"[17]

A debtors' prison of colonial times.

Starting in 1778, Wilson ventured into the acquisition of speculative real estate in New York, Pennsylvania, Virginia, the Carolinas, Georgia and the western territories. A vast empire, it gave the impression of immense wealth. But with deceiving appearances, his empire – constructed with borrowed money – stretched to the breaking point.[18] Among the creditors was the aforementioned Senator Pierce Butler, to whom Wilson owed $197,000, a huge sum for the time. Wilson became the only justice of the Supreme Court ever imprisoned for debt. Though

Second Thoughts — William T. Harper

Wilson's troubles ended in Edenton, North Carolina, they weren't limited to that location.

During his term as a Washington-appointee to the Supreme Court, Wilson did not achieve the success on the Supreme Court that his capabilities and experience promised in the eyes of his mentor. Indeed, during those years Wilson was the object of much criticism and barely escaped impeachment due to his attempt to influence Pennsylvania legislation favorable to land speculators.[19] Furthermore, contemporary history held him in such low esteem that his remains were not brought back home to Philadelphia, the site of his greatest legislative accomplishments, until more than a century later.

In Washington's retirement back at Mount Vernon, he heard the startling news about Supreme Court Justice Wilson's indebtedness and imprisonment. With the man who was "second only to James Madison" in the writing of the U. S. Constitution but who became "a fugitive trying to elude a swarm of creditors," who in the 220-year-plus history of the Court is the only Justice sentenced to jail for indebtedness, the former president may have had *Second Thoughts* about his nomination of James Wilson – languishing in a debtors' prison.

* * *

The Father of Our Country surely must have had second thoughts about the last of his nine Associate Justice nominees to join the Supreme Court. In less than two years after Samuel Chase took his oath of office on February 4, 1796, replacing Justice John Blair who resigned because of ill health, the government passed the Aliens and Seditions Acts (which Washington strongly opposed). One of the Acts treated scandalous and malicious writings or writings against any elected official as treasonous behavior. (In other words, if for instance, the Act had still been on the books in 1998 when President Bill Clinton was impeached for "high crimes and misdemeanors," it would be a treasonous act for anyone to report or write about it!) As the then junior member on the Bench, Justice Chase quickly became one of the Acts' most vocal and judicial supporters – in direct defiance of the wishes of the man who appointed him to the Court. Ultimately, articles of impeachment were filed in the House of Representatives against Justice Chase on charges of malfeasance in office, five years after Washington died on December 14, 1799. And, if Chase could be impeached, reasoned the Republicans, could not their arch-enemy, then Supreme Court Chief Justice John Marshall, be next?

Chase was impeached basically for three principal reasons. First, he gave a pro-Federalist charge to a grand jury in Baltimore in 1803 criticizing the Congressional repeal of the Judiciary Act of 1801 – which a vengeful Adams-based Congress had passed lowering the Supreme

Court's size to five members. A second charge came from his conduct in the 1800 treason trial of John Fries who was convicted and sentenced to hang for his part in an anti-tax rebellion. The third basis was his conduct in the trial of James Callender, who wrote that President John Adams was a tool of the British crown. Such a charge, ruled Chase, was an act of treason under the Alien and Seditions Acts.

But none of these actions matched those of Adams' avowed enemy, Thomas Jefferson, and his aversion to Supreme Court justices serving for life, thereby making the Judiciary too powerful. So, President Jefferson reasoned in 1804, if he could get Chase impeached, it might serve as a brake on future Justices' tenure. Chase then became the only Supreme Court justice, again in the 220-plus-year history of the Republic, to face such charges. The fact that the Senate eventually acquitted Chase on March 5, 1805 hardly alleviated Jefferson's angst.

The trial in the Senate turned into what today's pundits would see as a "media circus." As the Senate's presiding officer, Vice President Aaron Burr arranged a special gallery for ladies when the "grand inquest" began. Burr had killed Alexander Hamilton in a duel and New Jersey wanted him for murder, but nonetheless, he presided sternly, rebuking Senators who were eating cake and apples. "We are indeed fallen on evil times," said one. "The high office of President is filled by an *infidel*; that of Vice-President by a *murderer*."[20] So much for the required "fair and impartial jury."

Chase was a home-schooled student under the tutelage of his father, the Rev. Thomas Chase. He studied law later and became a signee of the Declaration of Independence, served in the Revolutionary War Congress, and was a noted judge in Maryland and the federal judiciary. The jurist, eventually termed by some biographers as the most brilliant Supreme Court justice ever, was deemed a more impressive legal figure than the famed Chief Justice John Marshall. Chase became one of the most important political and legal theorists at work in the new Nation.[21]

However, the Federalist (i.e., conservative) justice crossed swords with the Democrat-Republican (i.e., liberal) administration of Thomas Jefferson when Chase supported the above-mentioned and controversial Alien and Sedition Acts in the courtroom. Signed into law by President John Adams in 1798, the Alien and Sedition Acts consisted of four laws passed by the Federalist-controlled Congress as America prepared for a potential war with France. Adams *et al* felt then-Vice President Jefferson was pro-French and that his outspoken opposition to administration policies was dangerous to the country's security. Parts of the Acts were aimed at foreign aliens, who tended to support the Democratic-Republican Party, its leaders (Jefferson, Madison, Monroe, etc.) and their policies.

For instance, the Acts increased the residency requirement for American citizenship from five to fourteen years. They authorized the president to imprison or deport aliens considered "dangerous to the peace and safety of the United States," and they restricted speech critical of the government. Designed to silence and weaken the Democratic-Republican Party, these laws actually backfired on Adams and led, in part, to Jefferson's hotly contested election to the presidency in 1800. However, the Sedition Acts were enthusiastically enforced by the Adams' administration as more than two-dozen pro-Republican newspaper editors were arrested, fined, and imprisoned. While riding on and presiding over the onerous circuit courts during the Adams' presidency, Chase singled out Jeffersonian Democratic-Republicans for their anti-Adams criticism. In aforementioned Fries trial, he sentenced the Jefferson supporter to death. Fortunately, President Adams rescinded the sentence. Congress repealed the Naturalization Act segment in 1802; the other acts were allowed to expire.

As history has shown, spite and personal pique are often the impetus for actions taken throughout the government, especially in the relationships between the Executive, Legislative, and Judicial branches. Jefferson's spite and pique as President led him to encourage his Congressional majorities in the House and Senate to launch impeachment proceedings against Chase in the former, leading to a trial in the latter, charging him with "high crimes and misdemeanors."

Similarly, spite also came from the other direction. The lame-duck Federalist Congress passed a law just prior to Jefferson's inauguration lowering the number of justices on the Supreme Court in an effort to reduce the new President's chances of adding his Republican-Democrat-leaning candidates to the Bench. That Justice Chase sometimes missed or delayed his court hearings because he was busy on the stump campaigning for Adams in his 1800 presidential race against Jefferson, added spice to Jefferson's spite.

Most all of this contentiousness came from the earliest days of the Republic when the Federalists and the anti-Federalists (the Republicans) disagreed over a central government structure. The Federalists (John Adams, Alexander Hamilton, John Jay and even George Washington) wanted a strong central government to replace the weak government born of the Articles of Confederation. Conversely, the Republicans (Patrick Henry, Thomas Jefferson, George Mason, et al) were fearful of a return to an overpowering central government (i.e., King George III) and preferred instead that national power instead be vested in what came to be known as "states' rights."

The good news coming out of the Chase impeachment trial, historians agree, was his victory discouraged further attempts by the Legislative branch to bring similar charges against justices for purely political reasons, and in so doing, strengthened the federal judiciary. Even so, George Washington was dismayed by the passage of the Aliens and Seditions Acts because, as he wrote to Adams on November 15, 1794, "My opinion, with respect to emigration, is, that...by an intermixture with our people, they, or their descendants, get assimilated to our customs, measures and laws:—in a word, soon become one people."[22] Washington felt those aliens should also be free to pursue their happiness and have First Amendment rights; things he felt were violated in the Alien and Sedition Acts. Nonetheless, Supreme Court Justice Chase agreed with the Acts' intent – as witness by his Circuit Court judgments against those who claimed the Acts violated the Bill of Rights. Not only would have Chase's outspoken support of the Acts given Washington *Second Thoughts*, so too would they have done likewise with the first president's Federalist successor, John Adams.

* * *

Long before the term "senior moment" came into vogue for some of today's elder citizens, our First Citizen had one too. Among the eleven names President Washington submitted as justices of the Supreme Court throughout his two terms was that of Senator William Paterson. On February 27, 1793, Paterson's nomination reached the Senate. The next day, the President withdrew the nomination because he believed it was in conflict with Article I, Section 6 of the Constitution, which says:

> "...No Senator or Representative shall, during the Time for which he was elected, be appointed to any civil Office under the Authority of the United States, which shall have been created, or the Emoluments whereof shall have been encreased [sic] during such time; and no Person holding any Office under the United States, shall be a Member of either House during his Continuance in Office."

This simply means that a sitting Senator, for instance, cannot be appointed to a government office either created or had its salary (Emoluments) increased during the senator's term in office.[c]

---

[c] This was not the last time questions would be raised regarding the Constitution's emoluments clause. One hundred and sixty-four years later, President Franklin D. Roosevelt's 1937 appointment of Hugo L. Black to the Court was also in jeopardy because as a U. S. Senator, Black had voted in favor of a bill that guaranteed no reductions in the Supreme Court justices' retirement program. Black, too, was able to overcome the objections. The Supreme Court eventually ruled there was no violation of the emoluments clause because the bill only guaranteed there would be no reduction in the retirement plan, therefore, it was not an enhancement.

Unfortunately for Paterson – and in this case for Mr. Washington, too – Paterson had served as a U. S. Senator from New Jersey from March 4, 1789 until November 13, 1790, when he resigned, having been elected Governor of that state. Thus, Paterson had been a senator when the Judiciary Act of 1789 was adopted so, it was thought, he was ineligible for any civil office affected (such as by setting/raising salaries or other Emoluments) by this act for the extent of the "time for which he was elected" to the Senate.[23]

This lapse was entirely understandable. When the first batch of Senators took office on March 4, 1789, they drew lots to see who would serve two-, four-, and six-year terms to allow staggered six-year terms of service for future classes of senators, with no two senators from the same state being in the same term. Senator Paterson drew a four-year term, which technically ended on March 3, 1793. Paterson, as noted, resigned his Senate seat on November 13, 1790.

In his original letter nominating Paterson, the President must have believed that since his candidate was no longer in the Senate, there would be no restrictions on his qualifications for Court service. President Washington and his advisors might be forgiven for still not knowing all the ins and outs of the new Nation's emerging documents and protocols during the preceding four years. There were few if any precedents. In those early days of the Republic, just about every official act set a precedent of one kind or another. However, when advised of the Emoluments clause, Washington believed it disqualified Paterson. An apologetic President then wrote to the Senate as follows:

> *United States, February 28th, 1793.*
> *Gentlemen* of *the Senate:*
> I was led by a consideration of the qualifications of William Patterson [sic], of New Jersey, to nominate him an Associate Justice of the Supreme Court of the United States. It has since occurred that he was a member of the Senate when the law creating that office was passed, and that the time for which he was elected is not yet expired. I think it my duty, to declare that I deem the nomination to have been null by the Constitution.
> Go. [sic] WASHINGTON.[24]

Meanwhile, in yet another seek-and-ye-shall-find situation, Washington and his aides – who must have assumed the candidate's Senate term was the generally-thought-of for six years – quickly discovered the timing sequence error. Thus it was determined that William Paterson *was* eligible for nomination as a Justice to the Supreme

Court because his four-year Senate term (from which he had, as noted, resigned in 1790), would have officially ended on March 3, 1793. So again, five days after the previous withdrawal letter, the Senate received another missive from the President saying:

> United States, March 4, 1793
> Gentlemen of the Senate:
> I nominate William Patterson [sic[d]], at present Governor of the State of New Jersey, to be one of the Associate Justices of the Supreme Court of the United States....
> Go. Washington[25]

The Senate, in turn also aware of the "discovery," responded on the same day with its advice and consent to the Paterson nomination. (If only the Executive and the Legislative branches of the United States government interacted with such courtesy and alacrity all the time! But this current era of consideration between the Executive and Legislative branches lasted only seven more years and ended radically in November of 1800 – and it continues basically even to the present day. The animus between the Legislative and Executive branches started when President John Adams was defeated in his bid for a second term by his unrelenting rival, Thomas Jefferson. Sadly, even more dramatic changes in comity were to come a century and one-half or so later.) Thus nominated by a chastised President Washington and confirmed by the Senate, Paterson took his seat on the Court one week later where he served until his death in Albany, N.Y., September 9, 1806.

* * *

The President consistently had problems seating the new members of the Supreme Court – especially the Chief Justices. When John Jay resigned from the Court in 1795, Washington's first choice was the aforementioned John Rutledge who served a recess appointment until he was rejected by the Senate for a full commission. On January 26, 1796, Washington nominated William Cushing. This time, the Senate unanimously confirmed the nomination the next day. Washington signed and dispatched Cushing's commission. One problem: Cushing was

---

[d] Research finds no reason for this misspelling of Senator Paterson's name – other than to note that the city of Paterson, New Jersey often warranted two tees in those Colonial times. Likewise, misspellings were common in early documents, the most glaring of which was the misspelling of "Pensylvania" in the Constitution. Noah Webster's Elementary Spelling Book didn't come out until 1828. Rather than overload the reader with [sic] this and [sic] that, we have left many misspellings the way the writers wrote them.

unaware of the nomination until Washington introduced him as "Chief Justice" at a dinner party. After sitting for just two days – formally or informally – as Chief Justice, Cushing apparently had second thoughts himself and returned the commission to Washington claiming that his "infirm & declining state of health" prevented him from serving as Chief Justice. With a third try, a wizened Washington then nominated Oliver Ellsworth on March 3, 1796 to finally fill the Jay-slot on the Bench.

Yet, only Rutledge's – of all the nominations President Washington submitted while plowing new legislative and regulatory grounds and setting new precedents – was flat-out rejected by the Senate. Compare the first president's ratio of seated Supreme Court nominations to that of some his successors. Of President John Tyler's nine nominations, only one was confirmed! Civil War hero (to some) and President Ulysses S. Grant was successful in but five of his eight nominations – despite the fact that Grant's Republican Party had an average 52-14 post-war voting advantage in the Senate during his eight years in the Executive Mansion.

Thus it was that President George Washington did have regretful moments as a result of some of his Supreme Court selections, such as:

> John Rutledge's abrupt and insulting Senate rejection as
>   Chief Justice,
> William Cushing's opting not to serve as Chief Justice
>   because of ill health,
> James Wilson's nefarious financial dealings that landed him
>   in debtors' prison,
> Robert Harrison's refusal to serve at all,
> William Paterson's nomination, withdrawal and re-
>   nomination,
> and Samuel Chase's impeachment.

* * *

Chapter IV
A Bumpy Ride for the Adams' Court
(Term in Office: 1787- 1801)

The new U.S. Judiciary spent its first decade as the weakest of the three branches of government, failing to issue strong opinions or even take on controversial cases. At the time, the Judicial Branch had "neither the power of the purse" which the Legislative Branch had, nor the "power of the sword" which the Executive Branch had as reserved by the Constitution. In Chief Justice John Jay's view, "the young Supreme Court was an 'inauspicious' body, characterized by little work, dissatisfied personnel, and a lack of esteem...."[26] Further, the Supreme Court was physically homeless. In an almost afterthought, a room in the basement of the Capitol was set aside for the third Branch in 1800. The Court would sit in that rather undistinguished environment for eight years while Pierre L'Enfant's Washington City grew around it.

Required by law to meet twice a year, the Court began its first term with a crowded courtroom and an empty docket. Appeals from lower tribunals came slowly and for its first three years the Court had almost no business at all, other than its incessant and jarring circuit riding. Even the retired Chief Justice John Jay brutally took the Court's current operations to task. When President Adams asked Jay to return to the bench following the death of Chief Magistrate Oliver Ellsworth on December 15, 1800, Jay declined. The Court, he said, lacked "the energy, weight, and dignity which are essential to its affording due support to the national government."[27]

Five of the first twelve men to serve on the Court abruptly resigned and three other nominees either declined their appointment to the Court or their promotion to Chief Justice. The Court was hesitant to consider the constitutionality of laws passed by Congress. That situation changed dramatically when President Adams appointed John Marshall of Virginia to be the fourth Chief Justice (after Washington appointees Jay, interim Rutledge and Ellsworth). Confident that nobody would tell him not to, Marshall took clear and firm steps to define the role and powers of both the Supreme Court and the judiciary system.

For the first decade and a half of its existence, the Court had little to do other than ride the circuit. "During the first 10 years of its existence, the Court decided only a total of 60 cases – that is not 60 cases per year, but six cases per year," reported latter-day Chief Justice William

Rehnquist.[28] It should be noted that seventy-five years later, the Court's case load had sky-rocketed to 1,500 cases per year.[e] But back in that first decade, for instance, the Justices had so little to do that in 1794, five years after John Jay was appointed Chief Justice and while still serving in that capacity, President Washington asked him to go to Great Britain to negotiate various disputes that were still unsettled following the Revolutionary War [See Jay Treaty discussion in Chapter II]. "Jay spent a year in England, and there is no indication that he was missed in the work of the Supreme Court...."[29]

Upon Jay's return from England in 1795, he discovered that he had been elected Governor of New York in absentia. Answering his State's call and declining his Nation's, he resigned the Chief Justiceship to accept what he regarded as the more important office. Washington then nominated Oliver Ellsworth of Connecticut to be Chief Justice. He, too, would be sent on a foreign mission while holding that office – by John Adams, who succeeded George Washington in 1797. Adams named Ellsworth as one of a three-man delegation to go to Paris and negotiate an end to the 'undeclared war' between France and the United States. Like Jay, he was gone for a year, "and does not seem to have been greatly missed by his colleagues on the Court."[30]

Some of the first justices never wrote even one opinion. They spent most of their time riding the circuit, travelling hundreds, sometimes thousands of miles over bumpy and unkempt roads throughout the newly-formed states and adjudicating seemingly mundane matters. An example of the rigors of "riding the circuit" in the early 19th Century is illustrated in this account of one Supreme Court justice's difficulties in the absence of Interstate Highways and jet aircraft:

> "To get to Washington from his home in Frankfort, Kentucky, [Thomas] Todd had to travel over 500 miles on various forms of horse-driven transportation, over roads that were often inaccessible in the winter months. His route, which took him through southeastern Ohio and what would become West Virginia, involved crossing several rivers, and there is evidence that in one year, 1809, he set out for Washington only to find that accumulated snow and rain had washed out roads

---

[e] To modernize these numbers, the Supreme Court received 7,738 petitions for case review in the 2008-2009 Term. This represents about a 6.1% decrease in the number of cases submitted for the 2007-2008 Term, but 234.5% more than the 2,313 the Court received in 1960. Due to limitations on the amount of work a nine-Justice Court can handle, only 1-2% of these petitions are granted. The Court typically hears between 75-100 cases per year.

and bridges, forcing him to abandon the effort in Chillicothe, Ohio, one of the courthouse locations on his circuit."[31]

After jolting rides in a stagecoach many hours daily over savage roads of ruts and rocks or helping lift the stagecoach from quagmires of mud, the justices passed restless nights in crowded way stations. Battered and exhausted by the rigors of travel, justices often arrived at the circuit courts too late, too bruised, or too sick to hold a session. Unfortunately for those justices of yesteryear, there were no video-conferences as there are for today's circuit judges.

The travel was so grueling that some found it even deadly. Justice Paterson suffered an injury while riding circuit in 1804, from which he never recovered. He died in 1806. Justice Wilson, after his release from debtors' prison, died of malaria while on circuit duty in North Carolina. John Blair had to resign because a ringing and rattling sound in his ears got louder and louder and he could no longer hear the lawyers. Samuel Chase drove his carriage across the iced-over Susquehanna River in Pennsylvania and almost died when the ice broke. Sometimes the justices spent nineteen hours a day bouncing on the roads. North of Boston and south of Richmond, roads turned into trails and even mere footpaths.

Justice William Johnson termed his Supreme Court service "no bed of roses." Some justices resigned from or refused to serve on the Court because of the rigorous travel conditions. The only one to come close to beating the system was William Cushing who was able to find some relief to his hardships. He bought a horse-drawn coach that was as

Justices had to endure hazardous conditions while travelling over sometimes non-existent roads in jarring coaches such as these or, even worse, on horseback for, in one case, 10,000 miles a year.
Courtesy, Library of Congress

Second Thoughts — William T. Harper

close to a modern-day camper as the 18th century could provide and talked his wife into sharing his travels.

Even the Court's official housing left a lot to be desired throughout its early years. According to the Supreme Court Historical Society, when the seat of the federal government transferred permanently to Washington, D.C. in 1800, no provision was made for housing for the Supreme Court. Less than two weeks before the Court was to convene, Congress magnanimously resolved to let the Court use a room in the Capitol building below the Senate chamber because Monsieur Pierre L'Enfant had forgotten the Court in his design of the city. So much for equality among the branches of government. The Court moved into the Capitol building's Old North Wing, meeting in various rooms for more than fifty years, from February 1810 to December 1860. During the early years when construction displaced the justices, they had to meet in nearby homes or taverns – which may explain some of its rulings in those days.

Eventually the Court occupied a courtroom especially designed for it in the basement beneath the new Senate chamber. When the Court moved upstairs in 1861, the old courtroom became the law library for both Congress and the Court. The Supreme Court was housed in what is now called the restored Old Senate Chamber from 1861 to 1935. Although the chamber was more spacious and dignified than the basement one, there was no dining room (the Justices lunched in the robing room and had no individual office space for them and their staff. The justices often had to work at home).

It was a long way from the Senate basement in 1800 to this grandiose structure in 1935.

As Vice President, William Howard Taft began lobbying for a separate building prior to his election as President in 1912. He redoubled his efforts when he became Chief Justice (the only former president to so become) in 1921. Taft persuaded Congress to fund the nearly $10 million building, giving the Court its own home for the first time. The Court held its first session in the new building on October 7, 1935.

Second Thoughts — William T. Harper

The long absence of its own physical home – the necessity for which should have been abundantly clear under the separation of powers edict – can only be explained by the carryover from the Court's earliest days when the Judicial Branch was hardly even considered one of the powers.

In designing what former Chief Justice Taft envisioned as "a building of dignity and importance suitable for its use as the permanent home of the Supreme Court of the United States," according to the Supreme Court's Historical Society, not everyone liked the new building. Associate Justice Harlan Fiske Stone, who later became Chief Justice (July 3, 1941), at first called it "almost bombastically pretentious…wholly inappropriate for a quiet group of old boys such as the Supreme Court." One of the "old boys" reportedly said that he and his brethren would be "nine black beetles in the Temple of Karnak." Another – undoubtedly thinking of exotic pomp rather than domestic party symbols – remarked that the Justices ought to enter it riding on elephants. Even the Court's housing needs brought *Second Thoughts*.

* * *

Chapter V
The Court Comes of Age

In one of his last acts as president, John Adams named then Federalist Congressman John Marshall from Virginia as his Secretary of State on June 13, 1800. Then, with the presidential election of 1800 still undecided and with just six weeks remaining before turning the office over to his bitter rival for the presidency in the hotly contested election of 1800 – Vice President Thomas Jefferson – President Adams named his Secretary of State as Chief Justice of the Supreme Court, replacing the retired Oliver Ellsworth. The Federalist Senate confirmed the appointment by voice vote on January 27, 1801.

Looking back at that appointment a quarter century later, former President Adams in 1826 said, "My gift of John Marshall to the people of the United States was the proudest act of my life."[32] Later historians, looking the "gift horse in the mouth," took issue with Adams. One of them said President Washington's appointee Oliver Ellsworth, the second Chief Justice if John Rutledge is discounted, was "without a doubt, the most qualified man in history to lead the high court."[33] All quibbling aside, history would go on to assert that Marshall was without a doubt the most influential Supreme Court Chief Justice in terms of impact on the Court.

That Adams "gift," along with a number of other Adams' acts, infuriated the incoming president because it denied him the opportunity to name his own choice for Chief Justice. By the time President Jefferson finished his first term, his distant cousin Marshall had radically changed the direction of the Supreme Court via what came to be known as the landmark *Marbury v. Madison* case. It was Marshall who "began to pump blood into this court."[34] The new Chief Justice was so dominant in his role that some later historians refer to the John Marshall Court as "Snow White and the Six Dwarfs." The Supreme Court of the United States would never be the same again. Nor would the Nation.

President Jefferson's concerns about a "super" judicial branch were expressed in a letter to a friend wherein he said, "The question whether the judges are invested with exclusive authority to decide on the constitutionality of a law has been heretofore a subject of consideration with me in the exercise of official duties. Certainly there is not a word in the Constitution which has given that power to them more than to the Executive or Legislative branches."[35] *Marbury v. Madison* resulted in giving that authority to the Supreme Court and the battle was joined.

All of the Adams' and Federalists' machinations were overturned immediately upon Jefferson and the Democrat-Republicans assumption of office in March of 1801. The Judiciary Repeal Act of 1802 reversed

John Marshall, the "inventor" of the U. S. Supreme Court.

John Adams called Marshall his "gift" to America.

that of 1801. The Court returned to six members, the onerous circuit riding for Supreme Court justices was reestablished, and the circuit courts were eliminated. This kind of tit-for-tat maneuvering would continue:

- a seventh seat on the Bench in 1807
- an eighth and ninth in 1837, and
- a tenth seat in 1863.

It wouldn't be until after the Civil War when the Court's size was cut back to nine members in an effort to thwart the perceptions that President Johnson was sympathetic to the defeated Confederacy. That was in 1866 and the Court's size has remained at nine ever since. President Franklin D. Roosevelt would be the last to try to alter the Court's size in a failed effort to "pack the Court" in 1937 (about which more is discussed in Chapter XXIX).

Enraged at Adams' last-minute appointments, one Republican from Kentucky called them "the last effort of the most wicked, insidious and turbulent faction that ever disgraced our political annals."[36] Even though government was miniscule when compared to today's behemoth, it is probable that Adams never knew much about many of these appointees. Upon assuming office on March 4, 1801, new President Jefferson refused to honor some of those appointments. One of them, William Marbury, sued to get his job as justice of the peace.

Second Thoughts — William T. Harper

The suit ultimately wound up in the Supreme Court. Chief Justice Marshall faced a major dilemma. He knew that if the Court ordered the Executive Branch to comply with the Marbury *et al* demand, the Jefferson administration would ignore it, in effect, challenging the Court's authority – and maybe even its existence. But should the Court rule against the plaintiff, some would charge the Court "caved" and was as weak and ineffectual as many claimed it to be. Either road would be a denial of the basic principle of the supremacy of the law. Instead, Marshall found a common ground where the Court could chastise the Jeffersonian Republicans for their actions while enriching the Supreme Court's power.[f]

In the end, the Court's unanimous ruling enhanced the Supreme Court by showing it had the power to declare governmental acts unconstitutional, a position not previously validated. Just as important, the ruling emphasized the Constitution was the supreme law of the land and the Supreme Court was the arbiter and final authority of the Constitution. Marshall wrote: "The government of the United States has been emphatically termed a government of laws, and not of men. It will certainly cease to deserve this high appellation, if the laws furnish no remedy for the violation of a vested legal right." As a result of this ruling and perhaps through the Law of Unintended Consequences, the Supreme Court was then and forever deemed to be an equal partner with the Executive and Legislative branches of the government.

In essence, the Supreme Court's *Marbury v. Madison* opinion as written primarily by the Chief Justice himself said, the plaintiff having "this legal title to the office, he has a consequent right to the commission; a refusal to deliver which is a plain violation of that right, for which the laws of his country afford him a remedy." At the same time, the Court denied Marbury's petition, holding that the statute upon which he based his claim was unconstitutional. Thus, the Supreme Court was deciding what *was* and *what was* not constitutional.

So, John Marshall and the sitting Supreme Court of the United States said that Marbury and his associates were legally entitled to their jobs but the legality entitling them to such was unconstitutional. In other words, Marbury *et al* was right; and Marbury *et al* was wrong. Could Solomon himself have done better? Cut the baby in half.

With its monumental *Marbury v. Madison* ruling, the Court set forth the precedents that it (a) could overrule the Executive Branch and (b) it could interpret the Constitution. By setting these precedents, Marshall and his Court firmly planted the Judicial Branch of the United States on a course toward equal footing with the Executive and Legislative branches.

---

[f] (See http://supreme.lp.findlaw.com/supreme_court/landmark/marbury.html for a full Opinion of *Marbury v. Madison*.)

John Marshall served as Chief Justice for a record thirty-four years, more than three times longer than his three predecessors combined. Because of Marshall's longevity on the bench, none of Adams' illustrious successors – Thomas Jefferson, James Madison, James Monroe, and John Quincy Adams – had the opportunity to name a Chief Justice of the United States Supreme Court. President number seven Andrew Jackson

William Marbury (left) sued then-Secretary of State, James Madison.

named Roger Taney (pronounced, "Tawn-E) as Marshall's successor after Marshall died on July 6, 1835. However, Marshall, along with four Associate Justices who served with him for over twenty years each (Adams' appointee Bushrod Washington, William Johnson, and Gabriel Duvall and Joseph Story), started the federal judicial system down the road enroute to what many consider to be today's most powerful branch of government.[37]

* * *

Chapter VI
Politics Rears Its Ugly Head
(President Jefferson's Term in Office: 1801-1809)

John Marshall was not the only Supreme Court justice with whom President Thomas Jefferson had his problems [See *Marbury v. Madison* above]. In its 1806-1807 session, Congress voted an amendment to the Judicial Act of 1789 raising the size of the Supreme Court from six members to seven, thereby creating the Seventh District. It consisted of the newly-admitted states of Kentucky, Tennessee and Ohio. To fill that mandated expansion of the Court, President Jefferson chose Thomas Todd of Kentucky. For fifteen years (1786-1801), Todd had served as a government Clerk/Recorder, primarily engaged in record-keeping during the formation of the state of Kentucky via its separation from the Commonwealth of Virginia.

His biggest claim to fame: Legible Handwriting. Todd had been elevated to the Kentucky Supreme Court and eventually became its Chief Justice. Though the President never met the candidate before his nomination to the federal bench, Jefferson sent Todd's name up to the Hill simply because the Kentuckian was recommended as either the Number One or Number Two candidate by all the congressional representatives from the three new states – perhaps because of his penmanship. For Jefferson, it turned out to be a classic case of *Caveat Emptor*.

Todd actually started off on the right foot as far as the president was concerned. The new Associate Justice offered his first dissent of Jefferson's hated foe, Chief Justice Marshall, in the latter's opinion in *Finley v. Lynn*, a dispute between business co-owners. It turned out to be his first and only dissent. It was five lines long. The President's pleasure with Todd's anti-Marshall judicial dissent was short-lived. For the rest of his tenure on the Court, Todd concurred with every single one of Marshall's decisions, much to the President's elevated vexation.

Furthermore, Todd has the dubious distinction of being labeled by Judge Frank H. Easterbrook of the U.S. Court of Appeals for the Seventh Circuit in a 1983 edition of the University of Chicago Law Review as "the most insignificant U.S. Supreme Court justice."[38]

Of the almost nineteen years (1807-1826) he served on the Court, he missed five (some say six) entire sessions because of various illnesses, family matters, and the difficulties of travel while riding the circuit between Frankfort, Kentucky and Washington, D. C. In all of his years on the bench during which 644 cases were decided, he wrote not a single constitutional opinion. Surely the Master of Monticello must have had *Second Thoughts* about Todd's judicial prowess.

Thomas Todd labeled "most insignificant."

* * *

If Todd, the last of his nominees to the Supreme Court was disappointing to Jefferson, the very first of his three appointees to the Court had to be maddening. William Johnson was a very independent-minded judge from South Carolina who, unlike Justice Todd, developed a reputation for dissent. For Jefferson, that part was good – especially when the dissents were written against Marshall's opinions. The son of a blacksmith and patriot who was captured by the British during the Revolutionary War, Johnson graduated from New Jersey's Princeton University and later served in the South Carolina House of Representatives. That body then appointed him to his state's highest court.

While there, on March 22, 1804, President Jefferson nominated the thirty-three-year-old jurist to the U. S. Supreme Court. The Virginian believed the South Carolinian shared his views about states' rights being predominant in the Constitution. Jefferson initially was extremely happy with the nomination because it gave him his first opportunity to replace federalist Alfred Moore, one of the justices appointed by the hated John Adams. Moore was another of those who could not abide the rigors of circuit riding and his ill health caused him to resign from the Court after only four years of service.

Johnson, the first Democratic-Republican appointed to the U.S. Supreme Court, took the oath of office on May 7, 1804 and served for the next thirty years. Jefferson was pleased with his choice as Johnson quickly developed the label of "the great dissenter," voting consistently against Chief Justice Marshall and foiling Marshall's strong desire for unanimous opinions. During his Supreme Court years, Johnson wrote thirty-four dissenting opinions. Jefferson's pleasure was short-lived. Johnson was sympathetic to states' rights, but he nonetheless rankled the "my-way-or-the-highway" President Jefferson by encouraging cooperation between the federal and state governments. He defined their relationship in terms of concurrent powers rather than exclusive spheres. He simply believed that all government must serve the individual's welfare. "State rights, or United States' rights are nothing, except as they contribute to the safety and happiness of the people." The Virginian was not pleased by this developing heresy.

Johnson was considered a loose cannon. He was regularly vilified – by Federalists for his devotion to legislative energy, and by Jeffersonians for attacks on executive power and his radical states' rights theory. A slave-owner himself, Johnson opposed abolitionism as well as inhumane treatment of Africans. Some of Johnson's fellow justices weren't too personally happy with him either. He once referred to fellow colleague Justice Cushing as "incompetent" and he called Justice Paterson "a slow man."[39] As far as former President Adams was concerned, Johnson was "a restless, turbulent, hot-headed, politician caballing (secretive) judge."[40] Harmonious, Johnson was not.

In 1807, Johnson flip-flopped and zigged when he was expected to zag. He enraged the Democrat-Republicans by actually relying on the ramifications of Chief Justice Marshall's opinion in a Supreme Court decision. It was in a treason trial of two accomplices of Vice President Aaron Burr, the very man who ran with and against and subsequently lost to Thomas Jefferson in the 1800 presidential election which had to be decided in the U. S. House of Representatives.

Their differences in political philosophies notwithstanding, the fierce animosity between Chief Justice Marshall and President Jefferson (the latter called the former "a profound hypocrisy") reached its peak during Burr's treason trial in 1807. Burr was accused of planning to attack Mexico and having the new states emerging from the Louisiana Purchase secede from the Union to join Burr's alleged new nation. Two of Burr's so-called conspirators, Erich Bollmann and Samuel Swartwout, were arrested and Jefferson's Democrat-Republican Senate suspected the Adams-dominated Supreme Court would free the pair.

On March 30, 1807, Burr was brought before Marshall's Circuit Court and charged with, among other things, treason. Marshall allowed bail for Burr over Jefferson's opposition. Burr then demanded President Jefferson be subpoenaed to testify. Marshall agreed. Jefferson refused on the grounds of separation of powers. Marshall then excluded most of the government's treason testimony and the jury brought in a not guilty verdict. Later, the Supreme Court – with Justice Johnson voting with Marshall and against Jefferson – also ruled Burr's "accomplices," Bollmann and Swartwout, were similarly not guilty. Marshall wrote, "To support the charge against Bollman and Swartwout, war must actually be levied" and there was no such war at the time. Jefferson was outraged by the decision in general and he reportedly considered impeachment proceedings against Chief Justice Marshall.

Another burr under Jefferson's saddle was the *Gilchrist v. Collector of Charleston* case in 1808. Under the executive orders of President Jefferson's Embargo Act which ultimately almost ruined the country's economy, the Customs Collector of the Port of Charleston, South Carolina, refused sailing clearance to vessels engaged in trade with France and Great Britain. Those two countries were at war with each other and regularly raiding U.S. ships. When one of the owners of a grounded ship petitioned Justice Johnson in the Palmetto State's circuit court where he was presiding, the Associate Justice stated the executive branch's instructions "had no legal basis [because] Congress had not authorized the detention of ships, and the president held no executive right to enforce such acts that infringed on personal liberties." To say the least, "Jefferson was dismayed at this apparent betrayal by his appointee."[41]

He turned the matter over to U.S. Attorney General Caesar A. Rodney, who rebuffed Johnson's actions, stating that Johnson acted outside the Constitution when he ordered the ship to sail. Rodney, an aggressive Attorney General in the Jefferson (and Madison) administration, led the failed impeachment case against Associate Justice Samuel Chase. He later told President Jefferson that Johnson had been infected with "leprosy of the Bench." As Jefferson raged on about Associate Justice Johnson's actions, the Nation's third president may well have wished he had reconsidered his nomination of the South Carolinian. To make matters worse for the President, the opposing Federalists were overjoyed with Johnson's "heresy." At one point early in his term on the Court, Johnson – because he was dissatisfied with the Court's procedure – wrote to the President and told him service on the Court "was no bed of roses." He asked Jefferson to give him a new assignment. The president, much to his subsequent regret, declined.

Johnson later fell further out of step with his fellow Southerners over the slavery issue when he invalidated the Negro Seamen Act (*Elkison v. Deliesseline*), a South Carolina law designed to prevent slave insurrections by incarcerating Black sailors whenever they entered South Carolina ports. The press slammed him and South Carolina exercised what it claimed to be its state's right to ignore him.

Next came further enragement below the Mason-Dixon Line because of his ruling during the drawn-out and bitter Nullification Crisis

Second Thoughts William T. Harper

wherein South Carolina again attempted to put forth its perceived states' right to nullify a federal law. According to vice president John C. Calhoun, the Constitution was not the supreme law of the land, but a contract among states. Therefore, in Calhoun's view, states had the right to nullify or reject any federal requirements they believed to be unconstitutional. Johnson saw nullification differently. To him, it was a serious threat to the stability of the Union.

Johnson said the Palmetto State (and therefore any other state) could not nullify federal laws. Once again, the man enjoying his retirement at Monticello could not have been enjoying the rulings of his federalist-leaning Supreme Court nominee – even if said nominee did eventually publish a *Eulogy of Thomas Jefferson* after the Virginian's death on July 4, 1826. In one of history's great coincidences, it was the very same day his presidential rival John Adams died, fifty years to the day after the jubilation of their joint signing of the Declaration of Independence.

* * *

The second nomination sent up for and receiving Senate confirmation as a Supreme Court justice by the third President of the United States must also have been based on some more contemporaneous positive mutterings. In a Columbia University alumni magazine article for the fall of 2002 entitled "Living Legacies," there appears to be an indication of the impact President Jefferson's nominee, H. Brockholst Livingston, had during his sixteen years on the Supreme Court (1806-1823). The article reads:

> "Nine justices of the United States Supreme Court, including three chief justices, have had strong ties to Columbia, and nearly all of them played a substantial role in shaping American constitutionalism. The nine justices with strong Columbia ties are John Jay, H. Brockholst Livingston, Samuel Blatchford, Charles Evans Hughes, Benjamin Nathan Cardozo, Harlan Fiske Stone, Stanley Reed, William O. Douglas, and Ruth Bader Ginsburg."

Obviously H. Brockholst Livingston, who actually attended what became Princeton University but was Columbia's treasurer and one of its Trustees later in life, was one of those who played a less-than "substantial role in shaping American constitutionalism." Other than having his name appear under his portrait, Justice Livingston gets not another mention in the entire 3,300 words of that "Living Legacies" article. For that matter, neither do two other Columbia University "Living Legacies," Samuel Blatchford and Stanley Reed. The other six are praised glowingly and extensively. Livingston, Blatchford and Reed must have been considered as among absentees in the "nearly all" of the legends who contributed to shaping American constitutionalism.

In his early career, Livingston was a staunch Jeffersonian and successfully worked on his behalf to secure New York State's votes for the Virginian in the 1800 presidential election. However, just like Associate Justice Todd who followed him to the bench, Livingston fell under Chief Justice Marshall's spell, reverted to Federalism, and voted with the Chief Justice and thereby mostly against Jefferson.

Livingston did attain some measure of notoriety via his prominent proboscis which was legendary and often the talk of political social circles. It didn't escape George Washington's notice. It is reported that during a dinner at Mount Vernon in 1798, the General learned that Livingston had been engaged in a duel with a Federalist political opponent, James Jones. The then ex-President commented, "They say the shot Jones fired at his opponent cut a piece off his nose. How could he miss it? You know Mr. Livingston's nose and what a capitol target it is."

H. Brockholst Livingston – and his "capitol target."

This journey into anonymity for Judge Livingston may have been, as one biographer put it, because he "never left a mark." Furthermore, during his years on the Court, Associate Justice Livingston fell almost totally under the Federalist influence of Chief Justice Marshall, much to the dismay of Democrat-Republican President Jefferson during the remainder of his eighty-three years. With second thoughts, Jefferson ultimately no doubt felt the same insignificance as did the editors at Columbia University's alumni magazine.[42]

Jefferson's fervent hope that his three appointments would serve to break the Marshallian-Federalist stranglehold on the course of Supreme Court decisions was not realized....[43] Jefferson in his retirement in 1820 looked back on the Supreme Court – with his three appointees still serving thereon – and found it to be "a subtle corps of sappers and miners" consisting of "a crafty chief judge" and lazy or timid associates.[44] In his never-ending struggle between his Democratic-Republican beliefs and those of the Federalists, Thomas Jefferson surely went to whatever he believed to be a Higher Power on July 4, 1826, regretting his jurists' failure.

* * *

In a touch of supreme irony about the Supreme Court and H. Brockholst Livingston's service thereon, he was a part of the nine-man panel that still holds the record for the longest tenure of Justices without a change – February 3, 1812 when Justice Story joined the Court until March 18, 1823 when Justice Livingston died in office. That eleven-year-one-month-plus record was listed in the *Washington Post* on July 18, 2005 when the newspaper reported, "The next significant date for Chief Justice William H. Rehnquist and other members of the Supreme Court, barring another retirement, incapacitating disability or death in the interim, is Sept. 17. On that date, the present court will have the longest service without a change in membership of any Supreme Court lineup in history." The irony is that Chief Justice William Rehnquist died on September 3, 2005 – twelve days before his Court would have broken the record. Talk about *Second Thoughts*!

* * *

Chapter VII
If at First You Don't Succeed, Mr. Madison
(Term in Office: 1809-1817)

It was at the tail end of the presidency of Jefferson's successor, James Madison, that a significant change took place in the United States Senate. On December 10, 1816, the Senate Committee on the Judiciary was established and quickly became one of the most influential committees in Congress. It is responsible for oversight of key activities of the executive branch, and is responsible for the initial stages of the confirmation process of all judicial nominations for the federal court system.

The initial responsibility of the Committee focused on measures that remain under the present-day Committee's jurisdiction – the courts, law enforcement, and judicial administration. Among the first issues the Judiciary panel addressed were those of judicial nominations, judicial salaries, the creation of judicial districts, and legislation providing for the punishment of crimes within Indian territories. It should be noted that the new Senate Committee of the Judiciary had no hand in considering President Madison's nominations for the Supreme Court; its first action in this regard came in 1823 with President Monroe's appointment of Smith Thompson – about which more later.

However, within the five Supreme Court appointments made by President Madison, he had enough problems even without another Senate committee. One of his nominees was rejected, four were confirmed, yet only two served. Two of those who were confirmed and didn't serve were eminently qualified – by name at least, historically speaking – but each declined the honor. A third nominee should have followed the reticence

President James Madison's Nominees (in reverse order)					
Name	Replacing	Nominated	Vote	Result	& Date
Gabriel Duvall	Chase	Nov 15, 1811	V	C	Nov 18, 1811
Joseph Story	Cushing	Nov 15, 1811	V	C	Nov 18, 1811
John Quincy Adams	Cushing	Feb 21, 1811		D	Feb 22, 1811
Alexander Wolcott	Cushing	Feb 4, 1811	9-24	R	Feb 13, 1811
Levi Lincoln	Cushing	Jan 2, 1811		D	Jan 3, 1811

C=Confirmed D=Declined R=Rejected V=Voice Vote This chart lists only nominations officially submitted to the Senate, and does not include nominations announced but never officially submitted. Source: www.senate.gov/pagelayout/reference/nominations/Nominations.htm

of the other two. Thus did President Madison lose a chance to tip the Court to justices of his political persuasion for almost a year.

Second Thoughts   William T. Harper

When Associate Justice William Cushing died in 1810, the remaining six-man Court consisted of three Federalists (Chief Justice Marshall, Samuel Chase and Bushrod Washington) plus the three Democrat-Republicans named during President Jefferson's term (William Johnson, H. Brockholst Livingston, and Thomas Todd). With a new appointment available to Madison, the Democrat-Republicans would have a majority. However, it would take three swings of the proverbial bat – all of them considered foul balls by the President – before Madison could fill Cushing's seat on the Bench.

Former President Jefferson saw the possibilities of a home run (before there ever was one) when he wrote – with a rather callous opening phrase – to his protégé Madison on October 10, 1810 from Monticello: "Another circumstance of congratulation is the death of Cushing.... [It] gives an opportunity of closing the reformation, by a successor of unquestionable republican principles."[45] That "Era of Good Feeling" – the twenty-four-year Virginia dynasty in the Executive Mansion (i.e., Democrats Jefferson, Madison, and Monroe highlighted by Monroe's 1820 second-term, a smashing 231-1 Electoral College victory) – saw its first portent of waning as the slavery issue began to heat up.

Long before "Honest Abe" came along, trial lawyer Levi Lincoln, a leading Democrat-Republican, was involved in a series of landmark cases in the struggle against slavery. He served as a key adviser to President Jefferson, had served in the Massachusetts state House of Representatives, and in the U.S. Congress, 1800-1801. He served as Jefferson's attorney general and, on an interim basis, as his Secretary of State. Jefferson found words of high praise in recommending Lincoln to President Madison for the Supreme Court opening when he cited the New Englander's legal abilities, his integrity, and his unimpeachable character. Jefferson was persistent in his promotion of Lincoln. Ironically, Levi Lincoln found his calling in the field of law after hearing Jefferson's despised foe, John Adams, argue a legal case in Boston.

Levi Lincoln disappointed President Madison.

Lincoln later resigned from federal service and became lieutenant-governor of Massachusetts. He became governor upon the death of his predecessor but failed to win a full term in his own right in 1809. Then, President Madison nominated Lincoln, a man with "unquestionable republican principles," to the U.S.

Second Thoughts William T. Harper

Supreme Court on January 2, 1811. The Senate confirmed him a day later. However, as another "Honest" Lincoln, he disappointed the president by begging off from service because of failing eyesight and poor health. Even more regrettable for President Madison was Joseph Story, the man he chose and eventually filled the opening Lincoln had declined. He turned out to be a "closet" Federalist.[46] Story's story follows further in this chapter.

* * *

Still another fully qualified nominee declined Madison's invitation to serve on the Court and by so doing, may have changed the course of this Nation's history as well as that of the Supreme Court. As a measure of the personal esteem in which the Federalist-leaning candidate commanded, the nomination was offered to the son of former President John Adams and a future president himself, John Quincy Adams. After Levi Lincoln's disappointing turndown, Madison offered the post to Adams the younger. (How Thomas Jefferson must have groaned upon receiving that news!)

A graduate of Harvard College at age twenty, then President Washington's minister to Holland seven years later, U. S. Senator from Massachusetts, and ambassador to Russia for President Madison's – John Quincy Adams had it all. His contemporaries deemed him one of the most intelligent and thoughtful political figures alive. The Nation's fourth president had to be salivating at the prospect of having this illustrious son of John and Abigail Adams serve as an Associate Justice on the United States Supreme Court.

John Q. Adams declined an invitation and disappointed President Madison.

John Quincy was nominated on February 21, 1811 and confirmed by the Senate the very next day – even before Adams knew anything about it. He happened to be in St. Petersburg, Russia at the time in his ambassadorial role. Just one problem for President Madison: like that other candidate with a historically-significant name (Lincoln, Levi), Adams, John Quincy chose not to serve, claiming he didn't have the knowledge of the law the post would require. Such a genuine and personal evaluation was seemingly not always evident among candidates throughout the history of the Court – as witness 169 years later in the G. Harrold Carswell nomination.

Another factor, unstated at the time, was Adams had his eye on a different seat in the federal government – the one occupied by his father from 1797-1801. Adams the Younger went on to additional extremely high service to his country as the author (without credit some say) of President James Monroe's heralded "Monroe Doctrine." He did get to fulfill his dream and served as America's sixth president. Then he concluded his career as a brilliant Massachusetts Congressman in the U. S. House of Representatives where he died in the Speaker's Room inside the Capitol on February 23, 1848. On second thought, how would this Nation have been different if John Quincy Adams had accepted President Madison's Supreme Court nomination? On President Madison's mind must have been at least two *Second Thoughts* vis-à-vis Messrs. Lincoln and Adams.

* * *

The irony of the intriguing possibilities of the Lincoln/Adams appointments to the Court is the fact that they book-end Madison's disastrous nomination of Alexander Wolcott on February 13, 1811.

According to the U.S. Senate Art and History Office and as noted earlier herein, of the 160 Supreme Court nominees officially submitted to the Senate for review to date, 124 were confirmed. Unconfirmed, rejected, or declining to serve were thirty-six candidates. These rejections have been for a variety of reasons including the perception of personal or professional incompetence, inexperience, philosophical positions out of the mainstream of the public and/or Senate, and allegations of impropriety. Some justices have had attempts made to discredit them after they have served on the court, while others have been rejected once and later confirmed.[47]

Alexander Wolcott's appointment holds the dubious distinction of being rejected by the widest majority ever for a Supreme Court justice nomination. Not even John Rutledge, the man who publicly wished President Washington would die in office, received such an outright rebuff in his blatant quest for the Chief Justice post. Madison chose Wolcott based on his Democrat-Republican leadership in his home state of Connecticut. The media of the day immediately set off a howl of protest. "Oh degraded Country! How humiliating to the friends of moral virtue – of religion and of all that is dear to the lover of his Country!" the *New-York Gazette Advertiser* echoed others' wailing over the nomination.

Wolcott's qualifications to serve as an Associate Justice of Supreme Court were meager, to say the least. Some biographies say he "attended" Yale College, that he "studied" law, that he had a law practice in Connecticut and became a leader of the Democratic-Republican Party in that state. He also served as U. S. Customs Collector of the Port of Middletown. There he vigorously enforced the Jeffersonian federal statute of 1807 that prohibited all naval commerce to foreign countries hoping to avoid foreign entanglements. That enforcement didn't sit too well with the vast shipping interests throughout his native New England. As expected, Federalists greeted his nomination with contempt; called Wolcott depraved, and described him as a man of mediocre legal talent. Even Democrat-Republicans found it difficult to defend Wolcott. The media threw more editorial kerosene on the fire, as also shown in this quote from the *Boston Columbian Centinel* [sic] chiming in on Wolcott's nomination: "Even those most acquainted with modern degeneracy were astounded at his abominable nomination."[48]

Indeed and again, second thoughts....

Convinced that Wolcott lacked appropriate legal training and experience, the Senate rejected his nomination by the degrading 9-24 vote. Irving Brant, a biographer normally well-disposed toward Madison, wrote: "To nominate so well-hated a man for the Supreme Court, with no testimonial to his judicial fitness, was a first-rate political blunder."[49] John Randolph, a noted Virginia patriot from the Revolutionary War who served in the U. S. House of Representatives and later in the U. S. Senate, was a respected leader of the Democratic-Republican Party before he broke with Jefferson and formed a spin-off faction. He quickly noted Madison's embarrassment. Two days after the nomination was doomed, he wrote to a colleague, "The president is seen to have felt great mortification at [the Wolcott rejection] vote."

Then Randolph raised an even larger issue which Madison surely didn't want bandied about in public. It had to make the President deeply regret even more his nomination of the New Englander and the speculation it brought. "The truth seems to be," questioned Randolph, "that [Madison] is president *de jour* only. Who exercises the office *de facto* I know not, but it seems agreed on all hands that 'there is something behind the throne greater than the throne itself'."[50] There were those who didn't need to wonder about Randolph's modest "I know not," especially after his bitter split with Jefferson – Madison's mentor.

In the 200-plus-year history of the U. S. Supreme Court, no other nominee rejected by the Senate comes close to Wolcott's fifteen-vote thumbs-down. Not Rutledge in 1789, nor even G. Harrold Carswell, nominated by President Richard Nixon in 1970 and described by a senator of the President's own political party as being a representative of the "mediocre," suffered the margin of rejection as did Wolcott. "Only" fifty-three percent of the senators voted against Carswell while Wolcott's failure rate was a whopping, unprecedented and unsurpassed seventy-three percent. Wolcott's "mediocre legal talent" was further evidenced even after his rejection by the Senate. In the Connecticut State Constitutional Convention of 1818, he argued that *any* judge who declared a legislative act unconstitutional should be *expelled*. Future tsars and dictators may well have found inspiration from Wolcott's arguments. On the other hand, the members of the Senate and the President of the United States may well have had a number of *Second Thoughts* about Alexander Wolcott.

* * *

The ill-fated Alexander Wolcott's candidacy replacement, Joseph Story of Massachusetts, presented a new dilemma. At the age of thirty-two in 1811, he went on to become the youngest person in U.S. history to sit on the Supreme Court bench. Story, a Harvard graduate at nineteen, became a member of the Massachusetts bar at age twenty-two. He was a member of the Democratic-Republican Party; he served in the Massachusetts House of Representatives, as its speaker for two terms, and was a Representative in the U. S. Congress. Again, after the death of Justice Cushing, President Madison, despite strong urging from former President Jefferson not to, this time named Story in his fourth attempt to get Cushing's replacement. When finally serving on the Supreme Court, Justice Story would ride the New England circuit twice a year, holding court in Massachusetts, Rhode Island, New Hampshire and Maine.

While many were appalled by the supposed young radical's judicial oath-taking on February 3, 1812, Story's thirty-four years on the bench demonstrated he was one of the greatest legal minds produced by the United States of America.[51] Some legal commentators even believe Justice Story's treatises were as influential in the development of nineteenth-century U.S. law as were the earlier works of the English jurists Sir William Blackstone and Sir Edward Coke.[52] As a matter of fact, much of the success of the Marshall Court was surprising for some because the Chief Justice had minimal legal training, was not known for his legal research abilities but was better known for his political acumen. That success was due to Associate Justice Story, who was widely regarded for his legal scholarship.

However, even with Story's surprising support of the Federalist Marshall and the apparent positive nature of the Story appointment, it was not totally problem-free, especially regarding the thorny issue of the separation of church and state, among others. When it came to, "Congress shall make no law respecting an establishment of religion, or prohibiting the free exercise thereof…," President James Madison and the

Justice Joseph Story were on entirely different pages. Expressing his view, Story wrote, "My own private judgment has long been (and every day's experience more and more confirms me in it) that government cannot long exist without an alliance with religion; and that Christianity is indispensable to the true interests and solid foundations of free government."

The fourth President of the United States saw it quite differently. He argued that "history demonstrates that religion flourishes most freely when it is not supported by the state, and that the state should not impose religion on its citizens."[53] Justice Story was even more direct in his comments about President Madison's mentor and predecessor, Thomas Jefferson, whom some historians believe Story hated and the feeling was mutual. Speaking of President Jefferson, whom Justice Story believed to be "the head of the enemies of the judiciary," and commenting on his position on religion (rigidly secularist), Story wrote:

> "Mr. Jefferson has, with his accustomed boldness, denied that Christianity is a part of the common Law, & Dr. [Thomas] Cooper has with even more dogmatism, maintained the same opinion. I am persuaded, that a more egregious error never was uttered by able men.... Both of them rely on authorities & expositions which are wholly inadmissible. And I am surprised, that no one has as yet exposed the shallowness of their enquiries. Both of them have probably been easily drawn into the maintenance of such a doctrine by their own skepticism. It is due to truth, & to the purity of the Law, to unmask their fallacies."[54]

Madison's response to the controversy was:

> "The apprehension of some seems to be that Religion left entirely to itself may [enter] into extravagances injurious both to Religion and to social order; but besides the question whether the interference of Govt in any form would not be more likely to increase than Control the tendency, it is a safe calculation that in this as in other cases of excessive excitement, Reason will gradually regain its ascendancy. Great excitements are less apt to be permanent than to vibrate to the opposite extreme."[55]

Still further, what had to be even more upsetting to the nominating president was that his candidate, whom he felt would be a champion of the Democrat-Republicans state's rights argument, instead became another close ally of John Marshall and helped the Court to favor a strong federal government. Story was further opposed to Madison's predecessor when, as a member of the United States House of Representatives, he led a successful effort to put an end to Jefferson's Embargo against maritime commerce.

Worse yet for slave-holders of President Madison's southern states were Story's anti-slavery views. As early as 1819, he spoke out against "any comparison that would extend slavery into Missouri or any new states on the ground that it would violate the constitution and the principles of our government." He also drafted a town meeting resolution "condemning slavery as a moral and political evil." In a later ruling from the Bench outlining the brutalities of the slave trade, he held that it was "repugnant to…the dictates of natural religion, the obligations of good faith and morality, and the eternal maxims of social justice."[56] None of these positions could have sat well with many residents of Madison's Virginia and the other southern and slave-beholden states.

And still further, even before President Madison left office on March 3, 1817, Justice Story gave him a sour taste to carry back to Old Virginny. In the *Martin v. Hunter's Lessee* case of 1816 dealing with state-confiscation of private lands, the Virginia court of appeals ruled the state had that right. The U. S. Supreme Court voided that ruling and sent the case back to the court of appeals. The Virginia court, exercising its belief in states' rights, refused to obey the Supreme Court ruling, declaring the latter had no right to review the decisions of state courts under the U. S. Constitution.

When the case again came before the Supreme Court, Justice Story ruled that the Judiciary Act of 1789 granted the U.S. Supreme Court appellate jurisdiction over state courts in certain situations, *Martin v. Hunter's Lessee* being one of them. His decision affirmed the Supreme Court's right to review state court decisions. Once again, the advocates of states rights – President James Madison among them – found themselves on the wrong side of the law as interpreted by the Supreme Court. It was another blow to the solar plexus of states' rights advocated by the central government theorists. Worse yet, it became another mitigating force that ultimately led to April 12, 1861 and the firing on Fort Sumter, South Carolina.

Some of Justice Story's rulings must surely have made President Madison wish for a favorable Senate vote for the ill-fated Supreme Court nomination for Alexander Wolcott.

* * *

Gabriel Duvall, the fifth name President Madison sent to the Senate for its advice and consent, was named to replace the impeached but not convicted Justice Samuel Chase who died in office on June 19, 1811.

Second Thoughts — William T. Harper

Justice Duvall took his oath of office on November 23, 1811. Twenty-four years later, the Madison-appointed Associate Justice Gabriel Duvall retired from the Court and took with him the title, shared with at least one of his predecessors – Thomas Todd of Kentucky – as "the most insignificant justice of all time."[57] Circuit Judge Frank Easterbrook, who labeled Jefferson-appointee Todd "the most insignificant," scoffs at the thought of Madison-appointee Duvall sharing the title. Empirical evidence, the judge acidly wrote, demonstrates "that Thomas Todd made Duvall look like a titan of the bench." Others would vie for that dubious honor. Judge Easterbrook writing in the University of Chicago Law Review in 1983 puts Justices Clifford, Duvall, Livingston and McKinley among them.

In the annals of insignificance, Justice Gabriel Duvall ranks high in a tongue-in-cheek appraisal by David P. Currie, a constitutional scholar and professor, also at the University of Chicago Law School. Duvall served on the Court for almost twenty-four years (1811-1835) and, the professor notes, he is known to have offered exactly one opinion in constitutional cases, to wit in toto: "Duvall, Justice, dissented." That occasion was in *Trustees of Dartmouth College v. Woodward*, 17 U.S. (4 Wheat) 518, 1819. Currie further observes that three of Duvall's "colleagues had opinions totaling ninety pages to explain that the state had impaired the college's charter; Duvall managed to dispute them all in just three words."[58] Also worthy of mention in the realm of insignificance are the two justices Lamar [Joseph R. and Lucius Q. C.], "each so little known that their meager judicial output is commonly thought to be the work of one man...."[59]

So, President James Madison concluded his efforts to shape the Supreme Court of the United States, personally going 0-for-5 in the game of Supreme Court *significant* and supportive selections. Two esteemed gentlemen (Lincoln and Adams) declined his offer to serve. Many of these early thanks-but-no-thanks came from those who believed strongly in States' Rights and didn't want a Federal authority making rulings for said states. Others sent thanks-but-no-thanks because they felt the then-existing Supreme Court was an inferior branch of the government vis-à-vis the Presidential and Legislative branches.

One who accepted Madison's offer (Joseph Story) accepted only to engage in a bitter wrangle over the *church v. state* issue, who vehemently opposed slavery and – along with Duvall – moved the Court in the opposite direction from that which the President sought in the area of states' rights vs. federalism. And two (Wolcott and Duvall – the latter who ultimately earned the sobriquet, "Mr. I dissent") went down in a flaming pyre of insignificance or worse in the pages of judicial history.

* * *

Second Thoughts

William T. Harper

History has recorded James Madison as the shortest man in physical stature (five-feet-four-inches tall) ever to occupy the presidency. It seems he also came up woefully short in his selections for those he hoped would serve on the Supreme Court. There are Madison biographers who believe though "The Father of the Constitution" was a brilliant theorist when it came to government development; he was considerably less when it came to government operations.

He knew what he wanted; he just didn't know how to go about getting it. "There are those who *teach* and there are those who *do*," complain some whining high school dropouts. James Madison fell into the former category. When considering Supreme Court appointments, could any one president come up with five separate and distinct second thoughts?

James Madison, on the stage with President Washington, presents the final draft of the United States Constitution. (Notice Madison's height compared to Washington's.)

All this leads to another question of the day: How deep really was Madison's alliance to his mentor's anti-judicial/anti-Marshall/anti-central government/anti-religion stance? Story became a Supreme Court justice who abandoned Jefferson and became virtually unanimous in support of the third President's avowed enemy, Chief Justice John Marshall. Story was also a damned Yankee with beliefs completely out of tune with the slave-holding states from which the Jefferson-Madison-Monroe triumvirate came.

Second Thoughts — William T. Harper

It seems certain that nominee John Quincy Adams would not have been in Jefferson's corner in the match to thwart John Marshall. Levi Lincoln was questionable at best. Alexander Wolcott was a minus in many ways as was the closet Federalist Story. And Gabriel Duvall was "insignificant." Could a man as brilliant as Madison is acknowledged to have been be totally in the dark about the political philosophies of those he nominated to the Supreme Court? It'll be left here to Madison scholars such as Irving Brant to answer these questions and John Randolph's mystery about that "something behind the throne."

* * *

Chapter VIII
President Monroe's Only Candidate
(Term in Office: 1817-25)

James Monroe, who succeeded James Madison as the president of the United States, had few of the Supreme Court problems that plagued his predecessors. The reason? Monroe, through the eight years of his two terms, had only one chance to tinker with the makeup of the Court. On December 8, 1823, Monroe nominated fifty-five-year-old Smith Thompson as Associate Justice following the death of Henry Brockholst Livingston in March of that same year. On the advice of the Senate Committee on the Judiciary, the Senate *consented* the next day. Obviously the Senators were not *advised* of one detractor's opinion of the candidate. Even more obviously, Thompson wasn't too thrilled with the "honor." He accepted the post most reluctantly because he wanted to campaign for the 1824 Democratic-Republican Party's presidential election nomination against Andrew Jackson.

It should be noted here that the 1824 presidential election was a one-party struggle, that party being the Democrat-Republicans. The Federalists had been mortally-splintered and basically disappeared from the political scene, primarily because of its opposition to the War of 1812. The fact that there had been twenty-four consecutive years of Democrat-Republican presidencies didn't help either. Thus it was that John Quincy Adams defeated Andrew Jackson in the 1824 campaign with both carrying the Democrat-Republican label. That result was reversed four years later, again with both running as Democrat-Republicans. However, it wasn't until 1834 that those with similar centrist government views became a factor with the formation of the Whig Party, a coalition of National Republicans, Anti-Masons, and disgruntled, anti-"King Andrew" Jackson Democrats. It would be another 20-plus years before the Party found the label which it carries to this day – the Republican Party – with Abraham Lincoln being the first to be elected President under that banner.

Smith Thompson came from a wealthy New York state family, graduated from Princeton University, taught school, and began his legal career as a law firm clerk. He served one term as a New York State legislator and then on the state's Supreme Court. President Monroe tapped him as Secretary of the Navy. Starting in 1823 as a U. S. Supreme Court justice where he served for twenty years, Justice Thompson traveled the Second Circuit, consisting of New York, Connecticut and Vermont until he died in office in 1843. One of the principals of the law firm where Thompson started his career contemporaneously wrote that Thompson was "a plain, modest, humble, ignorant young man with narrow views and anti-federal politics. His mind did not expand and his principles became liberal very slowly."[60] The letter-writer obviously didn't appear at Thompson's confirmation hearings in the Senate.

Monroe, Madison and Jefferson, for the few years he then had remaining, had to be initially pleased with Thompson's performance on the Bench as he was a tireless opponent of the liberals' nemesis, Chief Justice John Marshall. Thompson was one of a 4-3 majority that forced Marshall into his sole constitutional dissent in *Ogden v. Saunders*, a case involving a New York insolvency law.[61] Otherwise, Thompson had only a slight impact on constitutional law. The Miller Center for Current Affairs website at the University of Virginia, in its listing for Smith Thompson, doesn't even mention his service as an Associate Justice of the United States Supreme Court! That oversight is baffling, if for no other reason than Thompson's role in the Supreme Court's handling of "The Trail of Tears" case.

Using some of the same "logic" of the infamous 1857 Dred Scott decision declaring no slave or descendant of a slave could be a U.S. citizen (a ruling that would rack the Nation two decades later) the Supreme Court's 1831 decision in *Cherokee Nation v. the State of Georgia* resulted in a national disgrace. Because gold had been found on the Georgia lands granted the Cherokee Indians by various treaties, the State ordered the Cherokees off their tribal land to make room for white prospectors. The Indian Nation appealed the State's decision to the Supreme Court. Claiming the doctrine of states' rights, Georgia refused to even send a lawyer to the hearing. On the other hand, luminaries such as Henry Clay, Daniel Webster, and Davy Crockett supported the tribal claims. Some historians claim it was Crockett's anti-states' rights stance among his Southern constituency that ruined his political career and sent him west to his fate at The Alamo.

As the Constitution says, the Supreme Court decides disputes brought by states against each other or by other nations against the various states. The Cherokee Nation claimed sovereignty and it sued the state of Georgia in an effort to retain its land. The Court, however, decided the Indians were neither citizens of the United States nor a properly constituted foreign nation. Therefore, the Court had no authorization to hear the dispute. The net result was the Indian Removal Act, which became history's dreadful "Trail of Tears."

Indian men, women and children were forced to march more than two-thousand circuitous miles from Georgia to Oklahoma by way of Illinois. The toll in human life from disease, exposure – and some say, broken hearts – was monumental as the Cherokees were forcibly relocated from their Georgia homelands. Regardless of the shame the decision led to, the affirmation of Georgia's states' rights must surely have pleased the Democrat-Republican President Monroe – until he read the

Second Thoughts — William T. Harper

Supreme Court's decision (later reversed) and saw that Smith Thompson, his only candidate sitting on that Court, voted in the minority against his views.

Almost 4,000 Cherokee Indians died during their forced-march Trail of Tears debacle.

In still another Supreme Court decision of notoriety on a par with the *Cherokee Nation v. Georgia* came in the famed *Amistad* rebellion case, decided a decade after James Monroe went to his final reward. That case – *United States v. Libellants and Claimants of the Schooner Amistad*, 40 U.S. (15 Pet.) 581 (1841) – must have made Monroe roll over in his grave. The case revolved around a rebellion of slaves aboard the Spanish schooner *Amistad* that ended up near Long Island, New York. (In 1997, Steven Spielberg made a feature film of this event.) The victorious defense attorney who won the case before the Supreme Court was none other than the anathema to all true Democrat-Republicans, former President John Quincy Adams, son the rabid Federalist president John Adams. And Monroe's "man on the bench" – Smith Thompson – was in the 7-1 majority voting for the despised Adams' son.

In the hereafter reserved for past Democrat-Republican Party presidents of the United States, the honorable Thomas Jefferson, James Madison and James Monroe must all have been having *Second Thoughts* about Supreme Court Associate Justice Smith Thompson's opposition to their avowed states' rights beliefs.

* * *

Chapter IX
King Andy's Reign – Deceit and Petticoats
(Term in Office: 1829-1837)

When "Old Hickory" rode into the "President's House" (almost literally-speaking in an infamous mob scene when muddy boots trampled the fine carpeting, crystal and china were shattered, and all the food and drink were quickly consumed in celebration of Andrew Jackson's inauguration in March of 1829), it marked a significant point in the history of the U. S. presidency. As noted, among his five presidential predecessors, only the Adamses were voted out of office after a single four-year term. After Jackson's eight-year term, none of the next ten U. S. presidents served two full terms until Ulysses S. Grant did – starting thirty-two years later. But during "King Andy's" eight years in office, he sent seven names (one of them, Roger Taney, twice) to the Senate for its approval of Supreme Court Chief and Associate justices' nominees. Every one of the candidates ultimately received the Senate's consent, although one (William Smith) declined the honor twice.

Jackson's judicial success came about even as national politics polarized around him, his newly-named Democratic Party, and the party of the opposition. That realignment, brought about by Monroe's amazing 231-1 Electoral College victory in 1820, begat two new political parties. Out of what was the old Democrat-Republican Party (which housed both J. Q. Adams and Jackson in the 1824 and 1828 elections) came the current-day Democratic Party. And what once was the Federalists' affiliation became the Whig Party which evolved twenty years later into today's Republican Party.

Primarily because of a needed two-seat expansion in the size of the Supreme Court in 1837 brought on by growth in the Country's size, President Jackson nominated more men to the Court than any other U. S. President except George Washington (eleven), Ulysses S. Grant, and Franklin Delano Roosevelt (eight each).g Grant's high number of

---

g Washington did, in fact, appoint only ten men but one of them (John Rutledge) he appointed twice. Some historians credit FDR with nine appointments, noting that he named the already-sitting Associate Justice Harlan Fiske Stone to the Chief Justiceship as the ninth. Jackson likewise made eight appointments but two of them were for the same man, Roger B. Taney as both an Associate Justice (denied) and Chief Justice (accepted). And in President Grant's case, though he appointed eight men, only four of them made it through the nomination process.

appointees was due to another Supreme Court expansion in 1869 and FDR's because of his extended and record-setting stay in the presidency.

President Andrew Jackson's Nominees (in reverse order)					
Name	Replacing	Nominated	Vote		Result and Date
John Catron	(new seat)	Mar 3, 1837	28-15	C	Mar 8, 1837
William Smith	(new seat)	Mar 3, 1837	23-18	D	Mar 8, 1837
Philip Barbour	Duvall	Dec 28, 1835	30-11	C	Mar 15, 1836
Roger Taney[18]	Marshall	Dec 28, 1835	29-15	C	Mar 15, 1836
Roger Taney	Duvall	Jan 15, 1835	24-21	P	Mar 3, 1835
James Wayne	Johnson	Jan 6, 1835	V	C	Jan 9, 1835
Henry Baldwin	Washington	Jan 4, 1830	41-2	C	Jan 6, 1830
John McLean	Trimble	Mar 6, 1829	V	C	Mar 7, 1829

[18] for Chief Justice   C=Confirmed   D=Declined   P=Postponed   V=Voice Vote
This chart lists only nominations officially submitted to the Senate, and does not include nominations announced but never officially submitted.
Source: www.senate.gov/pagelayout/reference/nominations/Nominations.htm

"Old Hickory's" first Supreme Court appointee was John McLean. The Ohioan saw previous government service as an examiner in the U.S. Land Office in Cincinnati, served two terms in the U. S. House of Representatives, was appointed to the Ohio Supreme Court. He was serving as U.S. Postmaster General when Jackson appointed him to the U. S. Supreme Court. McLean replaced the recently-deceased Robert Trimble, thereby transferring the "Kentucky Seat"[h] on the bench to the Buckeye State. President Jackson appointed McLean primarily to get him out of the postmaster general's post because McLean refused to permit political removals from post office positions.[62] To his credit, McLean refused to engage in the new President's development of the "spoils system," the conference of government jobs to people based upon political concerns rather than their fitness for office. Others believe he was given the job to quell his political ambitions.

Confirmed by the Senate's voice vote, McLean ultimately served thirty-two years on the Supreme Court and he continued to drift away from President Jackson's populist's views. But it was his first few years on the bench that caused personal havoc between him and his president. In 1829, Jackson picked McLean, a political power of the time, after McLean

---

[h] Assigned "seats" were later also designated for ethnic and gender reasons as well as geographic.

promised not to run for President. Once he was on the court, McLean broke his word and ran for President four times, including an 1832 campaign as the Anti-Masonic candidate against Jackson, the very man who had appointed him to his lifetime position on the Supreme Court.[63]

Sometimes called the "Politician on the Supreme Court" (no other sitting Supreme Court Justice has been similarly involved in such a relentless pursuit of the office of president of the United States[64]), McLean touched all the bases as he climbed the political ladder flirting with Jackson Democrats, anti-Jackson Democrats, Anti-Masons, Whigs, Free Soilers, and Republicans. In 1831 McLean was mentioned for the presidency for the first time at the Anti-Masonic Convention in Baltimore, and in 1833, several Ohio newspapers again began to press for McLean. It was at this point that he abandoned any connection with Jackson and his Democrats and joined the anti-Jacksonists, the Whigs.[65] And this was a man who "promised Jackson he would not to seek the presidency in return for a place on the Court."[66]

But an entirely different type of flirtation made Jackson have a second thought and ruefully wish, "If only I could do it all over again." The notorious "Petticoat Affair" really soured McLean's relations with his benefactor. The "Petticoat Affair" needs an explanation.

"Go back before Monica Lewinsky, before JFK's harem, before Nan Britton and Warren Harding, and you will find a woman named Peggy Eaton," wrote Florence King in 1998 about the "Petticoat Affair".[67] In a shocking sex scandal for its time and one that presaged Gary Hart's "Monkey Business" yacht embarrassment that ruined the popular Colorado Senator's presidential bid in 1988, the "Petticoat Affair" qualifies as similarly salacious and seamy.

Thirty-two-year-old Margaret ("Peggy") O'Neale owned the Franklin House in 1830. It was a favorite Washington, D. C. boarding-house/watering-hole frequented by many of the capitol's politicians, including Andrew Jackson when he represented the state of Tennessee in the U. S. Senate, prior to his presidency.

Second Thoughts — William T. Harper

In 1829, Ms. O'Neale married Jackson's Secretary of War, John Henry Eaton (who also lived at the Franklin House when he too was a U. S. Senator from Tennessee), after her first husband, John Timberlake, reportedly committed suicide eight months earlier in 1828 because he suspected she was having a sexual relationship with Eaton.

Tavern owner Peggy O'Neale had D.C. society awhirl.

The genteel ladies of the Capitol's society were up in arms, whispering not too quietly about Peggy's flirtatious behavior and even her second marriage without a "decent" passage of time following her first husband's death. Floride Calhoun, wife of Jackson's vice president John C., led the social snubbing inflicted by the outraged "respectable" ladies. The refusal of the wives of the cabinet members to recognize the wife of his friend John Eaton angered President Jackson. Living up to the nickname he attained during the War of 1812 because of his stern disciplinary actions, "Old Hickory" publicly sided with the Eatons, perhaps because Jackson's wife Rachel had also been similarly slandered with bigamy charges during Jackson's run for the presidency; and because Eaton had actually written the epitaph on Rachel's tomb.

Secretary of War John Eaton was enmeshed in "scandal."

Most of the Capitol's society took sides. Husbands and wives differed. So too did members of Jackson's own family. Jackson's niece, Emily Donelson, the widowed president's official hostess, snubbed Ms. Eaton at Jackson's inaugural ball. The two-year, tea room battle boiled over into the Cabinet Room when "the entire Cabinet resigned in 1831.

President Andrew Jackson took sides in the "Petticoat Affair."

Justice John McLean took the wrong side in the "Petticoat Affair."

The uproar consumed the first two years of Jackson's Administration, during which time the Nat Turner Rebellion and the birth of the abolitionist movement had gone unnoticed by all save [Vice President] John Calhoun, whose break with Jackson was also a break with nationalism."[68] States' right versus those of Federalism was percolating and beginning to boil over. Nullification, with its early threat of secession was in the air (see below). Jackson's political rivals likewise joined in on the attacks. The road to Fort Sumter, South Carolina was being paved.

Another who joined in against the President in the "Petticoat Affair," much to the chagrin of the tautly-tempered Tennessean, was Supreme Court Associate Justice John McLean. He opted for the anti-Eaton camp. It wasn't a good idea to get on the wrong side of President Andrew Jackson, as Congress found out when he vetoed twelve of its bills – more than all six of his predecessors combined. Thus, McLean also ended up in Andrew Jackson's dog-house. Jackson finally ended the debate when he sent Eaton and his wife Peggy off to assignments in the Florida Territory where he became governor, and later to Spain as United States minister. The fact that McLean, while serving as an Associate Justice of the Supreme Court cast covetous eyes from the dog-house to the President's House was another reason "Old Hickory" had *Second Thoughts* vis-à-vis John McLean.

* * *

Turning his attention back to Supreme Court matters, Jackson's thoughts went to his boyhood friend, William Smith. Reared and educated in South Carolina though born in North Carolina, Smith became a successful lawyer, served in the state senate for six years and was then elected to the state court of appeals. He later was elected to two terms in the United States Senate (1816-23, 1826-31). He was, however, as one biographer put it, "a bitter and vindictive enemy, witheringly sarcastic and never conciliatory, inclined to be opinionated and prejudiced." Despite this lack of judicial temperament, President Jackson had two chances to nominate Smith for the Supreme Court, in 1829 and 1837. Even after the second bid was approved by the Senate via a 23-18 vote, Smith declined both invitations, claiming in 1837 that he wanted to continue to comment freely on public affairs, such as states' rights.

Smith ultimately left South Carolina because of actions of President Jackson's Vice President John C. Calhoun, which peaked during the Nullification Crisis in 1832. Calhoun advocated nullification – the right of any state to nullify Federal laws applying to that state. Jackson did not. After Jackson ordered the U. S. Navy into Charleston harbor because he felt South Carolina was on the brink of insurrection, Calhoun resigned his vice presidency. He rejoined the Senate in a move of total support of the Palmetto State's belief in nullification. Although an ardent states' rights proponent himself, Smith felt nullification was going too far. The situation left Smith between the proverbial rock and a hard place: support South Carolina or his old friend Jackson. Smith compromised (for probably one of the few times in his adult life) and opted to move to Alabama where he ultimately prospered financially.

The rift between Smith and Calhoun became apparent as early as Jackson's presidential election in 1828. When it came to counting the votes that really count (those in the Electoral College), seven of the nine electors from Georgia voted for William Smith for vice president and thus against John C. Calhoun. However, the final count made little difference in the ultimate result and Calhoun was elected as Jackson's vice president. But the lines of antagonism were clearly drawn, leading to speculation that the real reason Smith refused Jackson's offer of a seat on the Supreme Court was because he didn't want to be beholden to any administration that involved Calhoun.

William Smith, "a bitter and vindictive enemy, witheringly sarcastic and never conciliatory, inclined to be opinionated and prejudiced," recognized his judicial short-comings more so than did President Jackson. By declining both offers to serve, he probably saved "Old Hickory" much future embarrassment as a Supreme Court justice.

* * *

President Jackson's second choice of a Supreme Court justice was another that could have posed second thoughts. After the November 26, 1829 death of President John Adams' Supreme Court appointee Bushrod Washington, Henry Baldwin was appointed an Associate Justice of the Supreme Court by President Jackson on January 4, 1830, despite the not-too-surprising objections from his ambitious vice president, John C. Calhoun, who favored an alternate candidate. The Senate consented two days later via an overwhelming 41-2 vote. Baldwin was another one of the President's good friends, a philosophical supporter who delivered his home state of Pennsylvania to the Tennessean in both the 1824 and 1828 elections. Although born in Connecticut, he later moved to Pittsburgh, Pennsylvania where he became publisher of *The Tree of Liberty*, a Democrat-Republican newspaper. He was a Yale University law school graduate at age seventeen, and he served six years in the U. S. House of Representatives representing a western Pennsylvania district before resigning because of ill health in 1822.

Getting that Supreme Court appointment was no easy task for both Jackson and Baldwin. Basking in the glow of the General's 1828 election in which the Keystone State's votes – brought forth in large part by Baldwin's efforts – he felt he deserved a prime position in the new Cabinet, Secretary of State, perhaps. He got nothing and went back to Pennsylvania quite miffed, to say the least. Not wanting such an influential enemy in the next go-round, Jackson offered the Supreme Court seat, which Baldwin accepted as much to "save face" from the previous snub as anything else.

One year after officially joining the Supreme Court, Baldwin actually considered resigning from it in 1831, finding himself at odds with the dominant personalities on the Court such as Joseph Story. Baldwin complained about the tradition of the members residing at the same boarding house during the Court's Term. Furthermore, the procedure of the Court until then was for the Justices not to publicize their disagreements, and Baldwin's decision to publish his dissents created a tremendous change in the relations among the members of the Court. Another factor came from the lack of communication between him and his mentor and because he felt like "a mere passing post, against which every puppy of the party raises his leg."[69] But Jackson persuaded him to stay. Despite suffering from paralysis in his later years, Baldwin continued to serve until April 21, 1844 when he died as a pauper – due to unfortunate land speculation deals (similar to one of his predecessor justices, James Wilson, at age sixty-four.

One of the reasons for President Jackson to have second thoughts regarding Baldwin was, some historians believe, he suffered from mental illness. During the 1831 term he dissented so often and his behavior became so unconventional that there was talk of his mind becoming unhinged. Insanity was not ruled out. Writer Robert Ilisevich speculated about more serious charges of "violent outbursts, insults, faulty reasoning, and jumping in his stocking feet." While on the circuit, he also exhibited bizarre behavior at times, often having coffee and cakes brought to him while he heard cases. He may have suffered from an obsessive-compulsive syndrome, exacerbated in his final years by his financial problems. His friends defended him by saying that he always had a crazy sense of humor, played practical jokes, and detested both formality and pomposity.

Whatever the explanation, Baldwin was a disruptive influence on the Bench, but no one suggested that he be removed and taken to the nearest asylum."[70] Fellow Associate Justice and antagonist Joseph Story said Baldwin was "partially deranged."[71] In his final years, he was even violent on the bench and could not be controlled.[72] Furthermore, Baldwin's abrasive individualism ran counter to and helped to break down Chief Justice Marshall's quest for unanimous decisions. In 1831 for example, Baldwin dissented seven times. In the words of one scholar, "His influence on American law was negligible and his presence on the Supreme Court was probably counterproductive."[73] Worse still, his collapse in 1833, which caused him to miss that term of the Court, signaled the onset of the mental condition that progressively incapacitated him.

Justice Baldwin was believed insane.

Roger B. Taney, Marshall's successor as Chief Justice in 1835, was reported to be so concerned about Baldwin's unpredictable behavior that he advised President Jackson not to take action against the Bank of the United States because Baldwin, as presiding circuit court judge over the case in Philadelphia, would be unreliable.[74] To his supporters, the President was reliable as he vetoed the re-chartering of the Bank of the United States, objecting to government involvement in a monster institution that, he believed, served the interests of the few at the expense of the many. When the issue got to the full Supreme Court, Justice Baldwin voted against President Jackson's position.

That instance was just one of several wherein issues that came before the Supreme Court on which, much to Jackson' angst, Baldwin voted directly (and some say, deliberately) against the President's position – even in one case where Jackson talked directly to the Justice about his interest in the case. One of those issues came shortly after the President's veto of the Bank of the United States bill. In *United States v. David Shive* (1832), the defendant pleaded for his acquittal of counterfeit charges because the bank had been declared unconstitutional by Jackson. Baldwin even took a swipe at his nominating President when he argued that the Court "cannot look to the construction given to the Constitution by the executive department as a guide."[75]

Another example of dissimilar views was *United States v. Arrendondo* (1832), in which Baldwin gave the Court's opinion reaffirming earlier rulings that claims to land titles must be protected…. Baldwin then admonished the government to have greater respect for treaties. It was a decision that many praised, but Jackson was not among them. Afterwards, he informed Baldwin of his disappointment. Jackson now realized how independent and unreliable Baldwin really was.[76] And when writing to a friend in 1829, just months before his nomination to the Supreme Court by Andrew Jackson, he complained that it "was his misfortune to have been a friend" of the President. Apparently, both men harbored *Second Thoughts* about each other.

* * *

Chapter X
Van Buren's Problems with a "Mediocre" Justice
(Term in Office: 1837-1841)

It would be hard to imagine that the Nation's eighth president, Martin Van Buren, didn't harbor some second thoughts about John McKinley, the first of his two nominations to the United States Supreme Court. Commentators and historians have disparaged McKinley's work as "lacking any legal significance." Some said "he was an unproductive and mediocre associate justice who wrote only twenty opinions for the Court during his fifteen years of service (1837-52).[i] He usually voted with the Court's majority and dissented only when joined by at least one other justice. He wrote no opinions that contributed significantly to the development of constitutional law."[77] His career on the Bench "was marked by absences from the Court and little contact with the major legal issues of the day."[78]

Upon McKinley's death Chief Justice Taney paid him the tellingly lukewarm compliment of having been "faithful and assiduous *when he managed to attend.*" Professor Currie was able in his monumental study of the period to conclude without qualification that in his entire career McKinley made "no significant contribution to legal thinking in any form."[79] Obviously, he was also another who vied with Thomas Todd for the "most insignificant" title.

John McKinley, the first Supreme Court justice from the state of Alabama, started out with beliefs similar to Henry Clay, the founder of the Whig Party. But after becoming a U. S. Senator from Alabama, that position didn't go too well with his constituents. So he later on switched over to President Jackson's Democratic Party. He did have one claim to (later) positive fame. He sat on the Court during the trial in which Joseph Cinqué (Sin-K) and forty-eight other African captives who were charged with murder and piracy in the take-over of the slave ship *Amistad* in 1839. One of the defendants' chief lawyers was none other than former President John Quincy Adams. The Court, in a 7-1 decision in which McKinley concurred, ruled in January of 1841 that the defendants were

---

[i] The reader should be aware that there are some seeming discrepancies in dates – such as this instance wherein it shows McKinley's term starting in 1837. On September 25th of that year his appointment was confirmed by the Senate. However, he wasn't actually sworn in until January 9, 1838. Also, during the earliest years of the Court, record-keeping was sometimes lax, as it was throughout the government and the Nation.

not guilty because they were held captive aboard the *Amistad* in violation of slave trade laws. The deranged Associate Justice Henry Baldwin, in the only dissent, said the slaves should be returned to the custody of the slave traders.

McKinley had – prior to his service on the Court where he filled a newly-opened seat in accordance with the Judicial Act of 1837 – served as a member of the Alabama legislature, a member of the U. S. House of Representatives, and had been elected to the U. S. Senate on two separate occasions. Nonetheless, he was so obscure that when he died in Louisville on July 19, 1852, the *New York Times* saw fit to give a sitting Associate Justice of the United States Supreme Court exactly one meager and condescending line of type as his obituary. Adding even further insult to injury is the fact that the prestigious Cave Hill Cemetery in Louisville, Kentucky in which he is buried, lists among its notable inhabitants Colonel Sanders of Kentucky Fried Chicken fame but not the twenty-third Associate Justice of the U. S. Supreme Court.[80]

The primary reason for McKinley being so "unproductive" was his requirement to spend so much of his time – as were all the Supreme Court justices of those days – riding the circuit. He was assigned to ride the newly-created Ninth Circuit (which included parts of Alabama, Louisiana, and Mississippi and all of Arkansas). In just one year, McKinley reportedly had to travel over 10,000 miles riding circuit. (That's 10,000 miles on horseback or in a jarring coach, not in a railroad's Pullman berth or a first-class seat in a jet aircraft.) In his later years he neglected his circuit-riding task. More than neglect, records show during his entire time on the Court he never visited his assigned state of Arkansas – which had only come into the Union in 1836, shortly before McKinley took his oath of office on January 9, 1838. He begged the U. S. Congress for relief, complaining bitterly but unsuccessfully about the difficulty and expense of the circuit travel and the threat of yellow fever. According to an 1839 Senate report, the following mileages were covered by the Justices in making their circuit rounds:

Justice	Miles
Baldwin	2,000
Barbour	1,498
Catron	3,464
McKinley	10,000
McLean	2,500
Story	1,896
Taney	458[j]
Thompson	2,590
Wayne	2,370
An astounding total of	26,776 miles

---

[j] Chief Justice's circuit encompassed only the states abutting Washington, D. C.

Second Thoughts — William T. Harper

The original Judiciary Act of 1789 required Supreme Court justices to also serve as circuit court judges. As we have seen, the justices complained sometimes angrily that circuit riding caused, among other things, serious physical hardships. The case of Associate Justice Samuel Chase, who drove his carriage across the iced-over Susquehanna River in Pennsylvania and almost died when the ice broke, is again cited here. McKinley's Southern circuit (and Catron's too) was particularly grueling because of poor and sometimes non-existent roads in that part of the country. And as Confederate generals were to find out in the early 1860s, a decade after McKinley had retired from the Court, dependable railroads were still in their infancy. The rails and the roads across the Southern states mostly ran east-and-west to the port cities and not generally north-to-south. Paved roads were practically unheard of and it didn't take much rain to turn the clay pathways into slippery slopes. Crossing rivers was extremely dangerous as bridges were far apart and ferries unreliable. Some justices of McKinley's times even agreed to take a reduction in salary if Congress would appoint separate circuit judges.

Not only that, the country was growing rapidly in both geographic size and population.

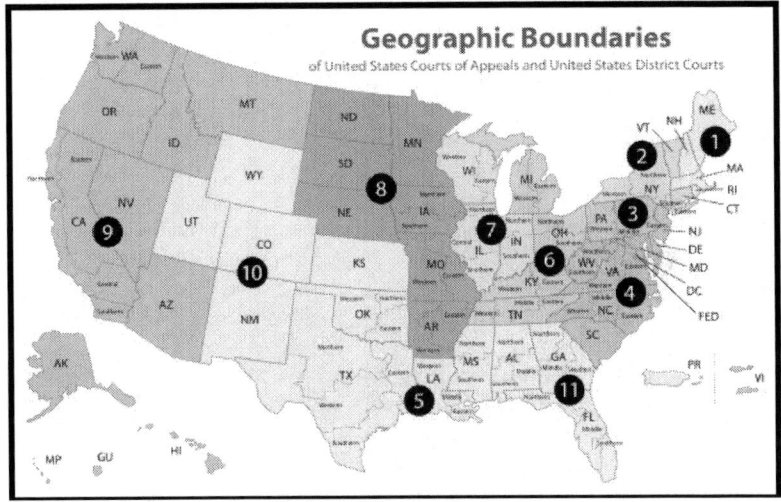

Today's District Courts

As seen herein, the first Supreme Court had six justices (including the Chief Justice) assigned to the original thirteen states populated by less than four million people in the late 1780s. By 1803, there were seventeen states so the Congress added one more associate justice, Jefferson appointee Thomas Todd. John McKinley was appointed by President

Martin Van Buren, President Jackson's hand-picked successor, with confirmation coming from the Senate on September 25, 1837. McKinley, along with President Jackson's last-day appointee John Catron six months earlier, filled the two new seats on the Court mandated by Congressional action that year. Together they brought the number of justices to nine serving the then twenty-six states in the Union. The 1840 census showed the U. S. as a nation had quadrupled its population over the previous fifty years to more than seventeen million people.

The first Supreme Court had one justice for approximately every 666,666 citizens. By 1837, the then nine Justices each had almost 1.8 million potential litigants to serve. That necessitated miles and miles of traveling for the beleaguered jurists.[k] In the last days of John Adams' presidency, he called upon John Jay, by then the retired governor or New York, to come back to the Supreme Court again as Chief Justice to fill a vacancy left by retiring Chief Justice Oliver Ellsworth. Mr. Jay's reply to the president indicated that he was too tired and in too poor health to attend the duties of the office. While previously in that office he had frequently complained about the rigors of attending the circuit court. Within six weeks of his note to the President, the Federalist-leaning Congress passed a measure that relieved the Supreme Court of all circuit court duties. Still, Jay stayed retired just the same.[81]

In another example of that Adams/Jefferson rancor and of the latter's disdain for the Court, the Jeffersonian Congress spitefully restored circuit riding for Supreme Court justices a year later. Almost seven decades after that, with the addition of even more new states, the Judiciary Act of 1869 finally established a separate circuit court judiciary, although the justices retained nominal circuit riding duties until the Circuit Court of Appeals Act of 1891. Congress officially ended the circuit riding practice altogether in 1911.[82] (However, there are those today who advocate the renewal of the requirement that Supreme Court Justices spend at least one week per year hearing cases on the United States Courts of Appeals.[83])

In any case and as previously noted, McKinley is not known for the volume of his writing opinions while on the Bench for fourteen years. But one of the few he did write turned out to be a stunning embarrassment midway through President Van Buren's single term in office. While riding the circuit in 1839 and hearing a lower court appeal on *Bank of Augusta v. Earle*, he ruled corporations could not operate within another state without the state's permission. If upheld by the full Supreme Court, such a ruling would have been devastating to the Nation's economy. The case made its way to the full Supreme Court where the

---

[k] By contrast, today's nine Supreme Court justices would have to geographically cover a nation of 300,000,000 citizens – or 33,000,000+ per justice, if they were still "riding the circuit."

famed barrister Daniel Webster argued against McKinley's circuit court ruling. How, one might ask, can a judge make a ruling in a lower court and then vote on the same case in the Supreme Court? Justice McKinley had the opportunity to recuse himself in the latter instance. He chose not to, as is allowed in the Federal court system. In so doing, he was not in violation of the Judicial Code of Conduct. He thereby chose instead to sit in judgment of his own ruling; perhaps more than in the merits of the case. The embarrassment was complete when the full Court ruled in favor of Webster's position via an 8-1 vote, the lone dissenter being, of course, McKinley.

* * *

Chapter XI
Tyler Bats a Sickly 1-for-9
(Term in Office: April 4, 1841-March 4, 1845)

Almost an entire book could be written about the Second Thoughts President John Tyler must have experienced with his nominations to the United States Supreme Court.

John Tyler was trained as a lawyer and rose through Virginia's political ranks as a member of its state legislature, the U. S. House of Representatives, the governorship of his home state, and into the U. S. Senate in 1827. After nine years in the Upper House as a strong states' rights activist, he resigned in protest against President Jackson's anti-nullification moves. Nevertheless, his anti-Jackson stance brought him the vice presidency in William Henry Harrison's Whig Party election victory over Martin Van Buren in 1840. Unexpectedly, his bolt from the Democratic Party to the Whig Party would shockingly come back to haunt Tyler all too soon.

When Harrison died just one month into his four-year term, Tyler ascended to the presidency taking with him the unflattering title of "His Accidency" – a word-play on the title "His Excellency." As the first Vice President to be elevated to the office of President of the United States, he didn't arrive there accompanied by a lot of good will or spendable political capital. What little of the two he had was quickly lost when he fought against a new national bank. At one point, even the newly-alienated Whigs in the House of Representatives tried unsuccessfully to have him impeached.

Tyler had a second strike thrown against him because of the widening factional split developing between newly formed, highly partisan political parties – the Whigs and the Democrats. And the third strike in his game of hoped-for harmonious relationships with Capitol Hill came when Tyler found himself as the first American president to preside over the country as it publically acknowledged its ideological split that led ultimately to the Civil War of 1861-1865. Naturally, the acrimony infiltrated almost all of Tyler's Congressional agenda, including his Supreme Court appointments.

With a term in office not yet two years old, Tyler had his first chance to fill a vacancy on the Supreme Court when Justice Smith Thompson died on December 18, 1843. Three weeks later, the President sent up his first nominee, John Spencer, for the Senate's advice and consent. Spencer, a fifty-five-year-old New York lawyer, politician and judge, was Secretary of War in Tyler's cabinet. It took the Senate just three weeks to vote down the Supreme Court nomination, 21-26, simply because Spencer was seen as a close ally of Tyler and any friend of Tyler's was a foe to the Senators – even those from his own Whig party. Railing loudest against all things Tyler, the influential Kentucky statesman and orator Henry Clay sneered about Spencer's unworthiness of the posts being offered and asked, "Does any man believe him true, faithful or honest?"

President John Tyler's Nominees (in reverse order)					
Name	Replacing	Nominated	Vote	Result	and Date
John Read	Baldwin	Feb 7, 1845		N	
Samuel Nelson	Thompson	Feb 4, 1845	V	C	Feb 14, 1845
Reuben Walworth	Thompson	Dec 4, 1844		W	Feb 4, 1845
Edward King	Baldwin	Dec 4, 1844		W	Feb 7, 1845
Reuben Walworth	Thompson	Jun 17, 1844		N	Jun 17, 1844
John Spencer	Thompson	Jun 17, 1844		W	Jun 17, 1844
Edward King	Baldwin	Jun 5, 1844	29-18	P	Jun 15, 1844
Reuben Walworth	Thompson	Mar 13, 1844	27-20	W	Jun 17, 1844
John Spencer	Thompson	Jan 9, 1844	21-26	R	Jan 31, 1844

C=Confirmed   R=Rejected   W=Withdrawn   N=No Action   P=Postponed
V=Voice Vote   This chart lists only nominations officially submitted to the Senate, and does not include nominations announced but never officially submitted.
Source: www.senate.gov/pagelayout/reference/nominations/Nominations.htm

On March 13, 1844, Tyler tried again to fill the Thompson vacancy. This time, the nominee was Reuben Walworth, a jurist and politician from upstate New York. The confirmation process this time took three months. However, in the interim, Associate Justice Henry Baldwin also died and Tyler then had two seats on the Bench to fill. Walworth was slated for Thompson and Tyler wanted future President James Buchanan for the Baldwin slot but the Pennsylvania Democrat declined the nomination. So, Tyler turned to Philadelphia lawyer Edward King on June 5, 1844 to replace Justice Baldwin. Walworth's bid ran afoul when it was alleged that "he was recommended by many distinguished members of the bar...merely because they are anxious to get rid of a querulous, disagreeable, unpopular" Yankee politician. King, initially a Federalist who turned into a Jackson Democrat and therefore distrusted by both sides of the Senate aisle, found his nomination in limbo as the Senate postponed action.

Second Thoughts   William T. Harper

That inaction led King to withdraw his nomination. The fact of the matter was, it didn't matter if Tyler reincarnated George Washington himself, the rancorous Senate was not going to give him anything.

Three times Reuben H. Walworth was chosen; not once elected.

Yet even in that atmosphere, John Tyler wasn't easily cowed. Two days after King walked away, the President came right back with renewed nominations of John Spencer and Reuben Walworth. That effort, made on June 17, 1844, did not even last twenty-four hours. The Senate refused again to take any action on Spencer's nomination. Walworth's name was withdrawn on the same day. Six months elapsed before Tyler tried again and once more he submitted Edward King's and Reuben Walworth's names. The problem this time was the 1844 presidential elections had come and gone. So had Tyler's presidency as the Democrat James Polk won the office. With the "out" party on its way in, the gleeful Senate was even more loath to give the "lame duck" anything at all. Two months later, both nominations were withdrawn.

One would think Tyler's hopes of naming anyone to the Supreme Court would be totally dashed. Everyone that is, but John Tyler. He was not done yet. Recognizing the handwriting on the wall, exactly one month before moving out of the Executive Mansion on March 4, 1845, Tyler submitted the name of Samuel Nelson. Nelson was a Democrat. The incoming President was a Democrat. Not surprisingly, the incoming Congress was filled with Democrats. Nelson's nomination was approved as Smith Thompson's successor fourteen months after Thompson died in office. As for Baldwin's successor, Tyler gave it one last gasp. He nominated John Read on February 7, 1845, three days after Nelson's successful bid. Read had served for four years as U.S. attorney for the eastern district of Pennsylvania. He went on ultimately to become Chief Justice of the Pennsylvania Supreme Court. But unfortunately for both Tyler and Reed, the southern-dominated Senate wouldn't even consider the Pennsylvanian because of his earlier stance against the expansion of slavery into the territories.

    And so it was: Two seats to fill. Nine nominations, four withdrawals, one permanent postponement, two total no-actions, only one flat-out rejection, and only one confirmation. And still one seat remained empty. Again the question arises: How many *Second Thoughts* could President John Tyler have had as he looked back over his Supreme Court appointments?

* * *

Chapter XII
Polk: "Ill-trained and Poorly Informed"
(Term in Office: 1845-1849)

One of the oddest of second thoughts regarding Supreme Court appointments must have occurred to President James K. Polk, said to have been the first "dark horse" to win the presidency (1845-1849). In September of 1845, President Polk's Secretary of State, James Buchanan, came almost begging for an appointment to the Court. The future fifteenth president of the United States, Buchanan had served ten years in Congress, a brief stint in Russia in 1832 as the United States Minister, a term as Ambassador to the Court of St. James, and had run for the Democratic presidential nomination in 1844, losing to Polk. Buchanan then worked hard to help the Polk campaign win the state of Pennsylvania in the presidential election of 1844 and as a result, Polk made Buchanan his Secretary of State. That's when the President's second thoughts started.

Buchanan would frequently upstage President Polk in matters of foreign policy. The President and his Secretary of State were constantly at war with each other over foreign affairs matters – in particular the War with Mexico (1846-1848) and the United States' territorial struggle with Great Britain over the Northwest Territories ("54.40 or Fight") which both countries resolved via a compromise agreement in 1846. Secretary Buchanan "never hesitated to oppose Polk, whom he considered ill-trained and poorly informed" in matters of state.[84] Their relations were constantly strained. Buchanan made frequent threats – either directly or through emissaries – that he would resign from the cabinet. After one of them, Polk "lambasted his Secretary of State with these scathing words: 'He cares nothing for the success or glory of my administration further than he can make it subservient to his own political aspirations'."[85]

Buchanan's condemnation of his president was more a negative reflection on his matters of state than of Polk's. The eleventh President of the United States, rated in the top ten of those holding that job by some current historians primarily because of his nation-expanding policies, was indeed extremely knowledgeable in matters of state. During Polk's term in office, three states were added to the Union – Iowa, Texas and Wisconsin. It was mostly during his presidency the United States fought and eventually won the Mexican-American War in 1848 and consolidated Texas' entry into the Union. He was a proponent of the Nation's "Manifest Destiny;" its territorial expansion "from sea to shining sea." Only Thomas Jefferson's Louisiana Purchase was a bigger growth factor for the U. S. than was Polk's. The Nation grew by more than 300,000 square miles in the Oregon Territory and another 500,000 via the Treaty of Guadalupe Hidalgo.

As shown in this map, the Treaty included parts of today's Colorado, Arizona, New Mexico, western Texas, Wyoming as well as all of California, Nevada and Utah. (The rest of Arizona and New Mexico were later peacefully ceded to the United States via the 1853 Gadsden Purchase.) Via this expansion during Polk's term as President, the United States emerged as a world power. So much for a man "considered ill-trained and poorly informed" by his potential Supreme Court nominee.

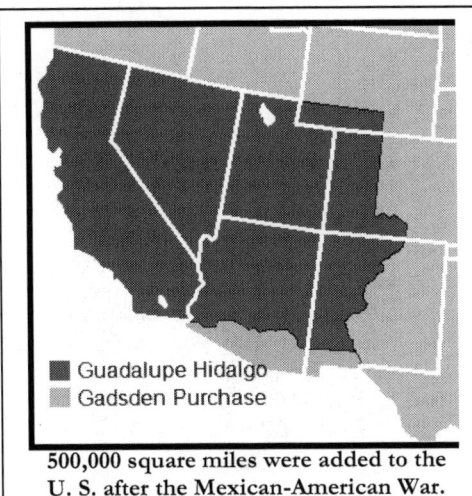

500,000 square miles were added to the U. S. after the Mexican-American War.

In any event, after asking Polk for the Supreme Court appointment to the seat left open by the death of Justice Henry Baldwin, Buchanan withdrew his request, fearful he could not win confirmation from the Senate because of his vacillating political positions. The Secretary of State also knew that no Supreme Court justice ever resided in the "President's House," a place to which he wanted to relocate. Still, he continued to vacillate even as he enlisted allies to promote his Supreme Court aspirations. In January of 1846, James Shields, U. S. Senator from Illinois and a contemporary from Missouri, Thomas Hart Benton, both recommended Secretary Buchanan for the Supreme Court. President Polk resisted the entreaties even though he believed Buchanan would soon be a candidate in the forthcoming 1848 presidential election – in which Polk would decline to enter. Even though he also believed "no candidate for the presidency ought ever to remain in the cabinet [because] he is an unsafe advisor,"[86] Polk retained Buchanan as Secretary of State.

On December 23, 1845, the President instead nominated George W. Woodward, a Pennsylvania Democrat and unsuccessful U. S. Senate candidate in 1844, for the high court seat. Because of internal squabbling among Pennsylvania Democrats, including Secretary of State Buchanan, the Senate rejected the Woodward nomination a month later. "Distressed at the news, Polk was quick to implicate Buchanan in the failure, charging that Buchanan could have prevented three or possibly four senators from voting against Woodward. On the next day, the president declared that if he could be certain that Buchanan had caused the rejection of Woodward, he would dismiss him from the cabinet."[87]

Eight months after the Woodward episode and with the Baldwin seat still open, Buchanan added to Polk's misery via a report that Buchanan himself was back again in search of the Supreme Court seat. "Polk was dismayed and distressed when he received word from Senators Cass and Benton that they were recommending Buchanan for appointment to the bench…. The negotiations therefore remained at an impasse until August 1, when Buchanan announced to Polk that he did not want to be named to the Court but instead preferred to remain in the cabinet…. In response, Polk informed Buchanan that he would nominate Robert C. Grier of Pittsburgh to fill the vacancy on the Court…thus bringing to a conclusion the sometimes acrimonious struggle between Polk and the Pennsylvania Democrats over the nomination to the Court."[88] Grier received Senate consent via a voice vote on August 4, 1846, the day after he was nominated.

The President had a Secretary of State who was antagonistic, quarrelsome, and garrulous; one who considered Polk to be "ill-trained and poorly informed," one who plotted to move into his office, and one who the President passed up a chance to gracefully move aside. For reasons little known to historians and biographers, "Polk has a chance to get rid of [Buchanan] then, and he doesn't take it."[89] On second thought….

* * *

Chapter XIII
Fillmore – Lots of "Advice" but little "Consent"
(Term in Office: July 9, 1850-March 4, 1853)

Vice President Millard Fillmore ascended to the Executive Mansion via the 1850 death of Zachary Taylor after the Mexican War hero spent only sixteen months in office before what was thought to be acute gastroenteritis killed him. Being the thirteenth President of the United States likewise didn't turn out to be very lucky for Fillmore, the last of the Whig Party chief executives – in a number of ways, Supreme Court nominations being one of them. He selected four candidates for the highest court in the land. Three of them did not make it through the "advice and consent" process. Two of those three failed because of states' rights and slavery issues and the third didn't make it because the Democrat-controlled Senate wanted to save the open seat for Fillmore's successor, Democrat Franklin Pierce. The only one that did get confirmed, Benjamin R. Curtis of Massachusetts, surely must have later given "The Last of the Whigs" some anguished second thoughts.

A self-taught lawyer, Fillmore had little to merit in what turned out to be his thirty-two-month presidency. One biography shows his "Profession" as an "apprentice to a cloth dresser, apprentice to a wool carder," and eight less-than-memorable years in the U. S. House as a Representative from New York State. As John Tyler's presidency was thought to be "Accidental," Millard Fillmore's was thought to be merely "Incidental." The New Yorker was put on the 1850 presidential ticket with General Taylor simply as a northerner to balance the general's southern, slave-holding constituencies. Fillmore was there to attract the abolitionist vote. He was there to merely fill in the seat of President of the Senate for the anticipated next eight years of the Taylor presidency. The Taylor-Fillmore ticket almost outdid itself in counter-balancing.

Not only were the pair poles apart on the primary political issues of the day, likewise was their upbringing and education. The general grew up in Southern aristocracy while his running mate lived in a log-cabin apprenticeship and abject poverty as a child. Their differences were practically irreconcilable – especially since they never even met once before their election to the highest offices in the land and the President didn't care much for his Vice President's counsel after their election. They were, in fact, the epitome of the ever-popular but herewith paraphrased quote: "strange bedfellows who make politics."

Nonetheless, the strange bedfellows of the Whig party squeezed by in the 1848 election. The first reason came about probably because Democrat President James K. Polk opted not to run for a second term, due in large part to health factors. The second reason was because former President and "Free Soil, Free Labor, Free Men" third-party candidate Martin Van Buren, once a Democrat, siphoned off ten percent of the popular ballots in a highly unsuccessful effort to return to the "President's House." The Whig Taylor/Fillmore slate garnered forty-seven percent of the popular vote versus forty-two percent for Democrats Lewis Cass and William Butler. But, had Van Buren's 291,000 favorable ballots gone to Cass/Butler, they would have outpolled Taylor/Fillmore in the popular vote by more than 153,000.

As Messrs. Taylor and Fillmore took up their seats at the head of U. S. government in March of 1849, almost immediately the many-faceted calamity of a looming Civil War gave them their first predicament. The Nation was already torn by the ideological differences in government and commerce between the North and the South. One of those differences, the Compromise of 1850 bill – the so-called Free State vs. Slave State four-year confrontation that threatened to bring on secession – was wending its way through Congress. The bill resulted from a variety of actions:

- the 1845 annexation of Texas,
- the expected future expansion of the United States as a result of the Mexican-American War and President Polk's geographic "Manifest Destiny" successes,
- and what to do about slavery in those new states joining the Union.

At the time of its adoption, the Compromise of 1850 did avoid secession or civil war. At the time....

The bill, a compromise indeed, therefore left both sides praising what it got and damning what it didn't. Somewhat surprisingly, as a Southerner and a slave-owner, President Taylor tried to implement the Northern policy of excluding slavery from the Southwestern expansion. When he died on July 9, 1850, another Vice President suddenly found himself in "the People's House" and he completely stunned *and* angered the Northerners by strictly enforcing the Fugitive Slave Law which required the capture and return of escaped slaves to their owners. Thus, in what seemed like an unheard of pair of role-reversals, the Southerner (Taylor) supported the Compromise of 1850's ban on the expansion of slavery but the Northerner (Fillmore) supported the Compromise's tough Fugitive Slave Law.

Less than two months after Fillmore entered the presidency, Associate Justice Levi Woodbury from New Hampshire died in office on September 4, 1851. Thus another problem faced the new President. He sent the name of Benjamin R. Curtis from Massachusetts to the Senate and he was confirmed three months later. Curtis, the first Supreme Court Justice to actually have a law degree (many have been nominated simply because they were FOPs – Friends Of the President), was chosen because Fillmore felt him to be a kindred soul on his views of the Compromise of 1850 and its Fugitive Slave Law. "The Last of the Whigs" was disabused of that thought when the Supreme Court issued its famous (infamous?) – *Dred Scott v. Sandford* decision in March of 1857. It, in effect, ratified those parts of the Fillmore-supported Compromise of 1850 which conceded that if slaves escaped from a Slave State to a Free State, a slave-owner could pursue the runaways across state lines and bring them back.

In *Dred Scott v. Sandford*, the Supreme Court however, under slavery supporter and Chief Justice Roger B. Taney, went even further than the Compromise when it declared all blacks, slaves as well as freedmen, were not and could not be citizens of the United States. Because Dred Scott was black, he was not a citizen and therefore could not sue for his release from slavery after he had lived – with his Army officer "owner" – in the free state of Illinois and the free territory of Wisconsin. The Taney Court stated blacks "had no rights which the white man was bound to respect; and that the Negro might justly and lawfully be reduced to slavery for his benefit. He was bought and sold and treated as an ordinary article of merchandise...."[90] The Court's vote was 7-2 in favor of Chief Justice Taney's majority opinion, thereby reinforcing the Court's support of Taney's claim that "Our founders believed that negroes were beings of an inferior order, and altogether unfit to associate with the white race; either in social or political relations...."

(It is ironic that the Taney Court's decision which declared a "free negro of the African race, whose ancestors were brought to this country and sold as slaves, is not a 'citizen' within the meaning of the Constitution of the United States."[91] But that fact was ignored three years later by the Courts in the trial of abolitionist John Brown and his co-conspirators for their raid on the Federal arsenal at Harper's Ferry, Virginia on October 16, 1859. In that trial, one of the accused – a freed Black named John Copeland – declared no United States court could try him because, according to the Dred Scott decision, Blacks were not citizens of the United States and only "citizens" of the United States could be tried in U. S. courts.)

The seven members of the Supreme Court voting in the majority in the *Scott v. Sandford* case (actually a mis-spelling of the slave-owner's name, Sanford) were not alone in their inner feelings about racial differences. It goes without saying that many of their fellow citizens felt the same way and that the justices were merely reflecting some of the mores of the times. That, however, is not – according to the strict constructionists' view of the Constitution – the role of the Supreme

Court. The Court is charged with ruling what it interprets were the Founders aims when they signed the Constitution in 1787. This gets us into the latter-day argument regarding "evolving standards" versus "strict constructionism (i.e., Framers' intent)" which continues on to this day and will not be argued in these pages.

It can be further said that "the will of the people" as expressed by the Supreme Court in the Dred Scott decision in 1857 was still held in great credence a half-century later. One of the most popular of American presidents, Theodore Roosevelt, expressed it as such when he said, "As a race...the [blacks] are altogether inferior to the whites...[and] can never rise to a very high place...I do not believe that the average Negro...is as yet in any way fit to take care of himself and others.... If he were...there would be no Negro race problems."[92]

Similarly, as an advocate of the Compromise of 1850, President Millard Fillmore on March 6, 1857 had to have been pleased with the Dred Scott decision which gave credence to his enforcement of the Fugitive Slave Act. At least, he was until he read that the most forceful of the two dissenting votes in *Dred Scott v. Sandford* was that of – none other than his only successful nomination of a Supreme Court justice – Benjamin R. Curtis. That had to give Fillmore more than *Second Thoughts*.

Having thoroughly alienated both the North and the South through his flip-flopping on the slavery issue, Fillmore soon became an anathema to both sides in the Congress. By August of 1852, the unpopular President was already perceived as a lame-duck for the coming November's election and just about everything he proposed was automatically doomed. Included in that "everything" were his next three Supreme Court appointments – Edward Bradford's on August 16, 1852, William Micou's on January 3, 1853, and George Badger's on February 14, 1853 – less than three weeks away from Franklin Pierce's presidency. There is little in the historical record to suggest the Senate had objections to any of these nominations. The Senate simply objected to Millard Fillmore.

President Fillmore approached President Tyler's fable of futility as he sent up four names, only one of which was accepted by the Senate. In comparison to Tyler, Fillmore's "batting average" was a slugging .250. (For the record and as another comparison, Franklin D. Roosevelt, ala Tyler, also sent up nine names to the Senate; every one of which was confirmed. No need to note FDR's batting average.)

* * *

Second Thoughts   William T. Harper

Chapter XIV
James Buchanan – the Great Procrastinator
(Term in Office: 1857-1861)

He who hesitates, they say, is lost. That surely was the case with President James Buchanan. Had he not hesitated in naming a replacement for Supreme Court Associate Justice Peter Vivian Daniel who died on May 31, 1860; had he not hesitated eight long months until February 5, 1861 to send up the name of one of the nation's leading lawyers, Jeremiah Black, he may not have lost the nomination. And even more disastrous for the President and his friend Black, Buchanan hesitated again in the election year of 1860 in naming Black to the Daniel seat. Instead, the President waited and gambled for another opening on the Bench – that of the eighty-four-year-old Supreme Court Chief Justice Roger Taney's whose resignation was expected because of his advanced age. Buchanan and Black lost out on both counts. One would have thought Buchanan had learned a lesson about hesitation as he watched President Polk's delay in naming him to the Court in 1845, a procrastination that denied Buchanan the post.

Justice Daniel, born in Virginia in 1784, appointed to the U.S. Supreme Court by President Martin Van Buren, took his oath of office on January 10, 1842. He was an extreme defender of states' rights, limited government, and slavery – as witnessed by his vote in 1857 with the 7-2 majority to uphold the Dred Scott decision wherein he claimed "that the African negro race never have been acknowledged as belonging to the family of nations" (about which, more to come herein). He was radical in his hatred for anything northern; refusing, for instance, to eat any food produced north of the Mason-Dixon Line or even set foot on Yankee soil. With such firebrand views, it is conceivable that had Justice Daniel lived, he may have bolted from the Supreme Court and returned to Virginia with the outbreak of the Civil War in 1861. Or, even more ominously, he may have stayed on the Bench and been an avowed obstructionist to the North's conduct of the "War of Yankee Aggression."

From December 17, 1860 to March 4, 1861, Jeremiah Black was U.S. Secretary of State in Buchanan's Democratic administration, prior to which he served as Buchanan's Attorney General. Some say the former Chief Justice of the Pennsylvania Supreme Court was the most influential of the President Buchanan's official advisers, especially in the growing trend toward Southern secession and the looming Civil War. He denied the constitutionality of secession, and urged Fort Sumter be properly reinforced and defended. He was an extremely hard-working, dedicated lawyer and public servant. According to *The New York Tribune* and *Harper's*

Weekly, "though you never meet the Attorney General at a ball or soiree, you can find him all day in the Supreme Court, and nearly all night at his office."[93]

As Buchanan's Attorney General (an appointment and nomination he never knew about until he received his letter of Senate confirmation), Black consistently enforced federal laws relating to the slave trade and to the return of fugitive slaves – even though he disagreed with them – but because "the law is the law." With views 180 degrees out of sync with Justice Daniel's – and that of the majority of Roger Taney's Southerner-dominated Court – some historians wonder what Buchanan's fellow-Pennsylvanian's influence on that Court would have been?

However, Buchanan – believing, no doubt, that he would be returned to office – procrastinated through eight of the nine months left before he would be defeated by Abraham Lincoln in election in November of 1860. Then, on February 5, 1861, with only a few weeks left in his term as president, Buchanan named Black to fill the now-dead-cold seat left by Justice Daniel on the U.S. Supreme Court bench. By that time and despite his qualifications and positions, Black didn't stand a chance of winning Senate consent – especially with Lincoln's famed and strident debate opponent, Senator Stephen A. Douglas, leading the anti-slavery Democratic opposition.

In the first place, the Republicans in the Senate didn't want to give Democratic president Buchanan the chance to put one of his people on the Bench; they simply wanted to wait four weeks or so to give their president, "Honest Abe," the opportunity to present his man. Similarly, although Black was an anti-slavery proponent, he wasn't deemed to hold strong enough views on the subject to satisfy the Senate abolitionists and the northern newspapers which agreed with that all-or-nothing position. Also in the interim, southern senators who might have supported Black were resigning from the Senate to go home and join the Confederacy.

As a consequence, Black's nomination was rejected by the Senate, 25-26, on February 21, 1861, less than two weeks before Lincoln's inaugural. Historians seem to agree that had Buchanan acted more quickly on the Black appointment – anytime before the highly-contested November 1860 election – Jeremiah Black would have sat on the Supreme Court – in place of Lincoln-appointed Samuel F. Miller.[94]

In an 1863 trial in which Black was co-counsel for the defense, the legal team argued against President Lincoln's suspension of *Habeas Corpus* during the Civil War and "the government's claim that during wartime Lincoln could suspend constitutional rights wherever and whenever he wanted."[95] In that context, one is only left to speculate how President Buchanan's exercise in hesitation on the eve of the American Civil War might have changed the course of the Nation's history!

Second Thoughts William T. Harper

Pondering *Second Thoughts*, President Buchanan could well have asked, "Why did I hesitate so long?" Or simply, "Why did I hesitate?"

* * *

Chapter XV
Lincoln's Schemers and Scoundrels
(Term in Office: March 4, 1861-April 15, 1865)

As already seen in these pages, there have been schemers among the justices of the United States Supreme Court. Smith Thompson ran for (and lost) the governorship of New York in 1828 while still sitting on the Bench. And John McLean ran four times for President, once even against Andrew Jackson, the man who appointed him to the Court. As President Abraham Lincoln, the first chief executive to bear the current political label of Republican, also found out via his Supreme Court appointments, there were also scoundrels sitting on the bench.

Resignation and death left three seats vacant at the Supreme Court in 1862. With the Civil War raging, "The Rail-Splitter" was totally engrossed in frustration over his vacillating generals in a war going badly for the North at the time. Because of those pressures, he too ignored the open seating on the Court for ten months after his inauguration. Now, he needed support from the Bench for some of his drastic, war-inspired moves – such as the trying of civilians by military courts-martial, and the suspension of the Writ of *Habeas Corpus*.

According to the Constitution, Article I, Section 9, "the privilege of the Writ of *Habeas Corpus* shall not be suspended, unless in Case of Rebellion or Invasion the public safety may require it." A Writ of *Habeas Corpus* is a judicial mandate to a prison official ordering an inmate be brought to the court so it can be determined whether or not that person is imprisoned lawfully and whether or not he should be released from custody. Surely, from April 12, 1861 to April 9, 1865, a major "case of rebellion" was running rampant throughout the land. But, there were still the purists who didn't believe suspension of the writ was justified. Anticipating such resistance, Lincoln needed a stacked deck in the highest court in the land to support his actions – and the War. Franklin Delano would have similar "Court Packing" ideas seventy-five years later.

With that in mind (among other considerations), Lincoln was faced with the need to fill those three open seats on the Supreme Court. His initial appointee was Noah H. Swayne, an Ohio jurist and politician whose claim to fame came on January 24, 1862 when he became the first Supreme Court justice elected carrying the new Republican Party label. The label stood him well as he sailed through the confirmation process with a 38-1 affirmative vote, and he filled the seat vacated by Justice John McLean. Then, as noted in the previous chapter herein, Martin Van Buren appointee Peter Vivian Daniel died on May 30, 1860 – an election year in which Democrat President Buchanan couldn't get a nomination for that seat past a hostile Republican Senate. In July of 1862, Lincoln named Samuel F. Miller of Iowa as Justice Daniel's replacement.

Yet a third justice, John A. Campbell, a favorite of Franklin Pierce, resigned on April 31, 1861, just weeks after the Civil War started so he could return to Alabama in support of the Confederacy. The President replaced him, but not until twenty months later, December 1, 1862, by nominating an old friend, David Davis. He was a fourteen-year Illinois state judge before whom the self-taught lawyer Lincoln had practiced in the 1840s and 1850s. Judge Davis became Lincoln's campaign manager in his successful run for the presidency of the United States in 1860. Not surprisingly, all three new appointees carried Republican-leaning credentials. Also not surprisingly, all three justices who were replaced had been appointed by presidents bearing a Democrat-oriented label.

* * *

It's hard to imagine that any candidate for the Court ever so actively campaigned for the job than did Noah Haynes Swayne, a devout Quaker and thus far the only member of that faith to serve on the Supreme Court. Born in Virginia, Swayne was admitted to the state bar at nineteen years of age. An ardent supporter of President Andrew Jackson, Swayne was elected to the Ohio state legislature in 1829. In 1830 President Jackson named him U.S. district attorney, a position he held for almost ten years. Though he started out politically as a Jacksonian Democrat in the Dominion State, his anti-slavery views caused him to move *post haste* to Columbus in the free state of Ohio. Those views also caused him to switch his political allegiance conveniently to the Republican Party in the early 1850s.

In a touch of irony, the death of his friend – the aforementioned, overly-ambitious Justice John McLean in 1861 – opened a seat on the Court that Swayne coveted mightily. In his campaign for the post, he quickly enlisted the support of his comrades ranging from the entire Ohio congressional delegation (including influential Senators John Sherman and Benjamin Wade) to New York attorney Samuel Tilden, a future presidential candidate himself. He even traveled to Washington to help orchestrate a campaign aimed at educating President Lincoln about his suitability for the post.[96] The onslaught convinced Lincoln, and Justice Swayne took the oath of office in the Taney Court on January 24, 1862. Lincoln was on his way toward getting a Court which would uphold his controversial and unprecedented conduct of the war. Helpfully, Congressional Republicans obliged by speedily confirming all his appointments – every one of them in less than a week's time – and even adding a tenth seat to the Bench.

Unfortunately, Swayne's potential greatness as a jurist did not materialize. He was, in fact, both the first and the weakest of Lincoln's five appointments to the Court. His tenure on the Court was "lengthy though undistinguished...."[97] Along with later Court colleagues Ward Hunt and William Strong, he was rated as a "lesser talent."[98] As a justice, Swayne had no inclination to withdraw from politics. He eagerly schemed to replace Roger Taney as chief justice in 1864. His "judicial career had promised much, but produced little."[99] Swayne broke with Lincoln in 1862 in a treason case in which he ruled domestic rebels could not be "enemies" within the meaning of the Constitution or Federal law. He argued wartime circumstances "should have no effect on the administration of the law...." Such an argument had to be a direct hit on Lincoln's waging of the war via the President's "controversial and unprecedented conduct."[100]

Known for his "charm and political scheming, Swayne was undoubtedly Lincoln's least effective appointment to the Court."[101] Surely, President Lincoln must have had some *Second Thoughts* about allowing himself to be sold such a bill of unfit goods, as Noah Haynes Swayne.

* * *

Had he lived long enough, Abraham Lincoln would also, no doubt, have had *Second Thoughts* about his fourth Supreme Court Associate Justice appointee, Stephen Johnson Field. Lincoln was an avowed opponent of the Supreme Court's Dred Scott decision – the position of the most radical states' rights Democrats, that Congress had a constitutional obligation to protect slavery in the federal territories and no power to ban it. Lincoln denounced it vigorously in 1858 during one of his debates with Stephen A. Douglas in their famed lecture series.

During the 1860 presidential election campaign, Lincoln railed against the decision and used it to show the differences between the two political parties. In Lincoln's words, "The Republicans inculcate, with whatever of ability they can, that the negro is a man; that his bondage is cruelly wrong, and that the field of his oppression ought not to be enlarged. The Democrats deny his manhood; deny, or dwarf to insignificance, the wrong of his bondage; so far as possible, crush all sympathy for him, and cultivate and excite hatred and disgust against him...."

With words like that in some sixty or more speeches, Lincoln's supporters in the election campaign expected him to take steps to overturn *Dred Scott v. Sandford*, "a national debacle," by appointing Northern, Republican, abolitionist-minded Supreme Court justices who would follow his lead. Seven of the nine 1857 justices voted against Scott:

Second Thoughts   William T. Harper

Chief Justice Roger Taney plus Associate Justices James Wayne, John Catron, Peter Daniel, Robert Grier, John Campbell, and Samuel Nelson. Only John McLean and Benjamin Curtis voted for the plaintiff and Curtis was so incensed with the majority view that he resigned from the Court in protest. When Lincoln took office on March 4, 1861, every one of the eight sitting justices was labeled a Democrat.

Then, with the death of Justice John McLean eight days before Fort Sumter was attacked on April 12, 1861, and with urgencies of the Civil War occupying almost 100 percent of his time, Lincoln didn't get around to replacing McLean, Daniel, and Campbell until 1862. The replacements – Swayne, Miller, and Davis were Republicans from Union states – Ohio, Iowa, and Illinois, respectively. That brought the Court back to its prescribed complement of nine justices. The political philosophies of the justices then consisted of six Democrats and three Republicans.

The size of the Supreme Court is not prescribed by the Constitution; it is set by statute and in 1863 it was raised from nine justices to ten – meaning President Lincoln had yet another opportunity to fill a seat. On March 3, 1863, he sent up the name of Stephen Johnson Field who was confirmed four days later. A Connecticut Yankee and the son of a Congregationalist minister, Field practiced law in his brother's New York City office for five years before catching "gold fever" and heading for California's hills in 1849. He quickly became mayor of Marysville, a little town north of the State Capitol of Sacramento, where he again practiced law from 1851 until 1857 when he was appointed to the state's Supreme Court. Two years later he was named Chief Justice.

In retrospect, why would anyone choose a career in the human interactive field of law when an early opponent of his wrote that "if analyzed," Field's life would be "found to be one series of little-mindedness, meanlinesses, of braggadocio, pusillanimity, and contemptible vanity."[102] Not only that, but – contrary to expectations of some Lincoln advocates – Field was a Democrat! At the time, one could ask, "Honest, Abe, what were you thinking?" One answer available was that "Field was a staunch supporter of the Union cause."[103] Another was that the President was seeking input from the new western states of the Pacific Coast where Field had the unanimous backing of the California and Oregon congressional delegations for the new seat.

If President Lincoln was still thinking about redressing the Supreme Court's abuses against the downtrodden contained in the Dred Scott Decision when he nominated Field, what he saw in the Californian was not what he got. Conversely, Field was an ardent proponent of totally-free enterprise unchecked by government regulation. He even went so far as to pervert the Fourteenth Amendment's due process clause protecting the property rights of businesses while opposing its use to defend individuals from the abuses of the powerful. He was often attacked as an apologist for the wealthy establishment, and his opinions were grounded more in his beliefs about natural law than they were in a close reading of the Constitution.[104]

His final years on the Court were marked by a slow descent into senility. According to legal historian David Garrow, the Lincoln appointee acted "like a madman" during some cases, and it became increasingly clear he could not understand the arguments made before him.[105] Obsessed with breaking Chief Justice John Marshall's then-record of thirty-four years, seven months of service on the Bench, the useless justice did just that – by forty-four days when he resigned on December 1, 1897.

Field had further cause to embarrass his Supreme Court mentor, although the events happened long after that fateful night of April 14-15, 1865 in Ford's Theater. Field had a long-standing, personal feud going with David S. Terry, also a former California Chief Justice whom Field had recently jailed for contempt during a long-running legal case involving Terry's wife and her former lover and purported first husband, William Sharon. He was a United States Senator from Nevada who profited greatly from the famed Comstock silver lode. It all turned into what was called the juiciest scandal of its time.

When Judge Terry assaulted Justice Field in a train station near Stockton, California on August 14, 1889, Field's bodyguard, U. S. Marshal David Neagle, shot and killed Judge Terry. Justice of the Peace H.V.S. Swain of San Joaquin County, California issued arrest warrants for both Field and Neagle under the California criminal code, charging them with Terry's murder.[106] Neither was convicted. Ironically, the case continued through the courts for years, finally ending up at the U. S. Supreme Court on which Field was sitting as an Associate Justice. He recused himself from the deliberations and was ultimately acquitted. Stephen Johnson Field holds the distinction of being the only member of the United States Supreme Court arrested for murder.

Personality traits notwithstanding, Field does have some modern-day support. Timothy Sandefer, senior staff attorney at the Pacific Legal Foundation, displays what might be parochial pride when he states:

> "Lincoln's finest appointment was surely Stephen Field, the larger-than-life '49er who became the first Californian on the Supreme Court. Field, a pioneer of substantive due process theory and a staunch defender of the property rights and freedom of contract that were fundamental to the Gilded Age, had a bigger effect on the law than any justice until Oliver Wendell Holmes. Even today, Field's precedents remain among the most important in history."[107]

Second Thoughts — William T. Harper

Lincoln, despite his strenuous objections to the injustices against the African-Americans as evidenced by the Supreme Court's 1857 denial of Dred Scott's claim his Constitutional rights had been violated, then went ahead and appointed Justice Field as the new, tenth Supreme Court Associate Justice. This was a man who later dissented in *Strauder v. West Virginia*, a case holding the exclusion of African-Americans from a jury that convicted African-American (no first name available) Strauder of murder, was a violation of the Fourteenth Amendment's Equal Protection Clause. Field also joined the majority on the Supreme Court infamous 1896 case of *Plessy v. Ferguson* that upheld the constitutionality of racial segregation even in public accommodations such as railroads under the "separate but equal" doctrine. Had it not been for John Wilkes Booth's bullet into the back of Abraham Lincoln's head on April 14, 1865 in Ford's Theater, how could the President not have had *Second Thoughts* about this nomination?

* * *

The pressures upon a president in considering Supreme Court appointments are now, and in most cases have been, immense since the inception of the Court in 1789. Those pressures come from all directions, not the least of which are the candidates' qualifications for filling the post. Other considerations for a president come from personal friendships, from influential friends and family members of potential candidates leaning on a president, from political debts owed (or presumed to be owed) to a candidate by the president, from political parties and considerations, to name but a few. Candidates and their surrogates angling for the honor further compound many of these factors. Nowhere are such pressures more obvious than they were upon President Abraham Lincoln when it came to appointing a successor to Roger Brooke Taney (of *Dred Scott v. Sandford* infamy) as Chief Justice of the Supreme Court after he died in office on October 12, 1864.

Historians generally agree there were four primary candidates President Lincoln seriously considered – all for different but compelling reasons. At one time or another, all were members of the president's cabinet. Alphabetically-speaking, they were:

U. S. Attorney General Edward Bates, 3/5/61-11/24/64
U. S. Postmaster General Montgomery Blair, 3/5/61-9/24/64
Secretary of the Treasury Salmon P. Chase, 3/7/61-6/30/64
Secretary of War Edwin M. Stanton, 1/20/62-5/28/68

President Lincoln is joined by his Cabinet members, notably Edward Bates extreme right of the picture, Edwin M. Stanton sitting extreme left, Salmon P. Chase standing arms folded, and Montgomery Blair (standing next to seated Interior Secretary Caleb Smith – with long white beard).

Secretary of War Stanton (who obviously did not get appointed to the Court as noted in his Cabinet office tenure dates above) wanted the job to get away from the pressures of directing what historian Bruce Catton later called "Mr. Lincoln's War." By 1864, three years of many failures and few triumphs by the Union Armies in the field had worn the Secretary down physically and mentally. He, too, as was his president, was deeply distressed by infighting and blame-gaming among Union Army generals reluctant to fight. In serving his country, Stanton had sacrificed the financial fortune he had acquired via a highly successful pre-war legal career. A lifetime salary as Chief Justice of the Supreme Court would have relieved him of further monetary woes.

Postmaster General Blair was the only member of the Lincoln cabinet who supported the President's decision to reinforce Fort Sumter prior to the Confederates' attack there that launched the Civil War on April 12, 1861 – less than six weeks after Abraham Lincoln took office as the Nation's sixteenth president on March 4. In a modern-day colloquialism, Montgomery Blair subsequently "took the bullet" for President Lincoln and he nobly resigned from the cabinet. He felt, and Lincoln agreed that his presence, as the only hard-liner in the cabinet when it came to emancipation policies, would help insure Lincoln rival,

General John C. Fremont. The general was another disgruntled Radical Republican opponent, ala Salmon Portland Chase, who did not get the Republican Party's 1864 presidential nomination. Constantly "at war" within the war among the Lincoln cabinet members over the Civil War's conduct, Blair strongly felt – as did his influential family members even more so – that the Postmaster General was entitled to the Supreme Court post due to his loyalty to the President.

Attorney General Bates, another cabinet member and potential rival of Lincoln for the presidency in 1860, often disagreed with the President on the conduct of the war but their relations remained warm and friendly. It was the Attorney General who had the responsibility for enforcing the Commander-in-Chief's orders (later overruled by the Supreme Court) to make military arrests of civilians deemed to be acting in any manner against the conduct of the war. It was the Attorney General, also ailing and contemplating an easier life away from the tribunals of war and into those of seeming lesser import as assigned to the Supreme Court vacated-office of Chief Justice Taney, who felt it would be a "suitable reward for his devotion and service."[108]

Secretary of the Treasury Chase, a former U. S. Senator from Ohio and twice-elected governor of the Buckeye State, spent his entire three years in the Treasury post unabashedly and often embarrassingly campaigning for the presidency and also for a position on the Supreme Court, even to the point of multiple threats of resignation as Treasury Secretary if he did not get the latter job. The president finally took him up on his bluff and accepted his resignation. Chase, ever the grateful one, then ran (unsuccessfully) against Lincoln for the Republican presidential nomination in 1864. Nonetheless, the president still felt obliged to fulfill a verbal commitment he had made at one point or another to Chase in the latter's quest for the Supreme Court appointment.

* * *

It was from this *Team of Rivals* (so named in Doris Kearns Goodwin's 2005 book), colleagues and friends President Lincoln had to choose the next Chief Justice of the United States Supreme Court. In the end, it was a somewhat surprising choice, one that left many of his contemporaries having second thoughts. Lincoln chose Chase even though he had committed the unpardonable political sin of seeking to wrest the Republican nomination from Lincoln in 1864 by use of the extensive patronage of the Treasury Department.[109] What perplexed many at the time was that Lincoln and Chase were enemies in the same tent. A Chase associate later wrote that "personal relations between Mr. Lincoln and Mr. Chase were never cordial. They were about as unlike in appearance, in education, manners, in taste, and temperament, as two eminent men could be."[110]

Chase's peripatetic political posturing had him as a former Whig, a former Abolition Party founder, a former Free Soiler, a former Know-Nothing, and a former Democrat turned Republican. He battled Lincoln – whom he called "incompetent" and "confused" – for the 1860 Republican Party presidential nomination and lost. He even sought to oust Lincoln from the presidency by organizing a secret effort to deny the President's re-election in 1864.

According to Indiana Congressman George Julian, "Early in January [1864] an organized movement was set afoot in the interest of Mr. Chase for the Presidency.... I found the committee inharmonious, and composed, in part, of men utterly unfit and unworthy to lead in such a movement. It was fearfully mismanaged. A confidential document known as the 'Pomeroy circular,' assailing Mr. Lincoln and urging the claims of Mr. Chase, was sent to numerous parties, and of course [it] fell into the hands of Mr. Lincoln's friends." The result was one of Chase's several offered resignations – which the president rejected – as he did with other suggestions that he should dismiss Chase: "Let him alone; he can do no more harm in here than he can outside."[111]

Another similar version of Chase's self-preoccupation was described in 2002 by then-Chief Justice William Rehnquist when he said: "For most men the Chief Justiceship would have been enough, but not for Salmon P. Chase. He was an able man, a devoted foe of slavery, but an egotist through and through. One of his detractors said that there were four persons, rather than three, in [Chase's] Trinity."[112] Another observer said, "His tenure in that office is generally considered to have been undistinguished. He could not overcome his lust for the White House and continued to involve himself in Republican politics even after his elevation to the Court."[113]

Lincoln selected Chase primarily for the Court to "get him out of the way." Furthermore, Lincoln had "...three reasons why Chase should be appointed and one reason why he should not be. In the first place, he occupies a larger space in the public mind, with reference to the office, than any other person. Then we want a man who will sustain the Legal Tender Act, and the Proclamation of Emancipation.... But he wants to be president [and he] can never be president."[114] Chase's desire for the presidency never left him. He became a presidential candidate at the Republican convention in 1868, and when that convention turned to U. S. Grant, he became a candidate at the Democratic convention.[115] Obviously, Chase sought the position of President – no matter the Party nor the philosophy.

The correspondence of the day and contemporary journals indicate the President finally had some *Second Thoughts* as he got tired of the Secretary's carping, of his second-guessing, of his whining, of his campaigning for the job, of his back-biting, and his other acts – some of which bordered on subversion. However, Lincoln also believed Chase would judicially sustain the war-mandated issuance of paper money to pay its costs and repay its debts. The first U.S. federal currency was printed in 1862, during Chase's tenure as Secretary of the Treasury. Thus, it was his responsibility to design the notes. In an effort to further his political career, his own face appeared on a variety of U.S. paper currency. Not too long after Lincoln's death, Chase's judicial opinion on that matter was exactly opposite of that which Lincoln had expected him to take. As Interior Secretary John Usher put it, Chase's "opinions as a jurist were the opposite his views as a statesman."[116] This was evident when as Chief Justice he would declare the Legal Tender Acts unconstitutional after having advocated it as Treasury Secretary.

The Supreme Court nomination for Chase was primarily a political decision made to placate the uneasy Radical Republican wing of the party – as was Blair's resignation – during a heated 1864 presidential race, the conclusion of which would dramatically affect the outcome of the war. Chase, whose nomination to the Court was consented to by a voice vote in the Senate, took office on December 15, 1864. He served there until death on May 7, 1873. In this particular case, Lincoln – though he had many second thoughts about Chase – didn't live long enough to have one about his nomination of Chase as Taney's replacement. Unfortunately for the President and the beleaguered Nation, Lincoln was assassinated exactly four months after he got Chase "out of the way" – an exile that may well have led to the speedy conclusion of The War Between the States. The President also didn't live long enough to see Chase make another u-turn back to the Democratic Party where he ran for president in 1868 and then seek the Liberal Republican nomination that went to Horace Greeley in 1872. Nor was Lincoln around to wonder when Salmon P. Chase was another Justice labeled as "the least qualified person to sit on the high court."[117]

* * *

Lincoln legal scholar John J. Duff described President Lincoln as "a man of pedestrian judgment, [who] came to conclusions slowly and carefully and only after due deliberation and sober, second thoughts…." No doubt, "Honest Abe" had second thoughts about some of his Supreme Court candidates.[118]

Among those presenting problems for the President was "his old friend, David. Davis." David Davis, a Maryland born (1815) ex-patriot who moved to Bloomington, Illinois where he established a law office after earning a Yale law degree in 1835. Elected to the Illinois legislature in 1844 and while as a state circuit-court judge (1848-1862) he became a close friend of another young barrister, Abraham Lincoln.

The difficulties started immediately upon Lincoln's election in November of 1864. According to Lincoln legal scholar John J. Duff, Davis – who did yeoman service as Lincoln's campaign manager – presumed on their friendship and his role in securing the presidential nomination for Lincoln. Davis wanted pay-back and his patronage demands grated on the President and Lincoln's newly-perceived remoteness grated on Davis. Their relationship suffered…. Davis accompanied the President-elect to Washington in February 1861 with visions of power and influence – none of which were realized. In fact there is evidence that Davis presumed too much on this trip, annoying the President…. Lincoln spoke after the inauguration about Davis with "extreme irritability," emphasizing "in the bitterest terms against Davis's greed and importunity for office, and summarized his disgust in these words: 'I know it is an awful thing for me to say, but I already wish I was back home…'." Instead, it was Davis who returned back home to Illinois.[119]

An attorney who knew both Judge Davis and President Lincoln said he didn't "think Lincoln held Davis very close to his heart: he was too loquacious - too vain - too vacillating in his friendships…[and] Lincoln never had any intention of appointing Davis to any office at all & was disgusted at Davis' hoggishness after office for himself, for his cousin and for all his personal friends…."[120]

It took sixteen months and the intervention of a mutual friend to get Davis to the Supreme Court but only after Lincoln had nominated two other candidates, Samuel Miller and Noah Swayne. Davis and Lincoln along with Miller and Swayne agreed slavery was wrong, which is one of the reasons why they were nominated to the Supreme Court. But, being on the Supreme Court didn't stop Justice Davis from giving the President unsolicited advice about politics and policy. For instance, he boasted about a conversation with the President urging him to reconstruct his cabinet, and change his emancipation policy, as the only means of saving the Country.[121]

Historian David M. Silver wrote: "Justice Davis did not hesitate to write to Lincoln about political matters and on several occasions intervened to support certain candidates for office or to obtain political favors. …At times Justice Davis brought friends to see the President, wrote him notes of congratulations, asked for political favors, and gave Lincoln advice - sometimes unsolicited and undesired. He particularly objected to the use of military courts when there were civilian alternatives and President Lincoln's 1862 suspension of *habeas corpus* for civilians held by Union military authorities…."[122]

Four years later, Davis wrote the Supreme Court's opinion in *ex parte Milligan* effectively overruling Lincoln's wartime suspension of *habeas corpus*. Davis reportedly disliked serving in the job of his dreams, the Supreme Court, and found the appellate branch disagreeable for the hard study and labor it required. As one commentator remarked on Davis' career on the Court, "...it is surprising that it took him so long to discover that he would really be better off in the Senate."[123] Another of the justices with his heart in the world of politics, Davis – while still on the Bench – was nominated for President by the Labor Reform party which was opposed to the policies of President U. S. Grant. Davis ultimately traded his robes for a one-term seat in the U. S. Senate.

It is reported the basis for the Lincoln/Davis friendship in pre-Presidential days came from Lincoln's love of story-telling and Davis' love of listening to stories. Some stories the President later told and some stories Davis heard during the Presidential days were more than enough to give both of them an abundance of "sober, *Second Thoughts*."

* * *

Chapter XVI
Frustration for the First President Johnson
(Term in Office: April 15, 1865-March 4, 1869)

Former Tennessee Senator and since March 4, 1865 Vice President, Andrew Johnson succeeded the assassinated Lincoln as President of the United States. Johnson ascended to his Vice President position only because as a Democrat who supported President Lincoln's war efforts, he was expected to secure the votes of the most avid abolitionists and thereby assure the Republican president's 1864 re-election. In retrospect, such a compromise doesn't seem necessary as the Lincoln-Johnson ticket – with the help of some significant military victories by the Union Army in 1864 – won the Electoral College vote in the then twenty-five states of the Union by a whopping 212-21 vote over former Union Army General George B. McClellan (the eleven states of the Confederacy did not participate in the 1864 presidential election[1]). The Tennessean took the presidential oath of office immediately following the death of the martyred president on April 15, 1865.

The seventeenth president of the United States instantly ran into widespread public disapproval (some even charging him with complicity in his predecessor's murder) and Congressional firestorms – not the least of which came with Supreme Court implications. Determined to not allow this new "Southerner" President to thwart efforts by those in the Senate and elsewhere who wanted to punish the breakaway states by destroying all vestiges of the Confederacy above and beyond slavery, the Reconstructionists quickly passed an 1866 Judicial Courts Act that reduced the size of Lincoln's Supreme Court from ten members to seven via attrition.

It meant the Senate would neither advise on nor consent to President Johnson's nomination of conservative Republican Henry Stanbery to the Court in 1866 following the 1865 death of Justice Catron. Via the passage of the obviously vindictive 1866 Judicial Courts Act, Congress effectively barred the Tennessean from naming any new justices at all. This was accomplished through a statute that forbade new appointments "until the number of associates shall be reduced to six," not including the Chief Justice. At that point, due to the death of Justice

---

[1] Although there are those who claim the Confederate States of America (CSA) consisted of thirteen states, only Alabama, Florida, Georgia, Louisiana, Mississippi, South Carolina and Texas – later joined by Virginia, North Carolina, Arkansas, and Tennessee – officially joined the CSA. Border states Missouri and Kentucky were sympathetic to "the cause" but did not join the CSA.

Catron, there were nine justices sitting on the ten-member Court. When Justice Swayne died of yellow fever in July of 1867, the Court dropped to eight members until Congress again intervened, after Johnson had left the White House and Ulysses S. Grant succeeded him as president. On April 10, 1869, Congress passed the Circuit Judges Act, amending the judicial system in part by increasing the number of Supreme Court justices, to take effect the first Monday in December of that year, and the size of the Court reverted back to the nine members, at which number it still stands today. That later left Johnson's successor, President Grant, with only one vacancy to fill and when Justice Grier resigned on January 31, 1870, he had two.

In retrospect, it's hard to imagine that President Andrew Johnson had any regrets with his nomination of Henry Stanbery as an Associate Justice on the United States Supreme Court other than, perhaps, to Mr. Stanbery himself for the embarrassment of the rejection the Senate put him through. He was a victim of circumstances and did go on to become Johnson's Attorney General. Ultimately he became a member of Johnson's defense team in the President's impeachment trial of 1868. But this entire process had a distinct bearing on the workings of the Supreme Court – the use of, or even the threat of, altering the size of the Court up or down to suit either the President's or the Senate's political agenda. There have been at least two occasions when Congress has altered the size of the Court strictly for political reasons. In the waning days of Federalist President John Adams' administration, a sympathetic Congress passed the Judicial Act of 1801. It reduced the size of the six-man Court by one in an effort to deny new Democrat-Republican President Thomas Jefferson the chance to appoint a like-minded Justice. Not to be outdone, the ensuing Democrat-Republican reversed the 1801 Act by passing the Judiciary Act of 1802 that brought the Court's size back to six.

After two later Judiciary Acts (1807 and 1837) raised the Court's size to nine – primarily because of the growth of the country's size – politics really reared its ugly head in the 1860s. The new Republican Party gave the new Republican President the Judicial Act of 1863 and a tenth seat on the Court in an effort to counter the Democrats' majority thereon. Then, after Republican President Lincoln was assassinated and the Democrat President Andrew Johnson took over, the Congress passed the Judicial Act of 1866 reducing the size of the Court to seven, assuring Johnson would not get the chance to appoint Justices who agreed with his stance in the Reconstruction of the Nation after the Civil War. And as soon as Johnson was out of office and Republican President Grant was in, the Congress passed the Judicial Act of 1869 that brought the Court's size back to nine – where it has stood ever since. President Johnson's frustration with the political system, something a lot more than the expected checks and balances, may have given him *Second Thoughts*. The

Second Thoughts   William T. Harper

jockeying for power between the executive and legislative branches of government, particularly in the early 1800s and the late 1860s, shows that politics truly is a game of hardball.

* * *

Chapter XVII
Grant's New Battlefield
(Term in Office: 1869-1877)

The man christened Hiram Ulysses Grant on April 27, 1822 was later termed "the greatest general of his age and one of the greatest strategists of any age" by historian J. F. C. Fuller. If the later-named Ulysses Simpson Grant had made the same mistakes in picking his Civil War generals as he did as U. S. President picking his Supreme Court justices, the War Between the States could very well have gone on for another four years.

President Ulysses Grant's Nominees (in reverse order)					
Name	Replacing	Nominated	Vote	Result	& Date
Morrison Waite[12]	Chase	Jan 19, 1874	63-0	C	Jan 21, 1874
Caleb Cushing[13]	Chase	Jan 9, 1874		W	Jan 13, 1874
Geo. Williams[14]	Chase	Dec 1, 1873		W	Jan 8, 1874
Ward Hunt	Nelson	Dec 3, 1872	V	C	Dec 11, 1872
Joseph Bradley	(new seat)	Feb 7, 1870	46-9	C	Mar 21, 1870
William Strong	Grier	Feb 7, 1870		C	Feb 18, 1870
Edwin Stanton[15]	Grier	Dec 20, 1869	46-11	C	Dec 20, 1869
Ebenezer Hoar	(new seat)	Dec 14, 1869	24-33	R	Feb 3, 1870

[12] –for Chief Justice   [13,14] -for Chief Justice, failed   [15] -Died before oath   C=Confirmed   R=Rejected   W=Withdrawn   V=Voice Vote. This chart lists only nominations officially submitted to the Senate; does not include nominations announced but never officially submitted. www.senate.gov/pagelayout/reference/nominations/Nominations.htm

  It is truly amazing, for instance, the difficulties President Grant had in filling the Supreme Court opening left by Chief Justice Chase's death on May 7, 1873. According to Chief Justice William Rehnquist in a May 15, 2004 dedication speech at the Ohio Judicial Center in Columbus,[124] Grant offered the post to:

1. Senator Roscoe Conkling of New York, an old political ally who turned it down.[m]
2. Associate Justice Samuel Miller was considered.

---

[m] See page 107 for the irony of this offer to Conkling.

3. Associate Justice Noah Swayne was considered.
4. Associate Justice Joseph Bradley was considered. Grant then decided he didn't want to give the Chief Justiceship to a current member of the Court.
5. Senator Timothy Howe of Wisconsin was offered the post and turned it down.
6. Senator Oliver Morton of Indiana also turned it down.
7. Secretary of State Hamilton Fish was offered the post but he turned it down because he felt he was not qualified.
8. Caleb Cushing, in an "interim" deal, was offered the Chief Justice post if he would agree to "resign" before Grant left office. That fell through when the rest of Grant's cabinet voiced strong objections.
9. Attorney General George Williams – nominated, but denied by Senate opposition.
10. Caleb Cushing suggested again and this time without "strings," but he also failed again – because, in large part, of his "treasonous" communication with Jefferson Davis prior to the Civil War.[n]
11. Morrison Waite – finally, finally made it through the process.

Thus, at least ten times, President U. S. Grant had *Second Thoughts*. And that, according to latter-day Chief Justice William Rehnquist, was just for appointing a successor to Chief Justice Salmon Portland Chase.

* * *

President Grant had another pair of opportunities to shape the Court to his judicial philosophy. Both failed. First he picked Ebenezer R. Hoar for the new Congress-mandated ninth seat. After an extended battle in the Senate, Grant's New England candidate was rejected 24-33 by the Upper House on political grounds. Almost at the same time and to the other open seat – that of Justice Robert Grier – President Grant named the bullet-proof former Secretary of War Edwin M. Stanton. In less than forty-eight hours, a raucous Senate in its advice and consent process, speedily approved the man who proclaimed on April 15, 1865 that the martyred President Abraham Lincoln "belonged [sic] to the Ages." Five days before Christmas in 1869, Stanton was confirmed as a Supreme Court Justice by a 46-11 vote. The only problem there for President Grant – among others – was that the newest Associate Justice of the Supreme

---

[n] See pages 114-5 for details.

Court never got to take his oath of office. He died four days later, on Christmas Eve. For President Grant, it was two up and two down. Thus, the two vacancies still existed. The hero of Appomattox suffered more setbacks in his Court appointments than he ever did on any Civil War battlefield.

* * *

There was one more second thought the Civil War hero could have had, but the fates intervened. It is said American Army generals who end up as Presidents are inclined to appoint old friends to the High Court. George Washington did. Six of his nominees served with him in the field during the Revolutionary War. Likewise, ex-General Grant appointed his Civil War direct boss, former Secretary of War Edwin Stanton, to the Supreme Court. As noted above, Stanton died before he could take his seat on the Bench. That act of God saved Grant from the embarrassment of later charges claiming his nominee was a conspirator in the Lincoln assassination plot in April of 1865!

In a deathbed confession on July 2, 1868, Colonel Lafayette C. Baker, head of the presidential protection detail (the newly-formed forerunner to the U. S. Secret Service) said that Stanton was involved in the plot to assassinate Lincoln. Baker implicated Stanton, eleven members of Congress, twelve U. S. Army officers, three U. S. Navy officers and twenty-four civilians.[125]

There were those who subscribed to the Conspiracy Theory in the murder of President Lincoln (and many did in its immediate aftermath and well into the next century). Those, like Otto Eisenschiml in his book *Why Was Lincoln Murdered*, found all kinds of clues leading back to the complicity of Lincoln's Secretary of War Edwin Stanton. It is a fact that Stanton was against Lincoln's mild post-war Reconstruction policies and wanted him out of office so a more radical and punitive Reconstructionist policy could be employed. Another fact is that General Grant and his wife Julia were expected to attend the play *Our American Cousin* at Ford's Theater with the President and Mrs. Lincoln on that Good Friday night, April 14, 1865, but the general declined at the last minute. Eisenschiml argued that Grant's absence was due to an order by Stanton to change his plans for that evening.

Among Stanton's numerous and seemingly mysterious behaviors and events were, according to Eisenschiml:

- Not alerting the security at the capitol's Navy Yard Bridge (over which the assassin John Wilkes Booth escaped),

- The mysterious interruption of telegraph communications,
- Secretly arranging to have Booth killed before being brought to trial (a theory later reiterated following Jack Ruby's murder of John F. Kennedy assassin Lee Harvey Oswald in 1963),
- And the suppression of evidence by removing pages from Booth's diary.[126]

It must be said here most history scholars of recent vintage dispute Eisenschiml's hypotheses. But the conspiracy viewpoint had not yet reached its peak when President Grant appointed Secretary Stanton to the Supreme Court. If the conspiracy theory had become louder among "the nattering nabobs of negativism" when Grant made the appointment in 1869, both he and the U. S. Senate approving it would surely have had *Second Thoughts*.

But undaunted, the former general who attained so much of his battlefield success "because he never looked back," maintained that stance as President when it came to picking his Supreme Court nominees. Trying again, on February 7, 1870, the dauntless President appointed both William Strong (to the Justice Grier seat) and Joseph P. Bradley (to the open seat Mr. Hoar failed to win). If ex-President Grant ever looked back at his Bradley nomination, he could not have liked much of what he saw.

* * *

President Grant selected Bradley (and Strong) in an effort to "pack the Court" and ensure the preservation of the contested Legal Tender Acts which were passed in an effort to pay off much of the Civil War national debt and (unsuccessfully it turned out) prevent a financial crisis during the Grant administration. Born in New York State in 1813, Bradley was an 1836 graduate of New Jersey's Rutgers College and a self-taught lawyer who was admitted to the New Jersey bar in 1839. With the help of his wife's father, William Hornblower, chief justice of the New Jersey Supreme Court, Bradley built a successful law practice with a large business clientele. He became an expert in patent and railroad law which gave him frequent contact with the federal judicial system. With the opening of a new seat on the Supreme Court as a result of the Judiciary Act of 1869, Bradley welcomed Grant's invitation to fill that seat and, as was expected, he voted in 1871 to uphold the Legal Tender Acts' constitutionality.

What happened two years later was surely not what was expected by President Grant. According to a book review published in March 2008 by the Richmond County Bar Association in Staten Island, New York: On

Second Thoughts   William T. Harper

Easter Sunday, April 13, 1873, "a small army of white ex-Confederate soldiers, enraged after attempts by freedmen to assert their new rights granted through the Emancipation Proclamation and several amendments to the U. S. Constitution, killed more than sixty African-Americans (some say as many as 150) who had occupied a courthouse to protect a duly elected white Republican judge." This Louisiana episode – known as "The Colfax Massacre" – culminated in a series of subsequent courtroom dramas.

    The perpetrators walked out when the first jury could not arrive at a verdict and a mistrial was declared in a court presided over by Fifth Circuit Judge William B. Woods, who would be named to the Supreme Court seven years later. The second trial was presided over by both Woods and the circuit-riding Supreme Court Justice Joseph P. Bradley. This time, all the defendants were acquitted of murder.

    Ultimately, the case wound up before the Supreme Court in the *U.S. v. Cruikshank, et al* (92 US 542 [1875]). Sixteen specific charges were brought against the ringleaders of The Colfax Massacre – all of them as Civil Rights Violations. Eight of the charges were dismissed preemptively as being duplicates of other charges. Only the third charge hinted at "an intent to deprive the same persons [the victims] 'of their respective several lives and liberty of person, without due process of law'." The highest court in the land totally fudged this issue with this typical response in one of the sixteen charges:

> Inasmuch, therefore, as it does not appear in these counts that the intent of the defendants was to prevent these parties from exercising their right to vote on account of their race, &c., it does not appear that it was their intent to interfere with any right granted or secured by the constitution or laws of the United States. We may suspect that race was the cause of the hostility; but it is not so averred. This is material to a description of the substance of the offence [sic], and cannot be supplied by implication. Everything essential must be charged positively, and not inferentially. The defect here is not in form, but in substance.

    As the Richmond County Bar Association article says in its analysis of the Supreme Court's judgment, it "ruled that protections offered to former slaves by the 14th Amendment against racial violence did not apply to the actions of individuals, but only to the actions of state governments. Judge Bradley's dismissal of the case was affirmed, and the Supreme Court held that the African-Americans must look to their state for protection. As a result of this decision, the Enforcement Act could not be used to protect the newly franchised African-American against groups such as the Ku Klux Klan or other white supremacist organizations.[127] Thus the Supreme Court upheld Justice Bradley's verdict of "Not Guilty" in this atrocity. It wouldn't be until the Civil Rights Act of 1964 that the effects of this ruling would be overturned.

In another case that surely went against President Grant's stated desire for universal suffrage, *Bradwell v. Illinois*, 83 U.S. (16 Wall.) 130, 21 L. Ed. 442 (1872), Bradley concurred in the decision to reject Myra Bradwell's bid to practice law in Illinois. Ms. Bradwell had studied law with her husband and had passed the Illinois bar examination. However, Illinois denied her admission to the bar because she was female. Ms. Bradwell appealed her case to the U.S. Supreme Court, claiming that the Fourteenth Amendment to the U.S. Constitution protected her right to practice in her chosen profession. The Supreme Court ruled otherwise. Bradley wrote in concurring *dicta* that God had created woman to be wife and mother, not lawyer.[128]

According to the online Law and Legal Reference Library, "Bradley's Supreme Court and circuit court opinions often fail the test of time. Although his contemporaries praised him for his keen intellect and legal acumen, many of his decisions are, by today's standards, objectionable in outcome and reasoning."[129] Even his colleague sitting on the same Bench, "the Great Dissenter" Associate Justice John M. Harlan, said Bradley had reasoned his way into a monstrous error. Bradley's opinion in the Civil Rights Cases, according to Justice Harlan, "proceeds, as it seems to me, upon grounds entirely too narrow and artificial. The substance and the spirit of the recent [A]mendments of the [C]onstitution have been sacrificed by a subtle and ingenious criticism."[130] Could not President Grant have wondered, "Who is this guy?" Others have.

* * *

Within six weeks of Edwin Stanton's untimely death and Ebenezer Hoar's Senate rejection, the Chief Executive brought his Supreme Court batting average up to .500 – two for four – as both of these nominees, Joseph Bradley and William Strong, made it to the Bench. Then, on November 28, 1872, the Grim Reaper called on Justice Samuel Nelson (a President Tyler appointee in 1845) and General Grant sent the name of Ward Hunt to the Senate for its advice and consent, which was received on December 11, 1872. For the Civil War general/president, that appointment became the greatest blunder since General Ambrose Burnside led the Union Army into a meat-grinder defeat at the battle of Fredericksburg, Virginia in December of 1862. If ever a Supreme Court justice gave his nominator a severe case of the *Second Thoughts*, it was Ward Hunt.

Ward Hunt, a native of New York State, active in politics as a member of the state assembly, and mayor of the city of Utica. Formerly a

Jacksonian Democrat, he actually went on to become one of the founders of the Republican Party in New York. Elected to the State Supreme Court, he became its chief judge. His political mentor was the abrasive but powerful New York state Republican Party boss Roscoe Conkling who had an affair with Kate Chase Sprague, the wife of a Senate colleague (and daughter of Supreme Court Chief Justice Salmon P. Chase).[131] Reportedly, Senator William Sprague unsuccessfully went after Conkling with a shotgun at the time.

Even so, Conkling also "was an avowed enemy of woman suffrage."[132] As a confidant of President Grant, Conkling convinced him to nominate 62-year-old Judge Hunt for a U. S. Supreme Court justiceship on December 3, 1872. (The fact that the Conkling protégé Ward Hunt actually sat as an Associate Justice on Chief Justice Chase's court for six months had to provide some second thoughts for both.)

For whatever reasons, Justice Hunt did not contribute much to the highest court in the land. According to the U. S. Supreme Court's media information site, "To say that Hunt accomplished little on the Court would be an overstatement."[133] In his book, *The Constitution in the Supreme Court*, Author David P. Currie described Justice Hunt (along with justices Clifford and Swayne) as "decrepit."[134] A third author wrote "...Hunt proved to be at once the most judicially loyal and least effective of Grant's appointees during his brief tenure of nine years on the Court."[135] Had such damnation preceded the appointment, it would surely have been enough to cause second thoughts for President Grant. But unfortunately, Ward Hunt quickly became an extreme embarrassment for the president as well as the nation's entire legal community.

It was in a mere matter of months, while Justice Hunt was "riding the circuit," his ineptitude became glaringly apparent. And it happened in no obscure nor minor way. The judge's negative notoriety became vividly showcased for the entire world to see in one of the most closely watched and argued trials of the 19th Century – that of famed and defamed suffragette Susan B. Anthony on charges of illegal voting. A leading historical light in the women's suffrage movement, Ms. Anthony's journey to legal fame began, according to Margaret Truman (President Harry S. Truman's only child) in her book, *Women of Courage*, with a newspaper editorial. Wrote Ms. Truman:

> It began on Friday morning, November 1, 1872. Susan was reading the morning paper at her home in Rochester. There, at the top of the editorial page of the *Democrat and Chronicle*, was an exhortation to the city's residents:
>
> > Now register! Today and tomorrow are the only remaining opportunities. If you were not permitted to

vote, you would fight for the right, undergo all privations for it, face death for it. You have it now at the cost of five minutes' time to be spent in seeking your place of registration and having your name entered. And yet, on Election Day, less than a week hence, hundreds of you are likely to lose your votes because you have not thought it worthwhile to give the five minutes. Today and tomorrow are your only opportunities. Register now!

Susan B. Anthony read the editorial again. Just as she thought, it said nothing about being addressed to men only. With a gleam in her eye, she put down the paper and summoned her sister Guelma, with whom she lived. The two women donned their hats and cloaks and went off to call on two other Anthony sisters who lived nearby. Together, the four women headed for the barbershop on West Street, where voters from the Eighth Ward were being registered.[136]

From such pop-guns, great battles begin.
The *United States v. Susan B. Anthony* was a criminal trial in the federal courts. In the federal election in November 1872, Ms. Anthony, the best-known advocate of woman suffrage in American history, registered to vote and did, along with fourteen other women in Rochester, N. Y. The government then charged her with the crime of voting without "the legal right to vote in said election district" because she was "then and there a person of the female sex." In 1872 and throughout the previous history of the Republic, that was illegal.
The Susan Brownell Anthony trial opened on June 17, 1873 before a jury of twelve men (naturally) and a packed courthouse that even included former president Millard Fillmore, in the village of Canandaigua, New York. The prosecutor in the case, U. S. Attorney Richard Crowley, had reason to be worried about Ms. Anthony's lectures delivered during the preceding weeks in Rochester and its surrounding communities pleading her case. He feared they might "taint" the jury pool. She simply asked, "Is it a crime for a citizen of the United States to vote?" (Obviously the suffragette wasn't alone in "riding the circuit." So too, as mandated, was Supreme Court Associate Justice Ward Hunt riding the circuit with travels bringing him to upstate New York.).
Her speaking engagements and a deluge of newspapers asking the same question – "Is it a crime for a citizen of the United States to vote" – circulated throughout Rochester's Monroe County. This led the prosecutor to believe his ability to get an "uninformed" jury pool was limited. Thus, the presiding judge ordered a change of venue to

Canandaigua, the Ontario County (N.Y.) seat, about thirty miles of rutted roads southeast of the "tainted" Rochester. The judge hearing the case was newly-elected Supreme Court Associate Justice Ward Hunt, presiding because this Federal case fell in his Circuit, the Second. Evidently, Judge Hunt also brought some "baggage" with him to the trial in the Canandaigua courthouse – and it wasn't just suitcases holding his clothing as he too "rode the circuit." Ward Hunt was presiding over his first criminal case in his new role as Associate Justice.

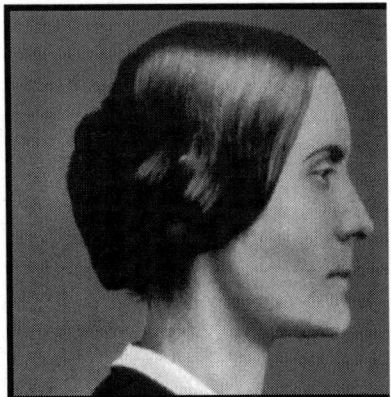
Defendant Susan B. Anthony

The following edited account of the trial is extracted from *The Life and Work of Susan B. Anthony* by Ida Husted Harper (no relation to this author).[137]

Supreme Court Justice Hunt

It was conceded that Miss Anthony was a woman and that she voted on November 5, 1872. [Defense counsel] Judge Henry R. Selden proposed to call Miss Anthony to testify...but the Court [Justice Hunt] held she was not competent as a witness in her own behalf. After making this decision, the Court then admitted all the testimony, as reported, which she gave on the preliminary examination before the commissioner, in spite of her counsel's protest against accepting the version which that officer took of her evidence. The prosecution simply alleged the fact of her having voted. Mr. Selden then addressed the judge and jury in a masterly argument of over three hours' duration, beginning:

The defendant is indicted...for "voting without having a lawful right, to vote. The only alleged ground of illegality of the defendant's vote is that she is a woman. If the same act had been done by her brother under the same circumstances, the act would have been not only innocent but honorable and laudable; but having been done by a woman it is said to be a crime...."

The district-attorney followed with a two hours' speech. Then Judge Hunt, without leaving the bench, delivered a written opinion to the effect that the Fourteenth Amendment, under which Miss Anthony claimed the authority to vote, "was a protection, not to all our rights, but to our rights as citizens of the United States only; that is, the rights existing or belonging to that condition or capacity." At its conclusion *he directed the jury to bring in a verdict of guilty.*

Miss Anthony's counsel insisted that the Court had no power to make such a direction in a criminal case and demanded that the jury be permitted to bring in its own verdict. 'The judge made no reply except to order the clerk to take the verdict. Selden demanded that the jury be polled. Judge Hunt refused, and at once discharged the jury without allowing them any consultation or asking if they agreed upon a verdict. The next day Judge Selden argued the motion for a new trial on seven exceptions, but Judge Hunt denied this.

Ms. Harper further wrote that Roscoe Conkling, an "avowed enemy of woman suffrage" and Justice Hunt's advocate vis-à-vis President Grant's Supreme Court nomination of Hunt, "had an interview with [Justice Hunt] immediately preceding this trial [and] Miss Anthony always has believed that he inspired the course of Judge Hunt and that his decision was written before the trial, a belief shared by most of those associated in the case."[138] Among those believers was Donna Lee Dickerson, who in *The Reconstruction Era*, also charged that Supreme Court Justice Hunt "pulled a piece of paper from under his robe, and began reading an opinion, which he had prepared before the trial started."[139]

Authors Carrie Chapman Catt and Nettie Rogers Shuler described the scene of that June 17th day in 1873:

"When the last word had been spoken, those assembled were shocked to see the presiding Judge draw from his pocket a written opinion, clearly prepared before he had heard evidence or argument. He directed the jury to bring in a verdict of guilty, and when Judge Selden protested at this unwarranted act, he refused to have the jury polled and in the midst of the controversy discharged it!"[140]

"...There was widespread condemnation of Judge Hunt's conduct of the case, and none were more outspoken than some members of the jury who boldly declared that had they had the opportunity they would not have voted guilty. The Albany *Law Journal,* though scornfully disapproving woman suffrage, admitted that the Judge usurped power in taking the case from the jury, and editorial discussion of the question "Can a judge direct a verdict of guilty" was frequent. Those who had sympathy neither with woman suffrage nor the effort to test the Fourteenth Amendment, pronounced Judge Hunt's assumption of authority a dangerous and menacing threat to free government...."[141]

Continuing from Ms. Harper's book, she reported that "scarcely a newspaper in the country sustained Judge Hunt's action." *The Canandaigua Times* thus expressed the general sentiment in an editorial, soon after the trial:

The decisions of Judge Hunt in the Anthony case have been widely criticized, and it seems to us not without reason....

The New York Sun scorched the judge as follows:

Judge Hunt allowed the jury to be impaneled and sworn, and to hear the evidence; but when the case had reached the point of the rendering of the verdict, he directed a verdict of guilty. He thus denied a trial by jury to an accused party in his court; and either through malice, which we do not believe, or through ignorance, which in such a flagrant degree is equally culpable in a judge, he violated one of the most important provisions of the Constitution of the United States....

The Rochester Democrat and Chronicle commented:

In the action of Judge Hunt there was a grand, over-reaching assumption of authority, unsupported by any point in the case itself, but adopted as an established legal principle. And the *Sun* proceeds to say that Judge Hunt "must be impeached and removed...."

The Utica Observer gave this opinion:

We have sought the advice of the best legal and judicial minds in our State in regard to the ruling of Justice Ward Hunt in the case of Susan B. Anthony [and it] is almost universally condemned....

The Legal News, of Chicago...made this pertinent comment:

"Judge Ward Hunt, of the Federal Bench, violated the Constitution of the United States more in convicting Miss

Anthony of illegal voting, than she did in voting; for he had sworn to support it, and she had not."[142]

Supporting the accused, in his inauguration speech on March 4, 1869, President Ulysses S. Grant – anticipating the growing clamor over the women's right to vote – proclaimed to the Nation and the world, "The question of suffrage is one which is likely to agitate the public so long as a portion of the citizens of the nation are excluded from its privileges in any State. It seems to me very desirable that this question should be settled now, and I entertain the hope and express the desire that it may be by the ratification of the fifteenth article of amendment to the Constitution."

Amending the Constitution depends largely how the U. S. Supreme Court deliberates and rules on such amendments. What could be the reaction of a president entertaining hopes of settling the burning universal suffrage question only to later find one of his appointees to that Court, Ward Hunt, tried to douse the flames of that fire and was thus being vilified thoroughly by the newspapers of the day? They said:

> "Judge Ward Hunt, of the Federal Bench, violated the Constitution...."
> "...the ruling of Justice Ward Hunt in [this case] is almost universally condemned...."
> "Judge Hunt "must be impeached and removed...."
> "[Justice Hunt] violated one of the most important provisions of the Constitution...."

As might be expected, Ms. Anthony was similarly incensed by Justice Hunt's predetermination of her "guilt." In her diary that night, Susan Anthony would angrily describe the trial as "the greatest judicial outrage history has ever recorded![143] She was writing about a man acting like a bull-headed anti-feminist refusing to admit he was wrong in his pre-determination of guilt and his deliberate judicial error in denying the defendant a trial by a jury of her peers. In a further embarrassment to President Grant, the role of judge was not enough for Ward Hunt in this case. He acted also as the jury and the executioner of the sentence.

Criticism of Justice Hunt's actions continued unabated. According to an article furnished by the Federal Judicial Center, "In January 1874, Anthony petitioned Congress for a remission of her fine because of the unjust character of her trial. Her congressional allies introduced her petition in the House and the Senate, and the judiciary committees of both houses debated the matter.... In the Senate, Matthew Carpenter...submitted a report condemning Justice Hunt's action. It was "altogether a departure from, and a most dangerous innovation upon, the well-settled method of jury-trial in criminal cases. Such a doctrine renders the trial by jury a farce. [Anthony] had no jury-trial, within the meaning of the Constitution, and her conviction was, therefore, erroneous."[144]

Even into the Twenty-first Century, there are those in the legal world who are still shocked by Justice Hunt's actions back in 1873. According to Michael McMenamin, an Ohio "Super Lawyer" and published author who writes frequently on free speech, "What the judge did was outrageous but, more importantly, it was unconstitutional. It wasn't his opinion that he arguably wrote ahead of time that is offensive," the counselor said as he opened another doorway of condemnation, "it's that it was a JURY TRIAL and he directed a guilty verdict. You can't do that. The Sixth Amendment says so.... In Susie's case, several jury members (who were not polled despite her lawyer's request) said they would have acquitted her. She only needed one...."[145]

Darrell A. Clay, a partner of McMenamin's, also noted that Justice Hunt's ruling "became the most controversial one in the case, eliciting sharp criticism in the press, among lawyers, and in Congress. In an unrelated case in 1895, the Supreme Court forbid the federal courts from directing a verdict of guilty."[146]

Well over a century ago, surely President Ulysses S. Grant must have had *Second Thoughts* relative to his 1872 appointment of Ward Hunt as an Associate Justice of United States Supreme Court. Justice Hunt provided second thoughts about a jurist who acts as both judge and jury, who determines guilt or innocence before hearing one word of testimony, and then violates the same sacred Constitution both of them swore to "protect and defend" by ordering a directed guilty verdict.

* * *

As noted, the hero of Appomattox with an administration caught up in what came to be known as America's "Gilded Age" of corruption and greed, found himself able to get only half of his Supreme Court nominees to the bench. When it came to his selections for the Chief Justice post after Salmon P. Chase died in office in May of 1873, his record grew dismal. A part of that dreary record was George H. Williams, a lawyer from the newly-admitted state of Oregon. Serving as U. S. Attorney General when the President sent his name up to the Hill for confirmation on December 1, 1873, he had been a U.S. Senator from the Beaver State. He had voted in 1868 for the impeachment of President Andrew Johnson. With an unremarkable term as Attorney General, his reputation was damaged by the events surrounding his failed nomination as Chief Justice.

There were allegations that Williams had participated in fraudulent activities involving voting in his home state. The organized bar on the East Coast also feared that as a frontier lawyer from Oregon, Williams was ill-prepared to preside over a Court that decided many complex commercial cases. A man of little formal education, he appeared too undistinguished to serve on the Court. Nonetheless, Grant nominated the inept [Attorney General] Williams...who had recently bungled the *Credit Mobilier* investigation.[147]

    Additionally, the Williams' appointment was shot down for a number of other reasons. One of them was that Williams had used department funds to purchase a carriage with exceptionally handsome horses, handled by a driver with brass-buttoned livery, although Mrs. Williams had purchased the buttons herself. But, Mrs. Williams had socially snubbed a number of senatorial wives, a fact that did no good when the vote came.[148] "Hell hath no fury," it is said. You just don't anger the wife of a Senator – especially one who will be voting on the nomination. President Grant had to withdraw the nomination.

* * *

The general, now midway through his second and last presidential term, turned next to personal friend (one of those historians who later would label as another "crony") Caleb Cushing as his Chief Justice choice the day after withdrawing Williams' name on January 9, 1874. Cushing served four separate terms in the Massachusetts House of Representatives, one in its state senate, and an eight-year term in the U. S. House of Representatives. In light of all this and as one who graduated from Harvard University at age seventeen and admitted to the Massachusetts bar at age twenty-one, Cushing was highly qualified for the post.

    He apparently was, however, ecumenical in his politics, having voiced views as a Republican-Democrat, as a Whig, as a Constitutional Conservative, and again as a Democrat. He was elected mayor of his hometown of Newburyport and served on his state's supreme court. Twice though he was nominated and lost the race for the Massachusetts governor's office. On the national scene, he had further mixed success. He was nominated Secretary of the Treasury in 1843 by President John Tyler but the Senate refused to confirm him. His most significant victory in politics came when another long-time personal friend, President Franklin Pierce, appointed him as U. S. Attorney General (1853-1857). Caleb Cushing had witnessed both winning and losing in the political battlefields.

    Cushing's see-sawing political views actually had him presiding at the 1860 Democratic Party Convention where one of its meetings led to the actual formation of the Confederate States of America and where he met and befriended soon-to-be Confederacy president Jefferson Davis. But then he supported the Union during the Civil War. It was this apparent vacillation and party-hopping throughout his life – plus the fact that he was seventy-four years old when nominated – that led to his downfall as another Supreme Court Chief Justice nominee.

It also didn't help when newspapers such as the *New York Herald* labeled Cushing as "incongruous," "objectionable," and worst of all in those times, "a pro-slavery Democrat." The *Nation* said the President had chosen "the worst man" in a small circle of eminent lawyers. The *New York Times* led its charge against this "turncoat and secessionist," viewing his nomination with "surprise and mortification," citing Cushing's lifelong support of the Democratic Party and opposition to many Reconstruction measures.[149] Adding to the furor of embarrassment for Grant, the *Nation* magazine noted that "the President has at last entered the small circle of eminent lawyers and then with great care has chosen the worst man in it."[150] That'll give you second thoughts.

Adding to the fires of discontent was the surfacing of a friendly letter of recommendation for a clerkship for a Texan named Archibald Roane that Cushing had once written to Jefferson Davis shortly before the Civil War broke out – creating only innuendo but not proof of disloyalty. And finally, the Senate could not decide what Cushing's political views were: a Whig, a Tyler Whig, a Democrat, a Johnson Constitutional Conservative, a Republican or something else. Those shifting allegiances once again caused President Grant to withdraw yet another nomination. This time, it only took four days. The Hero of Vicksburg was obviously having trouble with his vetting processes.

Six days after Cushing returned to his love of writing, on January 19, 1874, President Grant nominated Morrison R. Waite as his third choice for Chief Justice of the United States Supreme Court. The third time was, indeed, the charm. Two days later, a relieved Senate finally consented to the second runner-up for this supremely important post in the Third Estate – though not without some controversy over charges of cronyism. When Waite was confirmed in January 1874, President Lincoln's Secretary of the Navy Gideon Wells commented: "It is a wonder that Grant did not pick up some old acquaintance, who was a stage driver or bartender for the place." Another dissenting opinion declared "Grant's route to appointing Waite was a series of bungles that the *New York Times* described as 'humiliating' and 'scandalous'."[151] Years later, when Grant issued one of his few famous quotes, "My failures have been errors of judgment, not of intent," he may well have been revealing his *Second Thoughts* regarding some of his Supreme Court appointments.

* * *

Chapter XVIII
"Thanks, But No Thanks," President Hayes
(Term in Office: 1877-1881)

He had plenty of trouble getting the Republican Party's nomination in 1876; it took seven ballots. And then he had even more problems being elected president the following November; it took a Congress-mandated fifteen-member Electoral Commission to finally get him there even though he lost the popular vote. As it happened, Rutherford B. Hayes was another who had to have had *Second Thoughts* – at least when he later viewed the actions of William B. Woods, one of the two Supreme Court associate justices he managed to get confirmed by the U. S. Senate.

The presidential election of 1876 was one of the most disputed and intense presidential elections in U. S. history. Samuel J. Tilden, New York Democrat, defeated Ohio Republican Rutherford B. Hayes by 250,000 popular votes. Tilden also had 184 electoral votes to Hayes' 165, with 20 of those votes spanning four states in dispute. The resolution of the disputed states voting ended up in the House of Representatives where it went unresolved. So the House did what it always does – it created a commission. This was a fifteen-member Electoral Commission with five Democrat Senators and five Republican Senators and five Supreme Court Justices – two with each party's leanings and one "neutral." It wasn't until March 2, 1877 – two days before the Presidential Inauguration Day – that in what still is to many an unbelievable turn of events, all twenty of the disputed Electoral College votes from those four states were ultimately declared for Hayes. By a new 185-184 Electoral College vote, Hayes was finally declared the nineteenth president of the United States.

Many historians believe an informal deal was struck to resolve the disputed Hayes-Tilden election situation. Some say that in return for Southern (i.e., Democratic) acceptance of a Hayes victory, the Republicans would withdraw federal troops from the South, thereby ending the often feared and always hated Reconstruction in the former Confederacy. This deal, known as the Compromise of 1877, effectively denied the freed people access to governmental power; power they thought had been granted them by the Emancipation Proclamation and the Fourteenth Amendment to the Constitution (designed to establish civil rights for all) and the Fifteenth Amendment (the right to vote shall not be denied). In effect, the Compromise ended up barring them from voting via local poll taxes the poor could not afford, the "grand-father" clause (you could only vote if your grand-father had voted – and no slave grand-father could have), and other subterfuges limiting their access to the election process.

The newly-elected president – now tagged by some with the election moniker "Rutherfraud" or "His Fraudulency" or "Old 8 to 7" (the Committee vote) was – according to the Rutherford B. Hayes Presidential Center – a strong advocate in words and actions for the rights of Black Americans. His views are boldly stated in a radical, for the times, 1867 speech when he said of them, "Whether we prefer it or not, they are our countrymen, and will remain so forever." In public and private life, he never deviated from these principles.[152]

…As a congressman, the Hayes Center says, he enthusiastically supported the Fourteenth and the Fifteenth Amendments….[153] When running for governor three times in Ohio, he consistently campaigned for Black voting rights. As governor, he fought against those who would repeal his state's vote in favor of the Fourteenth Amendment to the U. S. Constitution. As President (1877-1881), Hayes continued to support the cause of the freed people through conciliation rather than confrontation. He hoped "to get from those States' governors, legislatures, press, and people pledges that the Thirteenth, Fourteenth, and Fifteenth Amendments…be faithfully observed; that the colored people shall have equal rights to labor, education, and the privileges of citizenship." Hayes' Southern policy envisioned full rights for all citizens [and that it would, among other things] eliminate acts of violence committed against Blacks in the name of politics.[154]

* * *

On December 14, 1880, the day after the retirement of President Grant-appointee Associate Justice William Strong from Pennsylvania, President Hayes sent Alabamian William B. Wood's name to the Senate for confirmation as Strong's replacement. In less than a week, the Upper House granted its 39-8 vote of approval. He thus became the first Supreme Court justice from the South appointed to the Bench since before the Civil War – leading some opponents to refer to him as a despised "Carpetbagger." Though the vote to approve was overwhelming, it was also questionable in that only forty-seven of the seventy-six eligible Senators from the then thirty-eight states cast a ballot. What those aye-voting Senators and the President thought they were getting – a Supreme Court justice who would be an advocate for granting its new and returning citizens from the Confederacy all the inalienable rights guaranteed by the Constitution – was not quite what they got.

Woods and President Hayes were both Ohio natives who served in the Union Army during the Civil War, both rising to brevet major generals. Woods fought alongside General William Tecumseh Sherman in his "March to the Sea." After the war, Woods moved to Alabama where he subsequently became active in Republican Party politics. President Grant later appointed him to the Fifth Circuit Court which was composed entirely of states along the Gulf of Mexico. While on that bench, Woods was a strong advocate for the rights granted African-Americans by the Fourteenth Amendment to the Constitution. The Thirteenth and Fourteenth Amendments to the U. S. Constitution were often in conflict – at least in how they were viewed and interpreted by the Supreme Court. The conservative view saw the amendments in narrow terms: the Thirteenth Amendment simply abolished slavery; the Fourteenth granted the freed people citizenship and a measure of relief from state discrimination. The more radical view believed the amendments helped secure all the rights to the freed people and others.

Moreover, the amendments gave the national government authority to protect citizens against both state and private deprivations of rights. Woods' decisions from the Circuit Court in answering the question – did the Fourteenth Amendment protect citizens from hurtful actions of private citizens, or only from hurtful legislation? – seemed to fall into the former category. Before being named to the Supreme Court, Woods agreed with the government's power to protect civil rights. "The rights," he said as U. S. District Judge for the Fifth Circuit, "enumerated in the first eight…[A]mendment[s] of the [C]onstitution of the United States are [*ipso facto*] fundamental privileges of the citizens of the United States…and *the states are inhibited from impairing or abridging them.*"[155]

However, after officially joining the Supreme Court on January 5, 1881, some of Woods' subsequent decisions were diametrically opposed to those he held as a Circuit Court judge. There, he voted the Federal government could punish private violations of civil rights under the Fourteenth Amendment. However, as a Supreme Court justice, he voted with the Court's conservative majority in negating the Civil Rights Act of 1875, saying it exceeded federal power. In another case, involving the Fourteenth Amendment, he struck down the Ku Klux Klan Act of 1871 on the grounds that protection of individuals from private conspiracies was a state, not a federal, function. Justice Woods' "shifting interpretations of the Fourteenth Amendment gave him the appearance of having a muddled judicial philosophy."[156] More than that, noted historian Henry Abraham rated Woods Supreme Court tenure as "mediocre at best…."[157]

Being muddled about the Fourteenth Amendment specifically, and thought of as mediocre in general, had to be enough to cause Rutherford B. Hayes to view Justice William B. Woods with some *Second Thoughts*….

* * *

Second Thoughts — William T. Harper

Never mind second thoughts. Did President Rutherford B. Hayes give *any* thought at all to his nomination of Stanley Matthews as an Associate Justice of the U. S. Supreme Court on January 26, 1881? If ever an appointment to the Bench was doomed to failure, it had to be this one. The odds against success in this case had to be greater than those of Samuel Tilden's winning the final outcome of the 1876 presidential race. How many omens did Hayes miss?

The first one surely had to be the timing of the Matthews nomination following the retirement from the Court by Justice Noah H. Swayne. When Hayes made the nomination, there were only five weeks left in his presidency. The then-sitting Republican President had to work with a 42-33 lame-duck Democrat-controlled Senate; one hardly inclined to give him anything in his remaining thirty-six days in office. On top of that, Matthews himself was seen as a reincarnation of the bubonic plague to many factions around the country.

Thomas Stanley Matthews – he ultimately dropped his first name – built himself a substantial set of credentials in his early years. In the Civil War, he rose to the rank of Colonel in the Union Army while serving under Kenyon College classmate General Rutherford B. Hayes in the Twenty-third Ohio Volunteer Infantry. After the war, he went on to a lucrative law career as a railroad and corporate lawyer. He adopted the Republican Party as his political base where he again prospered, even to the point of successfully arguing for Hayes in his presidential election dispute with Samuel Tilden in 1876.

With people asking "what-was-he-thinking," Republican President Hayes submitted a Republican name for a Supreme Court seat approval to a Democrat Senate. If that wasn't bad enough, the candidate was bitterly opposed by many labor-oriented organizations and their newspaper allies for his work with the "Robber Barons" of the times. Among those ultra-rich industrialists of the Nineteenth Century were eastern railroad magnate Cornelius Vanderbilt, his Western counterparts Leland Stanford and Collis P. Huntington, oilman John D. Rockefeller and the so-labeled prototype of all Robber Barons, financier Jay Gould (for whom Matthews was then working).

The *Louisville Post* asked, "Shall Stanley Matthews who sat in the Senate as an attorney for the Pacific railroads wear the silk gown as their attorney on the bench of the Supreme Court?" ...The *New York Times* argued that Matthews – who had served as president of the National Railway Convention in 1875 – was "superficial in his study and his thought" and was "carried to his conclusions by the intensity of his zeal rather than by the depth and accuracy of his reasoning."[158]

Being seen as wearing "the silk gown" for the railroad while sitting on the Supreme Court Bench likewise roused the wrath of various labor organizations which were just starting to feel their oats in the second half of the Nineteenth Century. One of the most vociferous was the Grange movement, which had reached its membership peak in 1875 (heading into the Hayes-Tilden election). Despite its origin as a fraternal order in 1867, the Grange was overtly political by the 1870s and through the 1880s. The Grange and its members were in a life-and-death struggle with the railroads which completely controlled the rates the farmers had to pay, exorbitantly and capriciously they felt, to bring their goods to market.

Much of the legislation the Grange had supported at the state level faced judicial review…and Grange opposition to Matthews was spurred in part by the fear that Matthews would be the decisive vote in striking down legislation regulating railroads. Thus the Grange realized that it had to lobby.[159] And lobby it did. For instance, the *Cincinnati Grange Bulletin* urged its readers "to dare to speak out" against Matthews' confirmation. The Pennsylvania State Grange petitioned the Senate Judiciary Committee on behalf of its 30,000 members.[160]

Another bloc opposed to the candidate arose after Matthews, though a Republican, helped engineer the Wormley Compromise of 1877. As part of the Hayes-Tilden settlement agreement, the Compromise resulted in the return of Democratic political control in the southern states. That meant the abandonment of "the freed people of the South to domination by vengeful, racist regimes, who within a generation would impose Jim Crow [segregation of schools, public places, transportation, restrooms and restaurants], economic servitude, political disfranchisement, and the political ideology of white supremacy."[161]

So now Hayes' nomination of Matthews was opposed by:

- The temporary, angry, lame-duck Democrat majority in the Senate,
- Many newspapers in the country,
- Democrats in general for the 1876 election result,
- The emerging American labor movement, and
- Abolitionists and other advocates for the freed people.

Support for the nomination seemed to be coming only from the railroad tycoons and other members of the "Robber Baron" class. Alarmed, Matthews wrote to Hayes and asked him to "help me out of the complications in the Senate which now seem to threaten my humiliating defeat." Hayes seemed surprised by the opposition, saying there had "been more active opposition than I had looked for."[162] (General George Armstrong Custer may have said the same thing at Little Big Horn five years earlier.) However, Hayes refused to back down and so did the Senate. It simply sat on the nomination, and Hayes' presidency ran out.

Compounding the situation was the fact that the incoming-President, James A. Garfield, re-nominated Matthews for the Supreme Court ten days after taking the presidential oath of office on March 3, 1881. It has been said Garfield was beholden to those same railroad interests and Robber Barons. Jay Gould and West Coast entrepreneur Collis P. Huntington were reported to have contributed some $300,000 to Garfield's campaign.[163] This time, the nomination passed two months later because the 1880 election changed the composition of the Senate from Democrat to Republican. Even so, many in the President's own Republican Party held their collective noses, and the Senate's consent was by a mere one-vote margin, 24-23 – the closest consenting vote in the history of the Court.

Although Matthews "could not understand how anyone could vote against [him]," as he later confided to his good friend President Hayes, the *New York Sun* expressed the widespread outrage at his confirmation and the appearance of a victory for the railroad lobby. "Mr. Jay Gould," said the newspaper, "under the name of Stanley Matthews of Ohio, has been confirmed by the Senate as a Judge of the Supreme Court of the United States."[164]

Never mind *Second Thoughts*. Once again the question comes to mind: Did President Rutherford B. Hayes give *any thought* at all to his nomination of Stanley Matthews as an Associate Justice of the U. S. Supreme Court on January 26, 1881?

* * *

Chapter XIX
President Arthur Is Also Snubbed
(Term in Office: September 19, 1881- March 4, 1885)

Throughout the 220-plus-year history of the U. S. Supreme Court, no candidate for a seat on the Bench ever gave *two* presidents cause for *Second Thoughts* – other than Roscoe Conkling, that is. Ulysses S. Grant and Chester A. Arthur both must have looked back on their nominations of Conkling and wondered why they had bothered. There was no doubt in Conkling's mind. He turned them both down.

In these days, when we think of political "bosses," we think perhaps of Frank Hague in New Jersey, Richard J. Daley, Sr., in Illinois, Huey Long in Louisiana, William H. ("Boss") Tweed in New York, Mark Hanna in Ohio, James Michael Curley in Massachusetts, et al. There were a whole host of others who officially and unofficially operated their political machines with a ruthlessness matched only by World War II Nazi SS troops running roughshod across Europe in the early 1940s. Roscoe Conkling was one of those bosses and had he been born eighty years later in Nuremburg, Germany, instead of Albany, New York, he could have been a Tiger tank commander disguised as an American GI at Bastogne during the Battle of the Bulge.

Conkling, a hard-charging, take-no-prisoners, partisan politico ran for and won seats in the U. S. House (1859-65) and in the Senate (1867-81). Before that, he too served as Mayor of Utica, New York, as did the aforementioned herein Supreme Court Justice Ward Hunt – whose seat on the Bench Conkling was supposed to fill upon Hunt's retirement in 1882. A leader of post-Civil War Radical Republicans, he also advocated severe Reconstruction positions seeking vengeance against the South for the Civil War. Some of his views included taking land from slave-owners and giving it to the former slaves.

As a firm believer in the populist patronage system during the "Gilded Age," he became absolutely convinced that "to the victor belonged the spoils." In his view, only the party that wins an election hands out the rewards, including monetary benefits and jobs, to its supporters – financial and voting. His entire political strength, which was considerable as one of the most powerful men in Washington, D. C. as well as in the New York State capital of Albany, was built on patronage. His empire in New York State and elsewhere came from his ability to reward his friends and punish his enemies through the granting of or withholding political favors, contracts and government jobs. His political machine came to be one of the wonders of the age.

Second Thoughts

William T. Harper

A king-maker and breaker, a close friend and political ally of Ulysses S. Grant, Conkling surprisingly turned into a bitter enemy of the General's immediate successors in the Executive Mansion: Republicans Rutherford B. Hayes, James A. Garfield and Chester A. Arthur. For instance, Conkling actually resigned his Republican seat in the U. S. Senate because he felt snubbed by President Garfield's appointment for the post of Collector for the Port of New York. The Garfield-Conkling split became so virulent that some even felt the former Senator from New York had to be involved in the assassination of President Garfield in 1881 because the assassin, Charles J. Guiteau, turned out to be a Conkling supporter.

Another of his bitter political enemies was likewise a fellow Republican and the perennial presidential office-seeker from Maine, James Gillespie Blaine. In a Senate debate on April 30, 1866, Blaine mockingly referred to Conkling's "haughty disdain, his grandiloquent swell, his majestic, super-eminent, overpowering, turkey-gobbler strut." Obviously, Roscoe Conkling was a man easy to dislike. He was an "egotistical coxcomb," according to President Lincoln's Secretary of the Navy Gideon Welles. Even his own biographer Donald Barr Chidsey said he was "haughty, supercilious, aloof." Contemporary historian Matthew Breen described Conkling as "vain as a peacock, and a czar in arrogance."[165]

His caustic remarks and strutting physicality managed to offend even his closest political allies. But, with a lot of negative help from Conkling, especially in the 1876 Republican Party's National Convention when he threw his favorite-son votes behind Rutherford B. Hayes and stopped Blaine's drive for the Party's presidential nomination, Blaine never attained his Executive Mansion goal. The Blaine-Conkling rivalry was of long standing and may have been the impetus for the infamous refrain that embarrassed and doomed Blaine's political career: "Blaine, Blaine, Blaine, the continental liar from the State of Maine." The chant was in reference to Blaine's involvement in unethical business deals with the railroad industry.

The New Yorker was instrumental in the presidential elections of General Grant and Rutherford B. Hayes in the latter's highly controversial contest with Democrat Samuel J. Tilden in the 1876 race (see previous Chapter). Even though as a Congressman he voted against President Grant's highly desired Legal Tender Acts, the old General repaid his debt to "Boss" Conkling by nominating him as Chief Justice of United States Supreme Court following the death of Salmon P. Chase in 1873. Claiming he could not be impartial enough in judicial decisions ("I do not know how to belong to a party a little," Conkling said he was more suited to be a politician than a judge), the nominee gave the nominator second thoughts when he turned down the honor and the position.

President Hayes' successor, James A. Garfield, an anti-patronage advocate and supporter of the civil service concept, died four months after being shot by the deranged Charles Julius Guiteau on July 2, 1881, as noted above. The assassinated president was succeeded by his vice president, Chester A. Arthur, who owed his place in the line of succession on the Garfield-Arthur ticket to help, much of it financial, from "Boss" Conkling. Former President Hayes even went so far as to claim the Garfield Administration would "undoubtedly be a Conkling Administration."[166] As expected, the new president tried to repay his political debt to the New Yorker by nominating him again to the Supreme Court, this time as an Associate Justice.

In a February 21, 1882 letter to "My Dear Mr. Conkling," President Arthur wrote: "It is my wish to send your name to the Senate for the vacant judgeship on the Supreme Court. If you will consent to this, it will give me more pleasure than I can tell you."[167] With no immediate answer, the President was forced to write another letter reiterating his invitation. On March 3, the day after the Senate had received Arthur's nomination and consented to it in a 39-12 vote, Conkling responded to President Arthur's invitation to serve with apologies for the delay in answering caused by travels.

In his letter, Conkling then wrote: "…It will be ever a matter of pride and satisfaction that you and the Senate deemed me fit for so grave and exalted a trust. But for reasons which you would not fail to appreciate I am constrained to decline." Mr. Conkling gave President Arthur no further word on the "reasons which [he] would not fail to appreciate."[168] So even before the president could congratulate his newly-confirmed Supreme Court justice, his newly-confirmed Supreme Court justice gave yet another chief executive *Second Thoughts* by simply saying again, "Thanks-But-No-Thanks" as he declined to serve.

Why did he refuse the job after the Senate confirmed him for it? The *New York Times* suggested the reason was the position paid too little money and did not carry any patronage. That proposition remains questionable because surely Conkling knew those things long before Arthur's invitation to serve. Ulysses S. Grant and Chester A. Arthur may have had, and historians are still having *Second Thoughts* about Roscoe Conkling and his two declined Supreme Court nominations.

* * *

Chapter XX
Cleveland-Harrison and *Plessy v. Ferguson* Decision
(Cleveland's Terms in Office: 1885-1889 & 1893-1897)
(Harrison's term in Office: 1889-1893)

President Millard Fillmore had to have been disappointed in Supreme Court Associate Justice Benjamin R. Curtis on March 6, 1857 when the *Dred Scott v. Sandford* decision came down. So too must have been Presidents Grover Cleveland and Benjamin Harrison when five of their appointees to the same Court also ruled thirty-nine years later that some of America's citizens likewise were less equal than others in their *Plessy v. Ferguson* ruling on May 18, 1896.

Homer Plessy, a thirty-year-old mixed-blood south Louisianan who could "pass" as white, became the principal in a planned protest against the state of Louisiana's "separate but equal" intrastate railroad facilities. On June 7, 1892 Plessy, with the railroad's permission, bought a first-class ticket on an East Louisiana Railroad train and took a seat in a "white" section coach for a ride from New Orleans to his home in Covington, Louisiana.

Homer Plessy tested "separate but equal"

Subsequently arrested, as planned in an act of civil disobedience, a Louisiana court found him guilty and fined him twenty-five dollars or twenty days in jail. The case went all the way to the U. S. Supreme Court, testing whether or not a state had the constitutional right to regulate, among other entities, railroad companies operating strictly within state borders. Plessy's defense counsel argued his client was being denied equal protection under the Fourteenth Amendment to the Constitution. Actually, the railroads of the time were hoping (though not too altruistically) for a Plessy victory knowing it would remove their financial burden of having separate but equal railroad cars for both Blacks and Whites.

The Supreme Court, in upholding New Orleans Criminal District Court Judge John H. Ferguson who first heard the case, ruled Louisiana had the right to regulate railroads within its state. The Louisiana Supreme Court had affirmed that ruling in denying Plessy's Writ of Prohibition. As U. S. Supreme Court Associate Justice Henry B. Brown wrote in the majority's opinion, "The object of the [Fourteenth] Amendment was undoubtedly to enforce the absolute equality of the two races before the law, but in the nature of things it could not have been intended to abolish distinctions based upon color, or to enforce social, as well as equality, or a commingling of the two races upon terms unsatisfactory to either." Justice Brown's interpretation continued: "If the civil and political rights of both races be equal one cannot be inferior to the other civilly or politically. If one race be inferior to the other socially, the Constitution of the United States cannot put them upon the same plane."

It might be noted here that the writer of this opinion, Associate Justice Henry B. Brown, was perhaps not the brightest of the Brethren sitting on the Bench at that time. In what could be construed as "damning with faint praise," the *New York Times* on December 24, 1890, referred to Brown prior to his appointment to the Court, as being "highly spoken of by those here [in Washington, D. C.] who know him, and they say he will make an excellent Associate Judge, without making any pretensions of brilliancy." Furthermore, reported *The Times*, "Brown was a social elitist [higher social standing than most] who held many of the prejudices prominent during his time toward blacks, women, Jews, and immigrants. He did not believe laws should require changes in social custom when strong public sentiments were against it."[169]

Summed up and paraphrasing, the Court's majority justified its position by proclaiming that both blacks and whites *were* treated equally under the law – in that whites were forbidden to sit in a railroad car designated for blacks. Furthermore, Justice Brown wrote, "If the two races are to meet upon terms of social equality, it must be the result of voluntary consent of the individuals." With that finding, Brown gave Supreme Court approval to the "separate but equal" concept. The ruling further paved the way for numerous state laws throughout the country to make segregation legal in almost all parts of American daily life, which resulted in discrimination.

Second Thoughts

William T. Harper

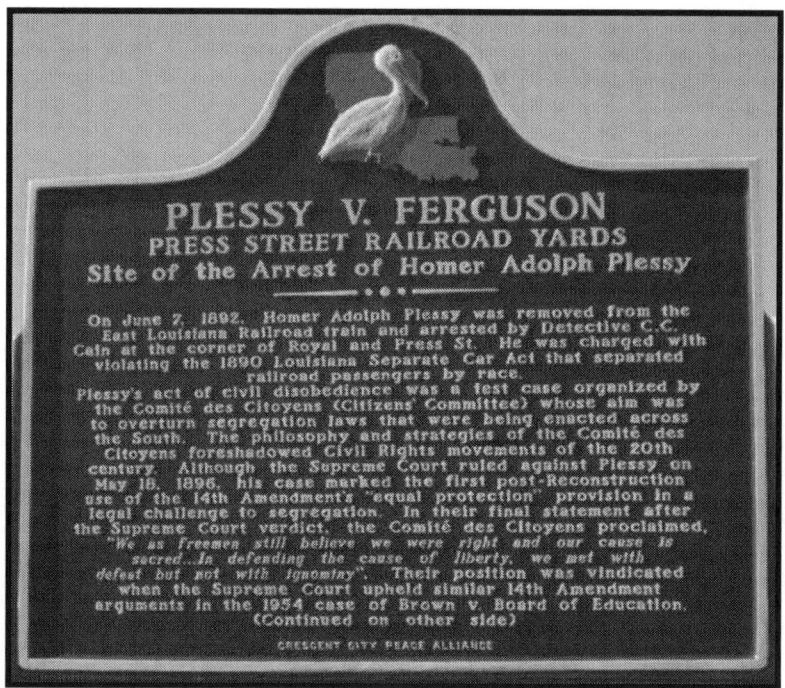

* * *

Grover Cleveland, the first Democrat elected president after the Civil War and the only President to have "the honor" of serving two non-consecutive terms (1885-1889 and 1893-1897), saw his first light of day in New Jersey on May 18, 1837 as one of nine children of a Presbyterian minister. At age forty-four, he emerged into a political prominence that carried him on a lightning-fast journey from an eleven-month seat in the Buffalo, New York mayor's chair, a two-year residence in New York state's governor's mansion, and straight to the President's House in Washington, D. C. In retrospect, it can be said Presidents Abraham Lincoln and Chester A. Arthur – wherever they were in the Great Beyond – as well as the man who interrupted Cleveland's two presidential terms, Benjamin Harrison, joined Cleveland in having *Second Thoughts* about some of the men each of them appointed to the Supreme Court.

On May 18, 1896, the United States Supreme Court was composed of:

Stephen J. Field	(appointed by)	Abraham Lincoln
John M. Harlan		Rutherford B. Hayes
Horace Gray		Chester A. Arthur
Chief Justice Melville W. Fuller		Grover Cleveland
David J. Brewer		Benjamin Harrison
Henry B. Brown		Benjamin Harrison
George Shiras, Jr.		Benjamin Harrison
Edward D. White		Grover Cleveland
Rufus W. Peckham		Grover Cleveland

Of the nine, Justice Brewer abstained and only Associate Justice Harlan voted against the Court's 7-1 ruling that, in effect, sanctioned what became known as "separate but equal" conditions among the races. An oddity about the *Plessy v. Ferguson* decision is that the lone dissent came from Justice John Harlan – the only Southerner and former slave-holder on the Court at the time. He argued the Constitution must be "color-blind."

Looking back at decisions such as *Plessy v. Ferguson* by the Fuller Court, it has been said that "history has not been kind so far to the Justices who served while [Melville W.] Fuller was Chief Justice. For decades the prevailing view of scholars has been that the Justices were mediocre and their jurisprudence was sterile. One distinguished observer wrote of the Fuller Court that it was a body dominated by fear – the fear of populists, of socialists, and communists, of numbers, majorities and democracy."[170] Adding confirmation to that assessment, legal scholar David Schultz noted that one of two legacies of the Fuller Court is described as "racist" and deserving of "a place of scorn and division."[171] These assessments are based not only on *Plessy v. Ferguson* but also on such as that Court's decision in *Lochner v. New York* wherein it decreed state-set maximum working hours were unconstitutional.

With six of the nine sitting judges being either Cleveland or Harrison appointees, both of those occupants of the Executive Mansion had to have had multiple second thoughts about the wisdom of five out of six of those appointees – Justices Fuller, White and Peckham (Cleveland nominees) and Justices Brewer and Brown (Harrison nominees) – in the *Plessy v. Ferguson* decision. Those regrettable thoughts would be based on ideas coming from Democratic President Cleveland's first inaugural address on a March 4, 1885 when, among his 1,681 words, he said:

> "In the administration of a government pledged to do equal and exact justice to all men there should be no pretext for anxiety touching the protection of the freedmen in their rights or their security in the enjoyment of their privileges

under the Constitution and its amendments. All discussion as to their fitness for the place accorded to them as American citizens is idle and unprofitable except as it suggests the necessity for their improvement. The fact that they are citizens entitles them to all the rights due to that relation and charges them with all its duties, obligations, and responsibilities."

* * *

Four years later, President Benjamin Harrison stood in the same place on the Capitol's East Portico. He got there in part because during the 1888 presidential campaign as the Republican candidate, he added election reform to his campaign platform. Born in Ohio and hailing from Indiana, Harrison was a Civil War veteran who declared the U.S. government had "an obligation solemn as a covenant with God to save [freedmen] from the dastardly outrages that their rebel masters are committing upon them in the South." During his campaign, he refused to "purchase the Presidency by a compact of silence" regarding black voting rights in the South.[172]

Once again, even in a losing effort to Cleveland during the 1892 campaign, Harrison readily accepted that segment of the Republican Party's plank that condemned "inhuman outrages" perpetrated in the South "for political reasons" (i.e., against black Republicans), and demanded the passage of laws protecting voting rights."[173]

After Harrison had given him a four-year "vacation" from the trials and tribulations of the presidency, in his second inaugural speech, this time of 2,012 words made on snowy and bitterly cold March 4, 1893, Cleveland again presented his belief about equality for all.

> "Loyalty to the principles upon which our Government rests positively demands that the equality before the law which it guarantees to every citizen should be justly and in good faith conceded in all parts of the land. The enjoyment of this right follows the badge of citizenship wherever found, and, unimpaired by race or color, it appeals for recognition to American manliness and fairness."

With views like these leading both Cleveland and Harrison to the White House, how could they not have had *Second Thoughts* about the votes in *Plessy v. Ferguson* by their Supreme Court nominees – Chief Justice Melville Fuller and Associate Justices Rufus W. Peckham, David J. Brewer, Henry B. Brown and Edward D. White (later to be Chief Justice)?

It must be said about many of both the praises and condemnations of various Supreme Court justices and their decisions discussed herein that they are made based on the mores of the times. For instance, the "separate but equal" doctrine is generally conceded as the "will of the people" – or at least a vast number of them – following the American Civil War. Conversely, that is absolutely not the case now. However, it can only be assumed – if one is to believe campaign rhetoric (?) – both President Grover Cleveland and Benjamin Harrison were against oppression of the freedmen and therefore had *Second Thoughts* when their Supreme Court appointees voted for "separate but equal" facilities in the *Plessy v. Ferguson* decision.

* * *

Chapter XXI
President Cleveland Learns "Senatorial Courtesy"

The American public is told time and time again – especially during our quadrennial election circuses – that it is selecting to the office of President of the United States someone who will be "the most powerful person in the world." That is certainly true when it comes to nuclear weapons, international relations, economic impact, etc. But not when it comes to Supreme Court nominations.

President Cleveland's Nominees - 2nd term (in reverse order)				
Name	Replacing	Nominated	Vote	Result & Date
Rufus Peckham	Jackson	Dec 3, 1895	V	C 12/09/95
Edward White	Blatchford	Feb 19, 1894	V	C 02/19/94
W. Peckham	Blatchford	Jan 22, 1894	32-41	R 02/16/94
W. Hornblower	Blatchford	Dec 5, 1893	24-30	R 01/15/94
W. Hornblower	Blatchford	Sep 19, 1893		N
President Cleveland's Nominees (1st term – reverse order)				
Melville Fuller[11]	Waite	Apr 30, 1888	41-20	C 07/20/88
Lucius Lamar	Woods	Dec 6, 1887	32-28	C 02/16/88

[11] – Nominated as Chief Justice.
C=Confirmed   R=Rejected   N=No Action   V=Voice Vote
This chart lists only nominations officially submitted to the Senate, and does not include nominations announced but never officially submitted.
Source: www.senate.gov/pagelayout/reference/nominations/Nominations.htm

  In 1893-1894, there were eighty-eight men sitting in the Upper Chamber of the U. S. Congress who were more powerful than the one man sitting in the Executive Mansion – at least when it came to their "advice and consent" roles. In another one of those strangely odd Congressional situations, one where the regulators write their own regulations, any one senator has the right to reject – without question – a president's Supreme Court nomination when the nominee is from the senator's home state. Under those circumstances and as explained below, any single senator can invoke "Senatorial Courtesy," deny a president's choice for the Supreme Court of the United States, and have no requirement to explain why.º

º Though started in President George Washington's first term, this practice no longer officially applies to Presidential Supreme Court nominations.

Second Thoughts William T. Harper

On September 19, 1893, Grover Cleveland in his second tour of duty at 1600 Pennsylvania Avenue, nominated William B. Hornblower as an Associate Justice of the Supreme Court. Why he did that is anyone's guess. He knew he was walking straight into a buzz-saw.

Before serving as president the first time (1885-1889), Cleveland was governor of the state of New York (1883-1885). His Lieutenant Governor was David B. Hill, an up-state party boss and big-time patronage purveyor. In the elections of 1884, both Cleveland and Hill went on to bigger things; the former to his unique split two terms as the president and the latter to the governor's chair in Albany, New York. As governor in 1890, Hill appointed the same William B. Hornblower, a lifelong Democrat, to a commission on state constitutional amendments.

Hornblower had impeccable qualifications for almost any legal or governmental office. He was the son of a Presbyterian minister and the great-grandson of a member of the Continental Congress. He graduated from Princeton University in 1871 and Columbia University's law school in 1875. He went on to practice law with a prestigious firm in New York City and later formed his own in 1888. William B. Hornblower did almost everything right; everything except – in 1891 he led an investigation into election irregularities for a seat on the New York Court of Appeals. Hornblower's investigation cost Isaac H. Maynard, Governor Hill's highly-preferred candidate, that Court of Appeals judgeship. What Hornblower obviously didn't learn at Princeton or Harvard was that you don't work to defeat a powerful party boss' choice; not even for dog-catcher. He didn't learn that you don't get into a cat-fight with a "hard-charging, take-no-prisoners, partisan politico."

Things subsequently went from bad to worse in the Hornblower-Hill feud. It turned into a three-way, Hornblower-Hill-Cleveland dog fight. Senator Hill wasn't just expressing Senatorial Courtesy in rejecting the nomination of William Hornblower (and subsequently, Wheeler Peckham) in 1894. He was also getting a huge measure of revenge against his political mentor – the man who put him in the same seat he occupied as Governor of New York State and his President, one and the same – Grover Cleveland.

Two years earlier it seems, in a bit of political sleight-of-hand, Hill moved into position to wrest away from Cleveland the Democratic Party's nomination for the 1894 election when a slate of his anti-Cleveland delegates from New York got the nod. Five months later, via some maneuvering at the convention, Hill marshaled the anti-Cleveland faction of the Democratic Party for a floor fight.

But the plot backfired when irate Cleveland backers from all around the country rallied to the former President's side. Not only did Hill lose that battle, but the proud party boss was extremely embarrassed by Cleveland thumping him in a 617-114 vote among the 1892 convention delegates. The failed plan by Hill and his henchmen caused the Senator a double-whammy because it was, in part, the reason Cleveland decided to leave his life of "retirement" and re-enter the presidential fray. Cleveland believed Hill wanted the Democratic nomination so badly he would sell out to almost anyone – even Republicans – to get it. So Cleveland put himself up for re-nomination and he got it.

Four months after Cleveland was re-inaugurated as President, Justice Samuel Blatchford died on July 7, 1893. As one of the aforementioned herein "absentees" from Columbia University's list of "living legends," Blatchford joined those who some eulogists damn with faint praise. In the charged atmosphere of the early 1890s, "Justice Blatchford's attempt to find and hold a solid center was strained at best. This may help explain the relatively restrained praise for Blatchford after his death. Seymour D. Thompson, the outspoken editor of the *American Law Review*, proclaimed, 'It is no great disparagement of him to say that he was probably a better reporter than judge.' During the Court's formal memorial service Attorney General Richard Olney said of Blatchford, 'If he was not brilliant, he was safe'."[174]

Meanwhile, split-term President Cleveland selected William Hornblower on September 19, 1893 as Blatchford's replacement. Senator Hill then extracted his full measure of revenge on both the nominee and the nominator. He used his prerogative of the so-called "Senatorial Courtesy." It requires care be taken by the president that, above all, the nominee to a high-level federal position is not personally obnoxious to a home-state senator (or other significant political personage) on pain of having him or her invoke that age-old, almost invariably honored, custom – an almost certain death knell to confirmation by the Senate.

The practice dates back to the first years of the Republic when the Senate recognized the need for solidarity to prevent a president from appointing a senator's political adversary to high office. Actually, the practice commenced in the very first session of Congress in 1789, when President George Washington nominated Benjamin Fishbourn as a naval officer in the port of Savannah, Georgia. Although apparently well qualified, Fishbourn was opposed by Georgia's two United States senators, and Washington withdrew his nomination when it was apparent that the Senate would side with its Georgia colleagues. Washington subsequently nominated someone favored by the two legislators, thereby enshrining the concept of senatorial courtesy perpetually. Senatorial courtesy enters into the Federal judiciary more pronouncedly and more predictably than for any other post over which the president has appointive authority because of the lifetime nature of judicial appointments, if confirmed.[175]

Second Thoughts William T. Harper

Senator Hill, with more rancor than a mere lifetime appointment would warrant, exercised his senatorial courtesy and Hornblower's nomination died in committee. But President Cleveland decided to push the ball a little further toward the end-zone. Three weeks later, the president again sent the already-rejected candidate's name back to the Senate. And, once more, Hill's "senatorial courtesy (?)" privileges sent the nomination right back – this time following a 24-30 rejection by the full Senate on January 15, 1894. But President Grover Cleveland was in no mood for backing off. And neither was Senator Hill.

A bit more than a month after the Senate's negative vote on Hornblower, the 24th president of the United States (who was also the 22nd) sent up another name as Justice Blatchford's replacement. This time it was that of Wheeler H. Peckham, a well-known New York lawyer who helped convict and topple New York politician William M. ("Boss") Tweed in 1873. Unfortunately for Peckham and President Cleveland, one political boss didn't look too kindly on the toppling of another. Peckham could have been a clone of Supreme Court Chief Justice John Marshall and Solomon himself but it would have mattered not to the New York senator/political boss. Behind Hill's spiteful influence, the Senate again rejected a nominee on the so-called "courtesy" basis and denied Peckham the New York seat on the Bench in a 32-41 negative vote on February 16, 1894.

By this time President Cleveland got the message; but he also got a measure of revenge himself. He simply took "the New York seat" out of the Empire State and gave it to Louisiana. He nominated Senator Edward D. White from the town of Thibodeauxville in the Pelican State's Deep South. Despite Hill's simmering campaign against anything President Cleveland was for, he could hardly battle the entire Senate against one of its own, and White's colleagues confirmed him by voice vote the same day as his nomination, February 19, 1894. President Cleveland was seen smiling that day.

As a post-script, it might be noted that yet another Supreme Court vacancy arose later in Cleveland's second term when Associate Justice Howell E. Jackson died on August 8, 1895 after contracting pneumonia that cut his term to a short two years. Once again, the stubborn President Cleveland actually gave considerable thought to naming – for a third time – William B. Hornblower! However, "Old #22-24" had second thoughts and turned to another member of the Peckham family, Rufus W., brother of the previously rejected Wheeler H. This time, Hill also had second thoughts about his continuing feud with the president, due to the Democratic Party's electoral losses, and he acquiesced to the Rufus W. Peckham nomination. The second Peckham took the oath of office on January 6, 1896. The ever-ambitious and still-

Second Thoughts   William T. Harper

seated Senator Hill ran again for Governor of New York in 1894. Once again, he lost.

* * *

Few Americans have enjoyed as extensive and diverse a public career as Lucius Quintus Cincinnatus Lamar. During the latter half of the nineteenth century, he served in all three branches of the national government, first as a member of the House of Representatives and Senate (Legislative Branch), then as Secretary of the Interior (Executive Branch), and finally as a President Cleveland nominee as an Associate Justice of the United States Supreme Court (Judicial Branch).

Born in Eatonton, Georgia, on September 17, 1825, Lamar graduated from Emory College and entered the U. S. House of Representatives in 1857. He resigned from Congress on the eve of the Civil War and served for two years as a Confederate Army officer including service as a Judge Advocate for the Army of Northern Virginia under General Robert E. Lee. In 1872 he was re-elected to the House of Representatives and five years later to the U. S. Senate. Lamar resigned that post during his second term to accept an appointment as President Grover Cleveland's Secretary of the Interior.

Following the May 14, 1887 death of Justice William B. Woods, *the New York Mail and Express* (considered a newspaper with Republican political leanings) editorialized on June 22 regarding the possibility of Interior Secretary Lamar leaving that post to accept the vacancy on the Supreme Court to be offered by Democratic President Cleveland. "We trust that the story be true.... In the first place, Mr. Lamar is a good lawyer.... We have hoped the President would find a Southern lawyer in every way worthy of a seat on the Supreme Bench, and no one has been named who so nearly approaches the high standard of the court as Mr. Lamar."

But not everyone was so favorably disposed to Lamar's nomination. Among legislators actively involved in the events leading up to the Civil War, one of the names ranked highest in unforgiving hatred was that of Senator Charles Sumner of Massachusetts. The New Englander spared no vehemence in denouncing slave-holders, and the sons of the South cheered mightily when he was brutally caned in the Senate chamber by a U. S. House of Representatives member from South Carolina, Preston Brooks. South Carolinians sent Brooks dozens of brand new canes, with one bearing the phrase, "Hit him again."

While not because of this incident, Sumner later moderated his views on the South and slavery. Lamar, a Mississippi Democrat who, like Sumner, had long advocated reconciliation after the war, later delivered a eulogy following Sumner's death in 1874. This was not what many bitter

Southerners wanted to hear, and they vented their never-ending grudge against Lamar during his Supreme Court confirmation hearings, even though he was to be the first ex-Confederate to serve on the nation's highest tribunal.

Opposition to his proposed nomination grew even louder but for far different reasons that political partisanship. His adversaries charged Lamar with being too old at sixty-two to serve, of having insufficient judicial experience, and of being in bed with the railroad companies – as well as some female acquaintances. He came under fire for accusations that he had had an affair and helped a woman get government employment in exchange for sex. Another charge was of a connection between then Secretary of Interior Lamar and a Miss Mary McBride, unfortunately under indictment for burning down her house to collect the insurance money. When sex and arson cropped up in what had been a routine political squabble, the newspapers gave their full attention to the controversy.[176]

Even though Lamar narrowly won Senate a 42-38 confirmation for a seat on the high bench as the first Southerner since 1853 and the first Democrat since 1862, certainly those latter charges must have caused President Grover Cleveland to have *Second Thoughts*, as he too had a sex-scandal of his own to live down. He was accused of fathering a son out of wedlock owing to his affair with Maria Halpin in 1874. This led to one of those infamous themes that sometimes brightened political campaigns: "Ma! Ma! Where's My Pa? Gone to the White House, Ha! Ha! Ha!" It's hard to imagine the President would have wanted his Supreme Court nominee's affair to come out in the public wash, thereby resurrecting that inflammatory controversy of his own.

* * *

Chapter XXII
McKinley's Man – "Unfit, "Slow, and Incompetent"
(Term in Office: March 4, 1897-September 14, 1901)

The legal profession has long been and still is the launching pad to the upper stratosphere of politics. According to the Congressional Research Service's 2008 year-ending profile report on "Membership of the 111th Congress," 204 of the then-current 535 members (thirty-eight percent) list law as their pre-election profession. In the 96th Congress (1979-1981), 257 members – almost half the body (197 Representatives and 60 Senators) – had a law degree. As the 51st Congress assembled on March 4, 1899, the percentage of those in that 355-member body with legal backgrounds was an astounding figure close to seventy percent.

One former member of Congress with a legal, though limited, professional background around that time was Joseph McKenna. He too had the distinction of serving in all three branches of the United States federal government – as a member of the House of Representatives, as United States Attorney General, and as a member of the United States Supreme Court. By the time the Civil War ended, McKenna had switched his career path from religion to law and his residence from Philadelphia to northern California where he passed the State's bar exam in 1866, according to the Supreme Court Historical Society records. One year later, despite little experience, he was elected district attorney for Solano County in the San Francisco Bay area.

He owed his rapid success to help from railroad baron Leland Stanford. In time and after two unsuccessful attempts, with Stanford's considerable financial help and introductions to the "right" people, he won a seat in the U. S. Congress in 1885 as a Representative from California's Third District. There he served four terms as a loyal party man adept at getting pork-barrel legislation for his district, such as a $400,000 appropriation for improving harbor and port facilities in the San Francisco Bay area. He was also adept at introducing private members' bills for railroad magnates such as Collis P. Huntington and Governor (and later U. S. Senator from California) Stanford. Not surprisingly, McKenna once blocked the California legislature's attempt to set railroad fares, arguing that the proposed rates were unfair to the railroads.

California politics then were virtually in the pocket of the Southern Pacific and Central Pacific railroads. In San Francisco, it was said the city was "swarming with keen, zealous, able agents of the railroad power...."[177] As a Congressman from California, McKenna opposed business regulations and he supported federal land grants to the railroads. Among other things, he also sponsored legislation that would have made

Chinese immigrants – the very labor force that provided two-thirds of the manpower necessary to build the western portion of the Nation's burgeoning intercontinental railroad system – carry identification cards.

An example of the legal battles being fought by the California railroad interests and supported by McKenna is reported in the following account "from a collection of six articles on the Pacific system of railroads, which appeared in Hampton's magazine" regarding a dispute between the federal government and the builders of the Central Pacific Railroad. The suit involved $27,000,000 in subsidy bonds which the railroad interests – Messrs Stanford, Huntington, et al – were not inclined to pay back.[178]

(The Ambrose Bierce cited in this account was a West Coast newspaper columnist, muckraker, cynic and a prolific author of short stories that were often humorous and sometimes bitter or macabre. He spoke out against oppression and supported civil and religious freedoms. Many of his works are ranked among those of other esteemed American authors' such as Edgar Allen Poe, Stephen Crane and Mark Twain.) According to the article:

> In 1896, the time for payment being close at hand, the debt to the government was [now] apparently more than $60,000,000, and the company's attorneys and representatives made no secret of its intention to default on this debt.... Mr. Huntington was still hovering about Congress with his agents and lobbyists. He prepared a bill that provided for the refunding of the debt into bonds bearing two per cent interest and payable a period estimated at eighty years from date.
>
> This bill was slated for passage by the Republican machine to which Mr. Huntington had always contributed liberally. Everybody knew that the bill was to be jammed through and Mr. Huntington was greatly pleased with the prospect. He had reason to be pleased. The bill settled all differences with the government and put off the day of payment so far that it probably would never come.
>
> Mr. Huntington's pleasure was of short life. It was presently upset by two men.
>
> At the request of [famed newspaper publisher] Mr. William Randolph Hearst, Mr. Ambrose Bierce went to Washington, and every day for one year he wrote an article exposing the rotten features of Mr. Huntington's bill. These articles were extraordinary examples of invective and bitter sarcasm. They were addressed to the dishonest nature of the bill and to the real reasons why the machine had slated it for passage. When Mr. Bierce began his campaign, few persons

imagined that the bill could be stopped. After a time, the skill and steady persistence of the attack began to draw wide attention.

With six months of incessant firing, Mr. Bierce had the railroad forces frightened and wavering; and before the end of the year, he had them whipped. The bill was withdrawn and killed, and in 1898 Congress adopted an amendment to the general deficiency bill, providing for the collection of the Pacific Railroad subsidy, debts, principal, and interest.

This may be held to be as wonderful a victory as was ever achieved by one man's pen, and, also, one of the most remarkable tributes to the power of persistent publicity. What it meant for California may be judged from the fact that when news was received of the death of Mr. Huntington's bill, the governor proclaimed a public holiday, and in the name of the state sent a telegram of thanks to Mr. Hearst.

Not even McKenna, by then serving on the United States Court of Appeals for the Ninth Circuit, could beat the power of the press.

Another of McKenna's benefactors, whom he met while serving in Congress on the Ways and Means Committee, helped him up the career ladder. A one-time lawyer, that fellow-congressman was named William McKinley, who left the House the year before McKenna did to become a two-term governor of Ohio. As a result of the national elections in 1896, fortuitously for Messrs McKinley and McKenna (with their roll call linkage in the House), McKinley was elected as the 25th President of the United States – and McKenna became U. S. Attorney General the day after McKinley was sworn in. It was currently reported in the newspapers, and not denied, that McKenna consented to accept the AG post on the understanding that when Associate Justice Stephen Field left the Supreme Court, McKenna would be appointed to succeed Field in the "California seat."[179]

On December 16, 1897, following the death of President Lincoln-appointee Justice Field, Joseph McKenna was in fact nominated by President McKinley as an Associate Justice of the United States Supreme Court. Conscious of his limited legal knowledge, McKenna took courses at Columbia University's Law School in the month between his appointment and his taking the oath of office on January 21, 1898 as an Associate Justice. "There is doubt that the last-minute tutoring had any measurable improvement on his ability as a justice," says today's Supreme Court "Oyez" media project.[180]

McKenna's nomination was also a blatant political foray by the Republican president into the increasing masses of Catholic voters emigrating from Western Europe into the burgeoning United States –

voters who generally were voting Democratic. He became the third member of the Court to occupy what had by then become known as "the Catholic Seat" on the bench – following Chief Justice Roger Taney in 1836 and Edward D. White in 1845. McKenna was McKinley's only Supreme Court nomination and, although it gave him great pleasure to name his long-time friend, the president's attractive personality could not have been ready for the firestorm of reaction the nomination ignited. The press of the day was brutal and unrelenting. The newspapers charges against Joseph McKenna said he was:

> "...unqualified for any judicial place of importance, much less for the highest place in the land."
> "...unfit."
> "...slow and incompetent...."
> "...a man of confused ideas, and his record on the bench is disgraceful...."
> "...a small man in every sense...."
> "...not of a mental caliber...."
> "...the tool of corporations...."
> And he was
> "...unfit by reason of a lack of learning...."

Imagine how President McKinley must have felt reading all that about his choice for a Supreme Court justice.

It wasn't only the newspapers piling on. Fellow members of the bar got their two-cents worth in also. "One extended petition from Oregon, signed by former United States Attorney General George H. Williams, and Judges Gilbert, Shattuck, Sears, George, Bellinger and many others including fifty members of the Portland (Oregon) bar, demanded the rejection of McKenna's appointment, on the ground that he was unfit.... The Hon. Jos. McKenna among his legal brethren has not been accorded a high place. On the contrary, the consensus of opinion has been and still is that he was not – either by natural gifts, acquired learning or decision of character – qualified for any judicial place of importance, much less for the highest place in the legal land."[181]

Ten days before President McKinley submitted McKenna's name to the Senate for its "advice and consent" on December 6, 1897, another petition signed by many prominent lawyers was sent from San Francisco to the Senate, saying: "we accuse the judge of being slow and incompetent. He is a man of confused ideas, and his record on the Bench is disgraceful...." That "disgraceful" opinion was seconded by later scholars, such as Professor Henry Abraham who, in 1974 wrote, "Before Justice McKenna went to the Court, he was a Ninth Circuit Appeals Judge where he served undistinguished or even incompetent years."[182] In a matter concerning one of the California railroads, McKenna was accused of "hemming and hawing over the simplest matters; questions that any other judge of the most mediocre ability would have passed on inside an hour." The petition concluded by referring to McKenna as "a small man in every sense, and a cunning politician...."[183]

Howls of protest were heard all the way eastward across the now 3,000-mile width of the expanding country. The *New York World* newspaper of Joseph Pulitzer and Nellie Bly fame was a journalistic ally of McKinley in his presidential election campaign against William Jennings Bryan in 1896. The *World*, in a circulation war with Hearst's *New York Journal American*, also attacked the President's choice. McKenna, said the newspaper, was "unfit by reason of his affiliations and actions as a lawyer and a judge. He has been the tool of corporations and the pet of plutocrats. His advancement has been due entirely to the favor of Stanford, Huntington and other multimillionaires of his section. Every important decision he made in corporation cases was clearly in the interests of his former clients.... To confirm him in a seat on the Bench of the Supreme Court would be an infamous betrayal of the people's trust."[184]

The day after McKinley sent McKenna's name up for confirmation, the *World* was at it again claiming the nominee was unfit "by reason of a lack of learning, a lack of capacity, a lack of fruitful experience and a lamentable lack of that high integrity which is the most essential qualification of a Supreme Court Justice...." Furthermore, the editorial charged, the candidate's "entire career has been one of servitude to the Pacific Railway robbers, trust magnates and their kind, and even his decisions as a judge upon the bench have been tainted by evidence of that subserviency. It is a shame to put this man upon the bench of the highest court in the land. It is a wrong to the nation and its people. It is an insult to widespread public opinion. It is a menace to the public welfare. It is a blistering disgrace to the administration which is responsible for it. The Senate's duty is clear. It should reject the nomination as shamefully unfit."[185]

"Other than that, Mrs. Lincoln, how did you like the play?"

Despite this blizzard of outrage in the media of the day and the pseudo-indignation exhibited by some transportation magnates competing with Stanford's and Huntington's California railroads, McKenna was what some Texans might call a "good, ol' boy, even if he was a damned-Yankee from up north" in Philadelphia. He was confirmed by the Senate in a voice vote on January 21, 1898. President McKinley had little time for *Second Thoughts* about his Supreme Court appointment that was so universally vilified by a vengeful media and an unrelenting legal community. On September 6, 1901 – less than a year after winning his

Second Thoughts William T. Harper

second term in office – President William McKinley was shot by anarchist Leon Czolgosz. He died eight days later.

* * *

Chapter XXIII
T. R. Prefers a Banana Split
(Term in Office: September 14, 1901- March 4, 1909)

Oliver Wendell Holmes is credited with contributing a number of later-to-be-common phrases in some of his Supreme Court decisions. For instance, in *Otis v. Parker*, he coined the phrase "due process of law." In *Schenck v. United States*, he wrote about the now-familiar "clear and present danger." He also proclaimed that the freedom of speech Amendment to the Constitution would not protect someone who "yelled fire in a crowded theater." Another of his lesser-known expressions came during the 1864 Civil War battle of Fort Stevens on the outskirts of Washington, D. C. Long before he came to the Supreme Court, he reportedly hollered at a man who unwittingly presented himself as a target to Confederate sharpshooters. "Get down, you damned fool!" he yelled – unknowingly at the battle scene observer: President Abraham Lincoln. The Supreme Court Associate Justice spent almost thirty years on the Bench – appointed in 1902 by President Theodore Roosevelt and serving almost until the 1932 presidential election of T. R.'s distant cousin, Franklin D. Roosevelt. During that time, it has been said Holmes was one who laughed at others far more easily than he laughed at himself.

"Teddy" Roosevelt was also adept at coining phrases. "Walk softly and carry a big stick," he famously said. He could be pithy: "The only man who never makes a mistake is the man who never does anything." He could be funny: "When they call the roll in the Senate, the Senators do not know whether to answer 'Present' or 'Not Guilty'." The twenty-sixth president of the United States could also turn an acerbic phrase every now and then – as he did when he had *Second Thoughts* about the first of his three Supreme Court nominees, the aforementioned Oliver Wendell Holmes.

Theodore Roosevelt was a governor of New York, a professional historian, naturalist, explorer, hunter, author, and soldier. He is most famous for his personality, his energy, his vast range of interests and achievements, his model of masculinity, and his "cowboy" image. As assistant secretary of the U. S. Navy, Roosevelt prepared for and advocated war with Spain in 1898. He organized and helped command the 1st U.S. Volunteer Cavalry Regiment – the Rough Riders – during the Spanish-American War. It was there he won widespread and ever-lasting fame for leading a charge of dismounted cavalry up San Juan Hill on July 1, 1898, in the bloodiest and most famous battle of the war in Cuba.

The war hero returned to New York and was soon elected governor. He wrote thirty-five books including works on outdoor life, natural history, the American frontier, political history, naval history, and his autobiography. In the presidential election of 1900, the incumbent William McKinley, Republican, chose Theodore Roosevelt as his running mate – much against the wishes and to the chagrin of other pols such as Cleveland industrialist, McKinley-backer, and king-maker, Mark Hanna.

Colonel Roosevelt (on horseback) leads his volunteer troops in the charge up San Juan Hill.

After the Republican ticket won the election, Hanna wailed, "Don't any of you realize there's only one life between that madman and the presidency?" Some of the Ohio political boss' coterie referred to Roosevelt as the "mad messiah."

Hanna's concern was realized less than a year later when President McKinley died on September 14, 1901 at 2:15 a.m. after two bullets were fired into his torso by assassin Leon Czolgosz eight days earlier. At 3:30 p.m. on that same day, Theodore Roosevelt – six weeks away from his forty-third birthday – became (and still is) the youngest man ever to hold the office of President of the United States. At that point, Hanna moaned, "Now that damned cowboy is president!" That "damned cowboy" ended up in the White House[p] and, along with presidents Washington, Jefferson and Lincoln, he also ended up on the Mt. Rushmore shrine in the Black Hills of South Dakota.

Long before the tragic death of President McKinley and right after the end of the Civil War, Oliver Wendell Holmes went back to Boston and to Harvard University where he studied law. He was admitted to the bar in 1866, and practiced admiralty and commercial law for fifteen

---

[p] At various times in history, the White House has been known as the "President's Palace," the "President's House," and the "Executive Mansion." President Theodore Roosevelt officially gave the White House its current name in 1901.

years. In 1882, Holmes became a professor at Harvard Law School and then became a justice on the Massachusetts Supreme Court. There he became chief justice in 1899, succeeding Horace Gray – one of those justices who voted in favor of the infamous *Plessy v. Ferguson* "separate but equal" decision by the United States Supreme Court in 1896. Six years later, on the recommendation of Massachusetts' then junior U. S. Senator and Holmes' cousin, Henry Cabot Lodge, President Roosevelt nominated Holmes to the U. S. Supreme Court, fulfilling a career-long dream for the Bostonian. However, it almost didn't happen at all.

In one of history's ironies, the above-mentioned Justice Gray, who preceded Holmes on the Massachusetts Court, was in failing health in 1902, and he agreed to step down upon an appointment of his successor by President McKinley. Alfred Hemenway, another Boston lawyer, was McKinley's choice. But before the President could act on it, he was, as noted above assassinated, an act which among many other things, deprived Hemenway of the post. That left the choice up to McKinley's successor, Theodore Roosevelt. When T. R. chose Holmes, the coincidence was startling because it again meant Holmes was filling a judicial chair left vacant by Justice Gray.

Nonetheless, Roosevelt almost denied the gods of fate their day because he developed severe reservations about Holmes (even though they both belonged to the same Porcellian social club as Harvard undergrads) despite the urging of T. R.'s friend, the powerful Senator Lodge. Because he was widely-read of happenings in his broad scope of interests, the President became aware of that which he perceived to be a slight made by Holmes in a speech. It led the President to believe the justice-to-be was not sympathetic with the Chief Executive's views on the status of the Philippines and Puerto Rico, territories the U. S. had acquired jurisdiction over in the aftermath of the Spanish-American War. Even though Lodge persuaded Roosevelt that Holmes was "our kind" and "safe" (i.e., favorable towards Roosevelt's progressive policies advocating such as popular control of government), it took a clandestine meeting between Roosevelt and Holmes for the latter to assure the former they shared common views on that and other issues. T. R. then felt "entirely satisfied."

On December 4, 1902, the Senate was unanimous in its consent and Holmes took the oath of office four days later. It is still believed that Holmes' Supreme Court appointment was one of the few not motivated by partisanship or politics, but strictly based on the nominee's contribution to law. (Urging by his highly influential cousin, Senator Lodge, didn't hurt his chances either.) At the time, the president might well have been uttering his famous cheer, "Bully!"

Roosevelt's optimism over his first Supreme Court appointment was short-lived and his "Bully!" cry was soon modified with the dropping of the last letter.

One of his first acts as President was to deliver a 20,000-word address on December 3, 1901, asking Congress to curb the power of trusts "within reasonable limits." Thus, the president quickly gained a reputation as a "trust-buster" by then forcing, among other entities, the great railroad combinations in the Nation to break apart. Trust-busting was defined as any government activity designed to break up trusts or monopolies. Trusts were large business entities that largely succeeded in controlling a market, thus essentially becoming a monopoly. In the late Nineteenth Century, trusts controlled much of U. S. economy. In a later-day analogy, large businesses (trusts) are called "too-big-to-fail."

As President, Roosevelt saw himself a representative of all the people, including farmers, laborers, white collar workers, and businessmen. He focused on bringing big business under stronger regulation. He sought to regulate, rather than dissolve, most trusts. Efforts continued over the next several years to reduce the control of big business over the Nation's economy and its workers. T. R. made "trust-busting" his activist slogan in answer to the peoples' demand for such control.

It just so happened that trust-busting was a basis for a case involving the merger of the Great Northern and the Northern Pacific Railroads run by James J. Hill and Edward H. Harriman, respectively. The bigs were getting bigger; too big for the trust-buster. Throw in the devouring interest of stock market manipulators like Jay Pierpont Morgan – the man behind a series of giant industrial consolidations and mergers that formed General Electric, International Harvester Company, and the U. S. Steel Corporation, the Nation's first billion-dollar company – and Roosevelt faced a powerful array of big business opposition. T. R., looking for a Justice Gray-replacement who would be sympathetic to his trust-busting views, thought he found that someone in Oliver Wendell Holmes. Later in his career on the Bench, Holmes became known as "the great dissenter," and was "one Justice, at least, [of whom Roosevelt] could be sure" to support the President's trust-busting efforts.[186]

It is said that above and beyond the entreaties of Senator Lodge, the most influential matter that convinced President Roosevelt he wanted Oliver Wendell Holmes on the Supreme Court was a Memorial Day speech the jurist presented in 1884. One of the most quoted Memorial Day speeches ever given, it was mainly about the uselessness of war. In it, the then-Justice of the Massachusetts Supreme Judicial Court, opened by noting, "Not long ago I heard a young man ask why people still kept up Memorial Day, and it set me thinking of the answer." In responding to that question, he spoke the most quoted line of this speech: "We have shared the incommunicable experience of war; we have felt, we still feel, the passion of life to its top."

While later considering Holmes' candidacy for the Supreme Court, Roosevelt read the speech and was deeply impressed, no doubt with its reference to his similar feeling about "the passion of life to its top." But what the President must have skipped over in the most stirring speech were some of the Justice's thoughts on the nation's economy. As he denigrated war and its glory to the fighters, Holmes also said, "The man who commands attention of his fellows [today] is the man of wealth. Commerce is the great power. The aspirations of the world are those of commerce." (Such thoughts could also have been the impetus for President Eisenhower's 1961 farewell address warning about "the military-industrial complex.") These ideas seem, in retrospect, to be a harbinger of some of Holmes' "to the victor belong the spoils" philosophy on which he based his dissent in the historic Northern Securities case.

As it turned out, that Justice tried to bust the trust buster, at least in 1904 when he joined the minority in voting against the President's position in *Northern Securities Co. v. United States*. The 5-4 decision upheld Roosevelt's position in what he called "one of the greatest achievements of my Administration." Holmes, in his dissent, took an approach diametrically opposed to Roosevelt's. He said, almost mockingly of the President's case, it was "because of some accident of immediate overwhelming interest which appeals to the feelings and distorts the judgment." The Justice said he believed "the strongest groups were entitled to the spoils of fair competition."[187] In other words, again, "to the victor belongs the spoils." Likewise, his dissent was a reflection of his feeling that "commerce is the great power." Obviously and despite the fact Holmes' dissent had no bearing on the final disposition of the Roosevelt-favored outcome, "Holmes, especially during his early years on the Court, was a 'bitter disappointment' to the president...."[188]

What particularly enraged Roosevelt was what he thought was Holmes' betrayal to the President's early analysis of the Judge's character. In considering Holmes for the Supreme Court, T.R. felt the candidate was "a judge who has been able to preserve his aloofness of mind so as to keep his broad humanity of feeling and his sympathy for the class from which he has not drawn his clients."[189] When Holmes voted for the Trust and against "the class from which he has not drawn his clients," the President had to be mortified by what appeared to be his inability to "size-up the man."

After hearing of Holmes powerful dissent in 1904, a furious chief executive had serious *Second Thoughts* about his Supreme Court two-year-old nomination of Oliver Wendell Holmes. As reported in the Supreme Court Historical Society's journal, "The decision brought an abrupt halt to what had been becoming a close friendship between the two men. Over the years the rift deepened. The bitterness that grew between them reflected more than a difference of opinion over law and economic principles; it reflected the type of disillusionment that comes only when a friend fails to live up to expectations."[190] The President even threatened to have the Justice thrown out of the White House if he ever found him in there. Roosevelt further and famously made his displeasure known when he blasted the Great Dissenter by saying, "I could carve out of a banana a justice with more backbone than that [of Justice Holmes]."

* * *

Chapter XXIV
Taft Tries to Empty the "Old Fools" Home
(Term in Office: 1909-1913)

Theodore Roosevelt had neither major problems nor second thoughts about his other two Supreme Court nominations (William Day in 1903 and William Moody in 1906), both of whom who were confirmed by Senate within days of the submission of their names. T. R., having sworn upon his victory in 1904 that he would not seek another term, practically "gave" the 1908 election to his rotund Vice President William Howard Taft against challenger William Jennings Bryan, "the Boy Orator" from Nebraska.

In a quirk of history, it was reported on the front page of the March 29, 1921 editions of *The New York Times* that in 1908 T. R. considered Taft for nomination as Chief Justice of the Supreme Court. Historians have fully recorded (and it is touched upon below) the falling out between the two leading to Roosevelt becoming the new Progressive Party candidate and actually running against Taft for the presidency in 1912 due to their differences in ideology and political philosophy. Unlike Roosevelt, Taft did not believe in the stretching of Presidential powers. Taft alienated many liberal Republicans by defending the Payne-Aldrich Act, which unexpectedly continued high tariff rates. He further antagonized Progressives by supporting his Secretary of the Interior, Richard Ballinger, who was accused of failing to carry out Roosevelt's conservation policies. The differences were many.

The *Times*' story noted above relates an informal dinner at the White House with Roosevelt imagining he had clairvoyant powers allowing him to see the future. There he saw something hanging over Vice President Taft's head. He couldn't be sure if he saw the Presidency or the Chief Justiceship. Mrs. Taft opted for the former. Her husband, who once said "I love judges and I love courts," quickly chose the latter. In time, both got their wish. But, imagine – in light of their subsequent falling out – the *Second Thoughts* Teddy might have had if he had made that Supreme Court appointment.

Following Taft's victory in the 1908 election, T. R.'s then-friend and his handpicked successor in the newly-named White House was a busy President vis-à-vis Supreme Court nominations. He sent six names (including that of sitting Associate Justice Edward D. White for Chief Justice) up for Senate approval and got it for all six within less than a month each.

President William Taft's Nominees (in reverse order)				
Name	Replacing	Nominated	Vote	Result & Date
Mahlon Pitney	Harlan	Feb 19, 1912	50-26	C 03/13/12
Joseph Lamar	Moody	Dec 12, 1910	V	C 12/15/10
Willis Van Devanter	White	Dec 12, 1910	V	C 12/15/10
Edward White[10]	Fuller	Dec 12, 1910	V	C 12/15/10
Charles Hughes	Brewer	Apr 25, 1910	V	C 05/02/10
Horace Lurton	Peckham	Dec 13, 1909	V	C 12/20/09

[10] – for Chief Justice   C=Confirmed   V=Voice Vote
This chart lists only nominations officially submitted to the Senate, and does not include nominations announced but never officially submitted. Source: www.senate.gov/pagelayout/reference/nominations/Nominations.htm

    The sextet still is the largest number of appointments made by any president serving a single term. Taft and Warren G. Harding, in their combined six-and-one-half presidential years, appointed ten justices to the Supreme Court. The rather bland Taft and the charming Harding served less than half as long as the fifteen years of the charismatic Teddy Roosevelt-Woodrow Wilson duo, but they appointed almost twice as many justices (10-6).

    William Howard Taft, who viewed the court room as "Heaven here on Earth," noted one of the reasons for such "productivity" within but two months of his presidency. On May 22, 1909, he communicated some of his unflattering impressions about those current members of the Supreme Court in a personal letter he wrote to Circuit Judge and soon-to-be Supreme Court Associate Justice Horace H. Lurton:

> The condition of the Supreme Court is pitiable, and yet those old fools hold on with a tenacity that is most discouraging…Really, the Chief Justice [Fuller] is…almost senile; [John] Harlan…does no work; [David] Brewer…is so deaf that he cannot hear and has got beyond the point of the commonest accuracy in writing his opinions; Brewer and Harlan sleep almost through all arguments. I don't know what can be done. It is most discouraging to the active men on the bench.[191]

    The Chief Justice, Melville W. Fuller, appointed by President Harrison in 1889, was seventy-five years old – as was Associate Justice John M. Harlan, appointed by President Hayes in 1877. Associate Justice David J. Brewer, appointed in 1889 also by President Harrison, was the "baby" of the threesome cited by Taft at seventy-one. The six other judges on the Bench when President Taft took the oath of office on March 4, 1909 were:

Name (age)	Birth Date	Confirmation Date
Edward D. White (63)	November 3, 1845	February 19, 1894
Rufus W. Peckham (70)	November 8, 1838	December 9, 1895
Joseph McKenna (65)	August 10, 1843	January 21, 1898
Oliver W. Holmes (68)	March 8, 1841	December 2, 1902
William R. Day (60)	April 17, 1849	February 23, 1903
William H. Moody (55)	December 23, 1853	December 12, 1906

A quick trip to an adding machine (or even an abacus as they may have been using during the first decade of the Twentieth Century) shows the ages of the 1909 Supreme Court totaled an average of just about sixty-seven years. The actuarial tables were working for President Taft. No President, in the 144 years between George Washington's inaugural in 1789 and Franklin Delano Roosevelt's in 1933 had such an opportunity to create a Supreme Court of the United States in his own image as did William Howard Taft.

Still, in spite of his carping about "those old fools" on the Bench, his first choice for a replacement of an Associate Justice became sixty-five-year-old Horace H. Lurton — the very man he had complained to about the senile, deaf, and sleeping old justices noted above he hoped to replace. Similarly, Associate Justice Edward D. White, one of only three Justices to have served in the Confederate Army and nominated for elevation to Chief Justice on December 12, 1910, had already celebrated his sixty-fifth birthday. Life expectancy tables for white males born in the United States in the year 1850 — as close as government records are available for the period in which the 1909 Supreme Court members were born — show only 38.3 years — a far cry from 76.5 years shown for 2004.[192] With the average age of the 1909 Supreme Court being 66.7 years, the Justices were, indeed, "living on borrowed time" and deserving of some of President Taft's condemnation as "old" fools.

Taft thought long and hard about the nomination of his friend Horace Lurton exactly because of his age. When he first floated Lurton's name as a possible candidate, the President ran into considerable opposition to the appointment on that basis. Protests came not only from members of the "Advice and Consent" Senate, but also from the then-sitting members of the Supreme Court. Those opposing the President's wishes proved right. Horace H. Lurton lived less than five years as a Taft-appointed member of the Supreme Court of the United States. Obviously, the President had *Second Thoughts* about four of his other nominees because they were all in their late forties and early fifties when they took the oath of office. And one of them, Willis Van Devanter, even stayed on the Bench right into the second term of the Franklin D. Roosevelt presidency, retiring in 1937.

When Chief Justice Melville Fuller died on the Fourth of July, 1910, President Taft was faced with a particularly poignant decision. As he mulled over the possible candidates, he ultimately chose sixty-five-year-old Associate Justice Edward D. White. Some say Taft had an ulterior reason for choosing the aging and overweight Justice – his own ascension to the post that he himself wanted more than anything else – even the presidency.[193] "It does seem strange," wrote Taft, "that the one place in government which I would have liked to fill myself I am forced to give to another."[194]

* * *

Chapter XXV
Wilson's Man – "Selfish, Prejudiced, and Bigoted"
(Term in Office: 1913-1921)

Unfortunately for both ex-President Theodore Roosevelt and his anointed successor President William Howard Taft along with the Republican Party, "Teddy" did have huge *Second Thoughts* about "Big Bill's" abandonment of T.R.'s progressive principles during the Taft presidency. Those differences between the two now-bitter enemies (they reconciled in 1918) split the Republican presidential vote in 1912. Taft got the Republican Party's nomination in 1912 and T. R. bolted the Party to run on the Progressive "Bull Moose" ticket against both Taft and their mutual Democratic opponent, Princeton University president/professor and New Jersey Governor Woodrow Wilson. Running for re-election, Taft got twenty-three percent of the popular vote; the "spoiler" Roosevelt got twenty-seven percent – and Wilson got elected – via a 266-vote majority over Roosevelt in the Electoral College.

    Wilson had only three opportunities to make appointments to the Court during his eight years in office. One of them came when Supreme Court Associate Justice and Taft-appointee Horace H. Lurton died on July 12, 1914 after just five years on the Bench. President Wilson was eager to replace him with a progressive-minded justice (in perhaps the Theodore Roosevelt mold) who would sustain government regulation of business. Sitting in the new President's cabinet was James C. McReynolds, a strong Wilson supporter in the 1912 election for which Wilson had previously rewarded him with an appointment as Attorney General of the United States.

    McReynolds had been extremely aggressive in his trust-busting activities, while at the same time being an embarrassment to the Administration because of his abrasiveness in the conduct of his AG duties. Nonetheless, "Wilson was satisfied that his man would stand up to what he liked to refer to as the Mr. Bigs [so he sent him to the Court] perhaps with a tinge of doubt but with sufficient confidence in his progressivism. History would prove [the President] utterly wrong...."[195] And McReynolds, who was confirmed by the Senate on August 29, 1914, "would become universally and justifiably regarded as all but a total on-bench failure."[196] He served on the Court as that "on-bench failure" for twenty-seven years.

    James C. McReynolds, a staunch conservative, proved to be anything but progressive. To the dismay of the president, McReynolds quickly became the most reactionary (and by all accounts, the most boorish and bigoted) member of the court.[197] McReynolds was often rude, impatient, and sarcastic. He detested tobacco and prohibited others from smoking in his presence. His attitudes toward women, especially female attorneys, were likewise intolerant.

Compounding such behavior, McReynolds proved to be intolerant of others' views and an anti-Semite. Examples abound. For instance, he refused to converse with fellow Justice John Clarke (also appointed by Wilson) because he felt Clarke was too liberal. McReynolds' nastiness toward Clarke helped prompt Clarke's resignation after just six years of service. McReynolds refused to sign the official letter expressing regret at Clarke's departure. And McReynolds made no secret of his anti-Semitism by refusing to speak to fellow justices Louis Brandeis (Wilson's next Supreme Court appointee) and Benjamin Cardozo because they were Jewish. Also, because the Kentucky-born son-of-the-South McReynolds refused to sit next to Justice Brandeis as required by the Court's seating protocol (which is based on seniority), there is no official photograph of the Supreme Court in 1924.[198]

McReynolds' bigotry was all encompassing – from his anti-Semitism with other members of the Supreme Court to even his prejudice with his personal household staff. Included therein were two black servants (Harry Parker, the messenger and general factotum, and Mrs. Mary Diggs, the housekeeper and cook) and John F. Knox, a white male, personnel secretary-law clerk, who held two law degrees, including an LL.M. from Harvard. As Knox remembered one occasion while engaged in a conversation with Parker, "the buzzer on my desk began ringing with an insistent hissing sound. Grabbing my shorthand pad, I walked in at once to the Justice's study."

> McReynolds said rather impatiently, "I don't want to dictate any letter, but I do feel that this is the time to speak about one thing. I realize you are a Northerner who has never been educated or reared in the South, but I want you to know that you are becoming much too friendly with Harry. You seem to forget that he is a negro and you are a graduate of the Harvard Law School. And yet for days now, it has been obvious to me that you are, well, treating Harry and Mary like equals.
>
> "Really," McReynolds continued, "a law clerk to a Justice of the Supreme Court of the United States should have some feeling about his position and not wish to associate with colored servants the way you are doing." McReynolds closed the one-way conversation by telling Knox, "I do wish you would think of my wishes in this matter in your future relations with darkies."[199]

McReynolds ultimately served on the Supreme Court through the administrations of Wilson, Harding, Coolidge, Hoover, and part of Franklin D. Roosevelt's. His bitterness and personal attacking style never left him. Imagine, if you can, what other second thoughts President Woodrow Wilson would have had had he been around when one of his Supreme Court appointees, James C. McReynolds, blasted a Wilson acolyte, President Franklin Delano Roosevelt by claiming, "I'll never resign (from the Court) as long as that crippled son-of-a-bitch is in the White House."[200] McReynolds didn't make good on that claim as he resigned on January 31, 1941 with "that crippled son-of-a-bitch (still) in the White House."

Even Wilson's bitter enemy from the 1912 presidential election, ex-President Taft and later the Chief Justice of the Supreme Court on which McReynolds sat, considered the Associate Justice to be a "selfish, prejudiced, bigoted person...and one who seems to delight in making others uncomfortable. He has no sense of duty!"[201] Furthermore, Taft called him "selfish to the last degree" and "fuller of prejudice than any man I have ever known."[202]

Wilson had still more reason for second thoughts. Not only did McReynolds shock the president almost at once by his vote against the constitutionality of a Kansas law outlawing yellow-dog contracts[q], he would *never* side with Wilson on any significant issue that involved government regulatory activity."[203] And apparently, much to Wilson's dismay in naming him to the Court, McReynolds "had the single-minded passion of a zealot in opposing federal legislation aimed at regulating the economy or achieving social ends."[204]

One final second thought President Wilson must have had about McReynolds was a bit of baggage the justice brought with him from his Attorney General's office. There, McReynolds had been lax in enforcing the Mann Act against the son of a prominent politician in California. The Mann Act, also known as the White Slave Traffic Act, is a federal criminal statute dealing with prostitution and child pornography. Enacted in 1910, the bill was introduced in 1909 by Chicago prosecutors who claimed that girls and women were being forced into prostitution by unscrupulous pimps and procurers. It was alleged that men were tricking, coercing, and drugging females to get them involved in prostitution and then forcing them to stay in brothels.

The President was most dismayed by his then-Cabinet member's disagreeable behavior. So, in an all-too-typical manner for politicians in general, Wilson – instead of outright firing McReynolds – merely got rid

---

[q] An employer-employee contract, no longer legal, by which the employee agrees not to join a union while employed.

of him via, unfortunately, shuffling him over to the Supreme Court. In turn, the former AG's laxness in the Mann Act case raised a bit of a fuss at Senate confirmation time, even though he was confirmed via a 44-6 vote. It also meant that Justice McReynolds had to recuse himself when the Court later acted on the case of *Caminetti v. United States*, the decision upholding even broader parameters for the Mann Act in covering the transportation of a sexual companion in interstate commerce.[205]

In reflection, President Wilson could not have been happy with McReynold's mishandling of the serious charges in the Mann Act case. As President as early as 1918, he announced his support for the Nineteenth Amendment – which established Women's Suffrage. The son and grandson of Presbyterian ministers, a professor at noted schools such as Bryn Mawr College for women and Wesleyan University, the father of three daughters, and a former President of Princeton University, Thomas Woodrow Wilson had to have had *Second Thoughts* about McReynold's mishandling of such serious charges when serving as Attorney General and his demeanor as an Associate Justice of the Supreme Court. All in all, regarding his nomination of James C. McReynolds to the Supreme Court of the United States, "Wilson himself was known to regret it."[206]

* * *

Chapter XXVI
Harding (Thankfully) Has a Second Thought
(Term in Office: March 4, 1921-August 2, 1923)

At least one President of the United States had surely had one huge second thought and reacted properly to it.

Warren Gamaliel Harding was only fifty-five years old when he was elected President of the United States in November of 1920. He never made it to his sixtieth birthday. Because of a heart attack he suffered in August of 1923, he was one of most short-lived presidents, serving a little more than twenty-eight months. Only Presidents William Henry, Zachery Taylor, James A. Garfield, and William McKinley served shorter terms. (President John F. Kennedy served thirty-four months in office.) Nonetheless, even with his limited tenure, Harding was able to appoint four men to the United States Supreme Court. He wasn't around long enough to form an opinion of some of his later-named "Four Horsemen" on the Bench so it's unknown whether or not he had any second thoughts.

Harding, the first President to ride to his inauguration in an automobile, won the presidential election by the then widest margin in history (sixteen million votes to nine million for the James M. Cox-Franklin D. Roosevelt ticket). His campaign capitalized on extensive newsreel coverage and the use of celebrity endorsements from Hollywood and Broadway stars such as Al Jolson, Douglas Fairbanks and Mary Pickford. However, to this day, he is generally ranked by historians as being last when it comes to an effective presidency.

According to an account presented in the Dictionary of Political Biography by the Oxford University Press:

> Harding was a disaster as President. His credentials for the job appeared to be that he looked presidential and would not go against his backers. His main attributes appeared to be those of ill-health (he suffered several nervous breakdowns during his publishing career), gambling, drinking, and adultery. He was lazy, preferring to play poker with his cronies rather than getting on with whatever job he was meant to be doing. His marriage was one of convenience and he had a child by his mistress Nan Britton (who later published a book about their affair). He was not a strong personality, wanting to get on with everyone, and had few ideas of his own. His wife was a driving force, influencing some of his decisions and apparently on occasion — like a later First Lady — taking advice from an

astrologer. Though popular in office, the scandal engulfing his administration — dubbed the Teapot Dome scandal — robbed his presidency posthumously of any credit. He was not cut out to be President....[207]

In the face of such a negative assessment, Harding – whose 1920 presidential campaign theme was a "Return to Normalcy" – turned out to be somewhat of a cardboard cutout of what a president was expected to be. The race to the White House was seen as a referendum between the progressive policies of Woodrow Wilson or a return to the *laissez-faire* years of the pre-Theodore Roosevelt era. As also happens in many parts of the world, the leader (Wilson in this case) who brings his nation to victory in an epic war, is quickly voted out of office when the war is won (i.e., Winston Churchill in Britain after World War II). The American people overwhelmingly opted for "the good old days" and Harding and/or the façade won the election by a landslide, 404-127 vote in the Electoral College.

With the ensuing scandals emanating from Harding himself (i.e., his mistress Nan Britton) and his Administration (the Tea Pot Dome fiasco), it's more than likely that "those old fools" Taft referred to had second thoughts about Mr. Harding and his Administration. Future President Herbert Hoover offered some insights as the rumors of scandal in the Harding Administration were bubbling forth. Looking wan and depressed, Harding journeyed westward in the summer of 1923, taking Hoover, his straight-laced Secretary of Commerce, with him. "If you knew of a great scandal in our administration," he asked Hoover, "would you for the good of the country and the party expose it publicly or would you bury it?" Hoover urged publishing it, but Harding feared the political repercussions.[208] The man who became President because, as some supporters said during the 1920 election campaign, "He looked like a president ought to," should have heeded Hoover's advice. As was shown in the Watergate scandals fifty years later, the cover-up can be worse than the crime.

Nonetheless, Harding did have – as noted at the outset of this chapter – one second thought about a potential Supreme Court nominee and he acted on it properly. When Teddy Roosevelt-appointee William R. Day retired from the Court on November 13, 1922, then-President Harding had to fill the gap on the Bench. One of those he considered, if only briefly, was Tennessee Senator John Shields. Imagine Harding's mortification had his candidate gone to Senatorial advice and consent hearings and the press probed the Senator's record which would have revealed Shields' explanation of why (using the distasteful vernacular of the day) he was opposed to giving "nigger women" the ballot. "You see,"

Second Thoughts — William T. Harper

Shields once said, "we couldn't treat the wenches as we do the men; we just club the niggers if they come to the polls."[209]

* * *

Chapter XXVII
Coolidge Finds What He Doesn't Want To
(Term in Office: August 2, 1923-March 4, 1929)

Calvin "Silent Cal" Coolidge, the thirtieth president of the United States, was so well-known and still is remembered for his absence of verbiage. It is said a woman sitting next to him at a dinner told him "I have a bet with a friend that I can get you to say at least three words." Coolidge's terse but typical response was: "You Lose!"

He didn't leave a litany of memorable quotes during his public career. But one of the few and maybe the most-remembered one was on January 17, 1925 when he reminded the Nation that "the chief business of the American people is business." Modern-day conservative commentator and syndicated columnist Cal Thomas quotes historian Arthur Schlesinger as saying, "for Coolidge, business was more than business; it was a religion; and...as he worshipped business, so he detested government."[210] Why then did he nominate a man for the Supreme Court who "sought to regulate business and working conditions"?[211]

The business-first sentiment was apparent from his presidential get-go when Coolidge told Congress, "The country does not appear to require radical departure from the policies already adopted as much as it needs a further extension of these policies and the improvement of details." One week after his "business of America" speech, Associate Justice Joseph McKenna retired, leaving Coolidge with his one and only chance to shape the Supreme Court. With the above sentiments being his credo, the puzzling question rises: Why did Coolidge nominate a liberal-leaning candidate – Harlan Fiske Stone – for a Supreme Court justiceship when that man's primary claim to public fame was his bulldog efforts to prosecute a then-sitting U. S. Senator for actions taken during President Warren G. Harding's scandals in the previous Harding-Coolidge administration?

Calvin Coolidge was a stubborn law-and-order man whose first public utterance to gain any national traction was "there is no right to strike against the public safety by anybody, anywhere, anytime." Why did the man who was then and still is regarded as the "the most articulate conservative who ever served as President,"[212] nominate a man who was considered "too liberal" for the Supreme Court by the man's friend and Coolidge's White House successor, Herbert Hoover? Why did Coolidge pick a man – Harlan Fiske Stone – who the Court's Chief Justice, William Howard Taft, feared "was not sufficiently conservative"?

The *Second Thoughts* persist. Why did he nominate a man who could not be defined in the media of the times as either "a liberal

Second Thoughts William T. Harper

conservative or a conservative liberal"? Why pick a justice-candidate who even before Coolidge's White House seat went cold, subsequently succumbed to his Democratic colleagues on the bench and joined "intellectual forces with those two celebrated dissenters of the bench, Justices [Oliver Wendell] Holmes and [Louis] Brandeis? With them he lined up, for example, against the [rest of the] Court's approval of wiretapping as a means of obtaining Prohibition evidence."[213] Why did the conservative Coolidge pick the liberal Stone whose political ideology was already established such that he later voted consistently to uphold President Franklin D. Roosevelt's "New Deal" programs – which would have been a total anathema to Coolidge? Why did Coolidge pick Stone who went on to be "a favorite of the New Deal liberals [and later] became a hero, lionized in the press and lauded by [FDR's] circle"?[214] Obviously, "Silent Cal" Coolidge was exactly that – Silent – when it came to questions such as these.

Nevertheless, the President nominated Harlan Fiske Stone, his former roommate from his days at Amherst College in Massachusetts, then serving as the nation's Attorney General. The Stone nomination should have sailed through the Senate. He was a diligent and independent university professor. Attorney General Stone was perceived to be beyond reproach in investigating various scandals lingering from the Harding administration.

The most prominent of those public outrages involved Stone's predecessor as Attorney General, Harry M. Daugherty. A lawyer, political advisor and friend of President Harding, Daugherty was suspected of profiting from the sale of government alcohol supplies, failing to enforce prohibition statutes, and the selling of pardons. Daugherty resigned under fire. Stone also showed no fear nor favoritism – nor, perhaps, political savvy – in the courtroom as evidenced by his taking on the Mellon family-controlled Aluminum Company of America – even while Andrew Mellon was serving as Coolidge's Secretary of the Treasury.

And still another question pops up in the Stone nomination: Is it possible that Coolidge misjudged the mood of the Senate and thereby the difficulty he would have in getting the advice and consent of that Republican-dominated body? Did the President, in making this choice, overlook the fact that, in addition to Stone's pursuit of Daugherty, he went after one of those very same Senators – Burton K. Wheeler of Montana – for his involvement in the infamous "Teapot Dome" scandal during the Harding administration? In his confirmation hearings, some senators expressed fear that Stone might be too protective of business interests because of his contacts on Wall Street. But conversely, once on the Court, Stone often sided with liberal justices upholding legislation regulating industry or attempting to improve working conditions.

Second Thoughts   William T. Harper

Perhaps the answer to some of these questions lies in the chameleon-like nature of Harlan Fiske Stone. His early career swung back and forth between several law firms and academia. After becoming Dean of Columbia University's Law School in 1910, the then so-called conservative lawyer proved to be most liberal in defending his faculty when the university decided to dismiss two professors because of their pacifist speeches. In 1923, his conservatism seemed to be reestablished when he resigned as dean to become a partner in a major law firm headquartered in the heart of New York City's financial district. His law-and-order views, like those of his president, were evident during his term as U. S. Attorney General as noted above. On the other hand, some have suggested the reason President Coolidge tabbed him for the Supreme Court appointment was to get him out of the Attorney General's office where his actions were bringing too much heat to the Administration. (If so, Stone would not be the first nor the last to make it to the Court via that path.)

Stone tried to balance a number of conflicting impulses coming from within him. As a child of limited circumstances he drew "toward the comforts of affluence, including fine wines and the arts, but he was fiercely determined not to let pleasure turn to extravagance. He could be humble, but he was confident of his abilities and could defend his opinions with tenacity. He was, by turns, proud or humble, open-minded or stubborn."[215] It was indeed difficult to label him as a Conservative-Liberal or a Liberal-Conservative. His 180-degree change of judicial philosophy again became evident after his appointment to the Supreme Court. In time, the liberal wing of the Court included Calvin Coolidge's old Amherst College classmate, Harlan Fiske Stone.

Obviously, neither President Coolidge nor hardly anyone else had any consistent idea where Stone might stand on an issue. On the one hand, in *Minersville School District v. Gobitis*, he voted against the Court's majority opinion that a state law could require public school students to salute the American flag and pledge allegiance to it and "the Country for which it stands." Three years later, he was in the majority in *West Virginia State Board of Education v. Barnette* (1943), which overturned the *Gobitis* decision. On the one hand, he voted as a liberal and on the other, as a conservative.

Historians agree one would pretty much know where "Silent Cal" stood, even if he didn't talk much about it. The Harlan Fiske Stone appointment may have been an exception to that expectation. Maybe President Coolidge should have had *Second Thoughts* about appointing an Associate Justice to the Supreme Court merely because he "wanted to get rid of him" or because he was an old college chum.

If President Coolidge didn't have reservations after January 5, 1925 when he nominated Stone to the Supreme Court, it could very well be said that many of those who followed him on the course to a Supreme Court appointment did. That's because during his confirmation process before the Senate Judiciary Committee, Stone asked if he might be allowed to answer questions in an unheard of manner at the time – *in person*. He thereby set the precedent for a still-existing practice that continues to bedevil some Court candidates to this day.

* * *

Chapter XXVIII
Hoover Wasn't Careful What He Asked For
(Term in Office: 1929-1933)

An old adage in life as well as in politics is, "Be careful what you ask for. You're liable to get it." Herbert Clark Hoover, thirty-first president of the United States, wasn't careful what he asked for in at least one of his four Supreme Court nominations. And his *Second Thoughts* must have been overwhelming.

President Herbert Hoover's Nominees (in reverse order)				
Name	Replacing	Nominated	Vote	Result and Date
Benjamin Cardozo	Holmes	Feb 15, 1932	V	C 03/24/32
Owen Roberts	Sanford	May 9, 1930	V	C 05/20/30
John Parker	Sanford	Mar 21, 1930	39-41	R 05/07/30
Charles Hughes[g]	Taft	Feb 3, 1930	52-26	C 02/13/30

[g]-for Chief Justice   C=Confirmed   R=Rejected   V=Voice Vote   This chart lists only nominations officially submitted to the Senate, and does not include nominations announced but never officially submitted.
Source: www.senate.gov/pagelayout/reference/nominations/Nominations.htm

     Slightly less than a year into his one-term presidency, Hoover was faced with a dilemma in naming a replacement for Chief Justice William Howard Taft whose ill health forced his resignation from the Court on February 3, 1930. Taft, the only former president ever to sit on the Supreme Court and about which he once said, "I do not remember that I was ever President," died five weeks later. Hoover's problem was that he wanted to elevate his good friend and a more progressive jurist to the Chief Justice seat – Associate Justice Harlan Fiske Stone. As seen in the previous Chapter, Stone was an eminently qualified jurist who, while disappointing his mentor (President Coolidge) by switching philosophical sides, knuckled under to no one. Stone's only other serious shortcoming – flip-flopping notwithstanding – seemed to be his inability to back away from an onrushing firestorm.

Harlan Stone looked "judicial."

Charles E. Hughes did too.

Even so, whatever diminished political instincts President Hoover had told him he should offer the job to Charles Evans Hughes. A twice-elected governor of New York, appointed by then-President Taft to the Supreme Court in 1910 from which he resigned in 1916 to become the losing Republican candidate for president against the incumbent Woodrow Wilson, Hughes was indeed ready, willing and able to report for duty back on the bench – this time as "quarterback."

His progressive credentials were similarly impressive. As governor of New York, he successfully promoted significant progressive legislation, including the enactment of the nation's first compulsory workers' compensation law, an eight-hour day for railway workers, and railroad safety regulations. Hughes' reputation as a progressive grew during his tenure on the Court from 1910-1916.[216] An offer to Hughes, his acceptance, the favorable advice and consent from the Senate, all seemed like a slamdunk in the cloakrooms of the District of Columbia's. Almost everybody thought it was a given, everybody except the man doing the giving – Herbert Clark Hoover.

The President had some deep but generally unarticulated reservations about the former Supreme Court justice. The differences between the two were long-standing, going back at least to 1922 when Hughes and Hoover were both serving in President Warren G. Harding's administration; Hughes as Secretary of State and Hoover as Secretary of Commerce. Their relationships, at best, were tenuous even then. Hughes retained relations of "wary, mutual respect impersonal civility" with Hoover "to shield himself from unpleasant encounters...."²¹⁷

Functionaries from both departments were feuding over turf and the credit coming out of various treaties with the conquered German nation following "the Great War."ʳ One reaction to the feud was that of William R. Castle, working under Hughes as the State Department's Chief of Western European affairs. "The secretary of commerce himself," reported Castle, "is not adverse to advertising [the departmental differences] and the various Jews who run the different divisions love it." Castle maintained that Hoover "appeared insanely ambitious for personal power."²¹⁸ As from the dawn of politics, it didn't take long for internal memoranda such as this to become external gossip. Hoover was not immune to gossip.

Hence, Hoover's 1930 dilemma. Does he accede to his own personal desires and nominate his friend Stone to the chief justiceship, or does he give in to overwhelming clamoring to bring his much less than personal friend Hughes back to the Court? Like many politicians, Hoover did what many of them do (sometimes even for the betterment of their countries): Solomon-like, he compromised. "Who gets to keep which half of the baby?"

At a meeting to discuss Taft's successor the President said, though it really wasn't what he wanted to do, he felt obligated to offer the position to Hughes. One of those present at the meeting told the President he was safe in making the offer because Hughes would have to decline. It would be because his son, Hoover's Solicitor General Charles Evans Hughes, Jr., would feel obliged to nobly resign his post as the Government's spokesman before the Court if his father became its Chief Justice. So Hoover called Hughes on the telephone and offered him the position of Chief Justice, fully expecting the New Yorker to graciously decline.ˢ After a short period of pitter-pattering small talk, Hoover said a polite goodbye. Then he slammed down the phone and boiled over: "The son of a bitch doesn't give a damn about his son's career."²¹⁹ The President's friend, Harlan Fiske Stone didn't get the job; The President's

---

ʳ "The Great War" (1914-1918) didn't become World War I until after the start of World War II (1939-1945).

ˢ In a later autobiography, Hughes is, according to author Laura Ray, painfully aware of the story that was circulated widely in the bestseller *The Nine Old Men* by Washington journalists Drew Pearson and Robert Allen. "To refute the story, Hughes marshals his evidence: that the offer came not by telephone, as the book reports, but in a White House conversation; that he at first declined on the grounds of age but was 'strongly urged' by Hoover to accept; and that the President himself had written a letter refuting the published account." See website http://works.bepress.com/cgi/viewcontent.cgi?article=1004&context=laura_ray

Second Thoughts — William T. Harper

adversary, Charles Evans Hughes, did. Hoover had gambled and Hoover had lost. Hughes, Jr., did resign his post after his father was sworn in.

As noted, Hughes' qualifications for the chief justiceship were impeccable. Even Chief Justice William Howard Taft strongly supported him. But to the surprise of all in the Hoover administration and to Hughes himself, none of them were prepared when both progressive Republicans and Southern Democrats vigorously opposed his confirmation. Still others saw him as the epitome of the social and economic elite class. Some attacked him for his advocacy of corporate business interests while states' rights proponents were fearful of his views on federal power. For those who couldn't elucidate specific criticism, they simply attacked his age, sixty-seven, as the oldest person ever appointed chief justice. Ultimately, the Senate confirmed Hughes by a 52-26 vote with eighteen wishy-washy abstentions.

Looking back, a second thought might well have made President Herbert Clark Hoover a little more careful about what he asked for in the future.

* * *

In an oddity of history, Charles Evans Hughes replaced former President William Howard Taft as Chief Justice – both of them losers to Woodrow Wilson in presidential elections (1912, 1916). Furthermore, as President, Taft first appointed Hughes to the Court as an Associate Justice on April 25, 1910 only to have Hughes succeed Taft as Chief Justice on February 13, 1930, appointed by President Herbert Hoover. If Hoover in later life did not regret his appointment of Hughes as Chief Justice, he surely had to be mystified by Hughes' actions during his second go-round on the High Bench. (In 1916, Hughes resigned from his first Supreme Court term to run for the presidency against Woodrow Wilson.)

What had to be confusing to President Hoover was Hughes' voting record as Chief Justice. When Hoover nominated Hughes in 1930, the candidate was, as expected, opposed by some in the Democratic Party who thought him too friendly to Big Business. Surprisingly, there were those in the Republican Party who opposed him on the same grounds. In a classic example of speechifying pomposity, Idaho Republican Senator William E. Borah blasted the nomination in grandiose terms. Putting Hughes back on the Court, Borah orated, would constitute "placing upon the Court as Chief Justice one whose views are known [on] these vital and important questions and whose views, in my opinion, however sincerely entertained, are not which ought to be incorporated in and made a permanent part of our legal and economic system."[220]

In spite of all that portentousness, Hughes was "incorporated in and made a permanent part of our legal and economic system." That's when things started to get confusing to Hoover, who by this time was regretting he had ever said anything about "a chicken in every pot and car in every garage." Much to Hoover's surprise, the jurist who was seen by both major political parties as being too friendly to Big Business, suddenly aligned himself with judicial liberals on the Court – such as Harlan Fiske Stone, Louis Brandeis and Benjamin Cardozo. But, the surprises didn't end there. On the one hand, Hughes led the fight against Hoover's successor, Franklin D. Roosevelt, in his attempt to "pack the court" with additional liberal justices. On the other hand, Hughes along with Stone, Cardozo and Brandeis, often ruled Roosevelt's New Deal measures to be constitutional.

And when nobody could definitively say how Hughes would rule, he wrote the opinion that invalidated Roosevelt's prized package, the National Recovery Act – an emergency measure intended to encourage industrial recovery and help combat widespread unemployment. Squaring this rejection of government entry into the world of Big Business was particularly confusing in light of his earlier vote as an Associate Justice when he voted for the Interstate Commerce Commission, saying it could regulate intrastate rates if they were significantly intertwined with interstate commerce (*Interstate Commerce Commission v. Atchison Topeka & Santa Fe Railway Company*).

* * *

Just a few weeks after Hoover saw Charles Evans Hughes sworn in as Chief Justice of the United States Supreme Court, on March 8, 1930, Associate Justice and President Harding appointee Edward T. Sanford died. President Hoover then nominated Fourth U.S. Circuit Appeals Chief Judge John J. Parker of North Carolina as Sanford's successor. Hoover's reason for choosing Parker was primarily to reward the South in general and specifically, the five Southern states that supported him in the 1928 presidential election. Furthermore, he hoped to hold on to and maybe even enlarge that support in the coming 1932 elections. Hoover's chances of continuing in office were already becoming slim-to-none as the effects of the five-month-old and growing "Great Depression" were starting to take hold. However, some senators saw through Hoover's foray into the Democratic "solid South," leading them to resent his political ploy.

Labor quickly identified Parker as its enemy because of his previous opposition to a United Mine Workers Union attempt to organize coal miners in West Virginia. Parker defended his so-called anti-labor judicial decisions by saying he had no choice in the matter, precedents for which had already been set by the U. S. Supreme Court. Had he decided any other way, he said he would have been "reversed and rebuked" by the Court for doing so. However, William Green, president of the American

Federation of Labor (AFL), likened Parker's decisions, in such as *United Mine Workers v. Red Jacket Coal & Coke Co.* in 1927, as being akin to the infamous Dred Scott decision in 1857. Green threw a couple of incendiary logs on the fire when he wrote "the effect of the Dred Scott decision was to perpetuate human slavery. The effect of [Parker's decisions were] to establish and perpetuate industrial servitude."[221]

The National Association for the Advancement of Colored People (NAACP) quickly joined the fight to defeat Parker when its research on the nominee came up with an article in the April 19, 1920 edition of the *Greensboro* (N.C.) *Daily News*. Parker, then running for governor of North Carolina, was quoted therein as saying, "…the participation of the negro in politics is a source of evil and a danger to both races and is not desired by the wise men in either race or by the Republican Party of North Carolina."[222] Now the battle was joined between the vocal opposition and the stunned White House.

While the AFL/NAACP opponents were quick to marshal their forces, do their information searches, and enlist other allies, the White House extended its *laissez-faire* attitude. It practically stuck its head in the sand and hoped Green and NAACP leader Walter White would "just go away." The charges went unanswered for weeks. According to writer Max J. Skidmore, it was "a reflection of his personality and his lack of political skill that…Hoover was unwilling to engage in the rough-and-tumble activity of politics and perhaps arrogantly considered political bargains to be beneath him. He soon paid the price for his aloofness."[223] In the view of some later historians, the Senate rejection of Judge Parker "is now all but universally regarded not only as regrettable but also as blunder."[224] The oft-quoted historian Henry Julian Abraham in his book *Justices, Presidents, and Senators* says on page 149 that Parker, the "so unfairly rejected [Supreme Court] nominee, was a jurist of outstanding credentials who unquestionably would have left a commendable record as a member of the Court."

This was at a time when Supreme Court nominees were new to being called before any Senate judiciary subcommittees to testify regarding their worthiness to serve. Hoover's advisers suggested Parker volunteer to do exactly that under the ruse of justifying his previous service on the federal bench, at which point he also could refute the AFL/NAACP charges. When the offer was put before Parker that he face down his accusers in a Congressional hearing, he was only grudgingly willing; he too felt it was beneath the dignity of a sitting judge to testify in his own behalf. However, because of some Congressmen's reticence at being labeled as supporting this judicial "target," hesitation brought on by the coming election fears, Parker was never invited to testify.

Late to the game, Hoover and his administration tried to fight back with attempts to say Parker was being quoted "out of context" in the

1920 report, but their efforts were almost amateurish in the face of the AFL/NAACP onslaught. They reiterated Parker's *Red Jacket* defense (i.e., "the Supreme Court made me do it"). When the opposition "leaked" to the press that Hoover's Vice President Charles Curtis was urging the President to withdraw the nomination, the White House countered with a meek denial that it was even considering such a move.

Another thing the politically naïve Hoover overlooked prior to making the nomination was the state of the nation's economy and its impact on the Congressional elections coming up later in that year of 1930. Many of Hoover's Republican allies in all walks of government were facing tight reelection battles in November. With the recession cartwheeling into a depression, any Republican lawmaker facing election was already on shaky ground and they deserted their president in droves, feeling that any anti-labor or anti-civil rights vote on their part would totally doom their chances. As the nation's economy sank into the depths of the Great Depression, so too did the election hopes of many Republican candidates, and with it, the President's clout on the Hill.

Despite the intensely negative lobbying by labor groups and the NAACP and the perceived ineptness of the Hoover Administration to salvage the nomination, Judge Parker lost by just one vote in the Senate advise and consent hearings. Many in the Republican-controlled 56-39 Senate were deeply resentful of the manner in which the administration had handled the nomination. It would have taken only one more Democratic senator to "cross-over" or one more of the seventeen negative-voting Republican solons to support his President. The 39-41 losing vote would have ended in a tie and Vice President Curtis' vote would have broken it, assuring the nomination. How many second thoughts must Herbert Hoover have had over this failure?

As this book's Chapter I noted, the struggle between the White House and the Senate in the confirmation process has developed into "one of the most contentious aspects of American politics." That has certainly been evident during the most recent half-century of the Court's existence. By comparison, from 1894 through 1967 – seventy-three years and forty-four nominations – only John J. Parker's nomination was rejected; a miniscule .023 percent failure rate. However, as shall be seen below, starting in 1968 the following seven of twenty-two candidates did not make it through the process:

Abe Fortas (Chief)	June 26, 1968	withdrawn
Homer Thornberry	June 26, 1968	no action
Clement Haynsworth	August 21, 1969	rejected
G. Harrold Carswell	June 19, 1970	rejected
Robert Bork	July 1, 1987	rejected
Douglas H. Ginsburg	October 29, 1987	withdrawn
Harriett Miers	October 7, 2005	withdrawn

This skyrocketing dissention ratio (7:22) over forty-seven years is an astounding 33-plus percent – in about one-half of the time! And this doesn't include the controversial, sometimes raucous 1991 hearings for the ultimately successful nomination of Associate Justice Clarence Thomas. The rules of engagement for getting candidates a seat on the Supreme Court bench have certainly changed as the U. S. has become markedly polarized along the liberal/conservative continuum.

* * *

Chapter XXIX
FDR – KKK, Liars, Internment – and More
(Term in Office: March 4, 1933-April 12, 1945)

One of those classic cases of having potential *Second Thoughts* for a president was the nomination of Hugo Lafayette Black as an Associate Justice of the Supreme Court by President Franklin D. Roosevelt. It didn't take long in FDR's first term for the inevitable conflict to rise between the politically liberal president and the conservative-leaning Supreme Court. When Roosevelt declared in his 1933 inaugural address "the only thing we have to fear is fear itself," he wasn't thinking about the Supreme Court. However, he had every reason to fear a voting block of justices called by some the "Four Horsemen" – Pierce Butler (serving from 1923-1939), Willis Van Devanter (1911-1937), James McReynolds (1914-1941), and George Sutherland (1922-1938). That foursome (all of whom served on the Bench during the famed Notre Dame University "Four Horsemen" football backfield of the mid-1920s) subscribed to the idea that Congressional powers were limited by the Constitution. They also believed in the Coolidge-Hoover dictum: "The business of America is business," which was definitely contrary to the new President's thinking. His philosophical allies on the Court were Justices Louis Brandeis (serving from 1916-1939), Benjamin N. Cardozo (1932-1938), and Harlan Fiske Stone (1925-1941). Charles Evans Hughes (1910-1916 and 1930-1941 as Chief Justice) and Justice Owen J. Roberts (1930-1945) were the swing votes. Often during FDR's first term, the Supreme Court votes didn't swing his way.

Roosevelt's first chance to alter the makeup of the Court did not come until after he had completed his first term. On June 2, 1937, Justice Van Devanter, a President Taft appointee in 1911 and the Court's most conservative member, resigned. Roosevelt was reveling in his second presidential term. His victory over Kansas Governor Alfred M. Landon – losing only Maine and Vermont while picking up more than sixty-percent of the popular vote and 523 electoral college votes versus Landon's eight – allowed many Democratic candidates to ride into Congress on his sizeable coattails. The new Senate contained seventy-six Democrats, "so many that a dozen would have to cross the aisle and sit in the traditionally Republican section."[225] The President deemed he had a mandate and it included a re-order in the Court.

Irking FDR (to put it mildly) were several of the Court's decisions. One, in 1935, saw the high court invalidate the NIRA (the National Industrial Recovery Act) authorizing the President to regulate banks in an attempt to stimulate the United States' economic recovery from the Great Depression. Another, in 1936, rejected the AAA (Agricultural Adjustment Act) granting subsidies to farmers. FDR was acutely aware that the Court could well invalidate the Social Security Act and the National Labor Relations Act, two pillars of New Deal legislation.[226]

The Judiciary Reorganization Bill of 1937 (called the "court-packing" bill by its opponents) became the vehicle for reorganizing the Court. Roosevelt and his advisors drafted a secret plan that would (a) limit the Court's jurisdiction, (b) require a two-thirds vote by the Court to overturn an act of Congress, and (c) allow the President to appoint an extra Supreme Court Justice – to a maximum of six – for every sitting Justice over the age of 70. (Just about the only thing the President and his advisors didn't ask for was that every new member of the United States Supreme Court have the surname of "Roosevelt"!)

L to R Standing: Owen J. Roberts, Pierce Butler, Harlan Fiske Stone, Benjamin Cardozo; L to R Sitting: Louis D. Brandeis, Willis Van Devanter, Charles Evans Hughes, James McReynolds, and George Sutherland.

At the time the "court-packing" bill was drafted, its 70-years-of-age factor included six of the nine then-sitting justices:

- Louis D. Brandeis, born in 1856, was 80
- Willis Van Devanter, born in 1859, was 77
- James C. McReynolds, George Sutherland, and Chief Justice Charles Evans Hughes, all in 1862, were 74

- Pierce Butler, born in 1866 and the "baby" of the septuagenarian group, turned 71 on March 17, 1937.

With the exception of the "baby" Butler, every one of these Justices entered this world before the end of the United States Civil War. And at the time of FDR's 1937 court-packing bill, World War II was only two years away from starting. How short is the span of American history!

The Judiciary Reorganization Bill of 1937 caused a firestorm of opposition – even, surprisingly, among members of Roosevelt's own Democratic Party – as well as some segments of the press of the day. In an editorial published in the *New York Herald-Tribune* on February 8, 1937, the newspaper charged, "President Roosevelt has brought forward a proposal which, if enacted into law, would end the American State as it has existed throughout the long years of its life.... He ingeniously conveys

Editorial cartoonist Lute Pease in the *Newark* (N. J.) *News* had this view of FDR's "court-packing" plan[227]

the impression that all he seeks is a routine and moderate effort to speed up justice and improve the whole Federal bench. Yet, beneath this veneer of politeness, the brutal fact is that President Roosevelt would pack the

Supreme Court – which he called 'government by senility' – with six new justices of his own choosing.

"No President of the United States," the paper contended, "ever before made the least gesture toward attempting to gain such a vast grant of power.

"Mr. Roosevelt demands it, calmly, artfully. By one legislative act, availing himself of the one loophole in the Constitution – the failure to specify the number of members in the Supreme Court – he would strike at the roots of that equality of the three branches of government upon which the Nation is founded, and centralize in himself the control of judicial, as well as executive functions."[228]

The following letter was typical of at least one small businessman's public opposition to the so-called Court-Packing Plan:

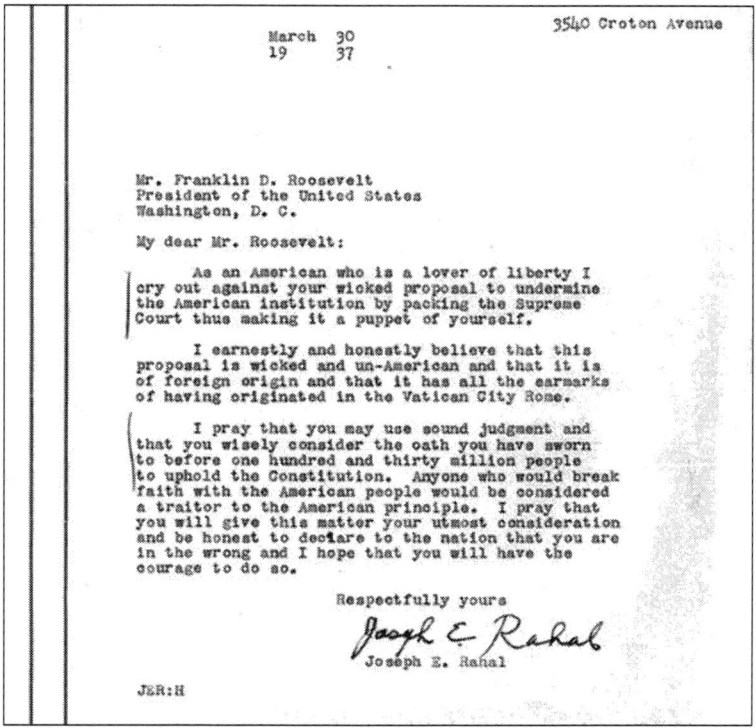

Courtesy: Franklin D. Roosevelt Library

Roosevelt resorted to the age-old political ploy of spending "three or four hours a day… listening, flattering, humoring, persuading and pressing party leaders to fulfill his wishes – and leading many of them to believe, in many cases, that his initiatives had been their idea."[229]

Roosevelt purported to justify such legislation on the questionable ground that the federal courts were behind in their work, and that a large number of active judges over seventy could not carry a full load. The President's camouflage fooled no one.[230] The ploy, obviously an inducement to get some of those "old fogies" off the bench, actually did work for the President – but only after his "court-packing" scheme failed. The bill was seen as a power-grab and it ultimately went down in flames.

Roosevelt wanted to continue the fight in the Congress of the United States. After the Court overturned two key pieces of New Deal legislation, FDR condemned the Justices' "horse and buggy definition of interstate commerce." But one of his closest advisors, James F. Byrnes (who himself would later be appointed to the Supreme Court by FDR), told the President that based on actuarial tables, the first of life's "sure" things (death and taxes) would solve his problem with the Court. And, Byrnes asked after the resignation of the aging Justice Van Devanter, "Why run for a train after you've caught it?"[231]

* * *

The national outcry against the court-packing scheme forced FDR to wait patiently until death or resignation gave him the opportunity to remake the Court in his own image. He didn't have to wait long. Death and resignation packed the Court for him. By 1943, eight of the nine Supreme Court justices were Roosevelt appointees, including Coolidge-appointee and liberal-leaning Harlan Fiske Stone who Roosevelt named Chief Justice in 1941. And even the ninth was swing-voting Justice Owen J. Roberts, a Hoover-appointee. Hugo Lafayette Black was the start of Roosevelt's Supreme Court dream team.

Hardly anyone had doubts about Black's qualifications for the Supreme Court judgeship when FDR appointed him on August 12, 1937. A high school dropout, he nonetheless entered the University of Alabama Law School, from which he was graduated in 1906. His subsequent distinguished service in Birmingham, Alabama courtrooms was interrupted by a one-year hitch in the U. S. Army as a captain during World War I. In 1926, largely because of his oratorical skills, he was elected a U. S. Senator from the Cotton State. As an early and ardent supporter of Roosevelt's "New Deal" and a vocal critic of the then-sitting, conservative-leaning U. S. Supreme Court, it didn't take long for him to gain the President's favor. Similarly, as a member of "The Most Exclusive Club in the World," he had almost complete backing from his fellow members of the Upper Chamber.

Some contemporary reports noted the President sent Black's name to the Senate merely as a means of "getting back" at that body for rejecting his Court reorganization bill. He thus replaced the arch-conservative Associate Justice Van Devanter with an ultra-liberal, avowed New Deal-supporter. There was, however, one thing that surely gave FDR some *Second Thoughts* after sending Black's nomination to the Senate. Following the Judiciary Committee's approval of Black's nomination, 13-4, the scene shifted to the full Senate which gave its advice and 63-16 consent. Black took his oath of office on August 19, 1937. The entire process took only one week.

President Franklin Roosevelt's Nominees (in reverse order)					
Name	Replacing	Nominated	Vote	Result	& Date
Wiley Rutledge	Byrnes	01/11/43	V	C	02/08/43
Robt. Jackson	Stone	06/12/41	V	C	07/07/41
James Byrnes	McReynolds	06/12/41	V	C	06/12/41
Harlan Stone[7]	Hughes	06/12/41	V	C	06/27/41
Frank Murphy	Butler	01/04/40	V	C	01/16/40
Wm. Douglas	Brandeis	03/20/39	62-4	C	04/04/39
F. Frankfurter	Cardozo	01/05/39	V	C	01/17/39
Stanley Reed	Sutherland	05/15/38	V	C	01/25/38
Hugo Black	Van Devanter	08/12/37	63-16	C	08/17/37

[7] – for Chief Justice   C=Confirmed   V=Voice Vote   This chart lists only nominations officially submitted to the Senate, and does not include nominations announced but never officially submitted.
Source: http://www.senate.gov/pagelayout/reference/nominations/Nominations.htm

Then the bombshell exploded.

The *Pittsburgh Post-Gazette*, one of the Hearst chain of newspapers (no friends of FDR were they) revealed the Court's newest Associate Justice, Hugo Lafayette Black had, on September 13, 1923, joined the Ku Klux Klan in Alabama! Black later answered the charges by saying that his two-year Klan membership was short-lived, that he only joined because he thought it would help his budding political career, that he was only peripherally active in the Klan, and that he spent most of his time therein trying to get the Klan to change its violent ways.

On the other hand, the new Supreme Court justice accepted a life membership in the KKK in 1926 and told that organization that, "This passport which you have given me is a symbol to me of the passport which you have given me before. I do not feel that it would be out of place to state to you here on this occasion that I know that without the support of the members of this organization I would not have been called, even by my enemies, the 'Junior Senator from Alabama'."[232] To some, he remained as "Justice KKK Black."[233]

FDR had to have been stunned by this revelation – mostly because it threatened his "get-even" with the Senate via his nomination of Black. In making that appointment, the President did it gleefully in an effort to punish the Senate members who had blocked his attempts to "pack" the Supreme Court. Roosevelt knew of the "Senatorial Courtesy" tradition wherein Senators almost never blocked a presidential nomination of "one of their own." He also knew many members of the Upper House totally despised Hugo Lafayette Black's abrasive, prosecutorial tactics as a Senator from Alabama. When Black's name was submitted for the Court vacancy, some "Senators churned with rage and revulsion," reported Jeff Shesol in his book *Supreme Power*, while FDR chortled, "They'll have to take him" even knowing the President "wanted to get back at" his opposing Senators and "stick it to them." As Shesol wrote, "Black, in short, was the perfect choice for a president who wished to antagonize rather than assuage his opponents."[234]

However, the entire vengeful plot almost blew up in Roosevelt's face, which would have been devastating for him – both personally and politically. Public disclosure of Black's KKK membership came shortly *after* his appointment to the Supreme Court was confirmed by the Senate. "The resulting public uproar would probably have doomed his Court appointment if the disclosure had come just a few weeks earlier."[235] In light of Roosevelt's stunning and public defeat in his Court "packing" attempts, to have his very first Supreme Court nomination fail – another public slap in the face – would have been the most disappointing event of FDR's life other than his polio disability.

However, unlike his predecessor Herbert Clark Hoover, Franklin Delano Roosevelt was an extremely astute politician and after four years in the White House dealing with Congress and the national media, FDR knew how to get things done. Hugo Black likely could have been the Grand Wizard of the entire Ku Klux Klan and he would still have had the President's total support. The Alabamian rode out the storm and found Port of Refuge on the Bench. While serving on the Court, his liberal philosophy influenced it through the third longest tenure on the Court, thirty-four years of social change. Roosevelt needed Black and Black needed Roosevelt. About that, there were no *Second Thoughts* – other than Black's failure to tell Roosevelt, *if he did not*, about his KKK involvement.

* * *

Felix Frankfurter was born in Vienna, Austria in 1882, arrived in New York City twelve years later and became a U.S. citizen when his father was naturalized in 1898. Felix was graduated from the College of the City of New York in 1902 and from Harvard in 1906, after which he joined a New York law firm. In 1907, he joined the staff of the U.S. Attorney. In

1914 he returned to teach at Harvard Law School. There he stayed for the next twenty-five years.

During that time, he was one of the original founders of the American Civil Liberties Union; he served on the NAACP's Legal Advisory Committee, and became identified with several progressive (seeking social reform through government intervention) causes such as the distribution of wealth, and criminal trials of the time. One of those cases was *Commonwealth v. Sacco & Vanzetti*, 225 Mass. 369, 151 N.E. 839, decided May 12, 1926. The infamous trial of Ferdinando Sacco and Bartolomeo Vanzetti, two left-wing radicals and Italian anarchists who were convicted in 1921 for the 1920 armed robbery and murder of Alexander Berardelli and Frederick A. Parmenter, a pay-clerk and a security guard in Braintree, Massachusetts. Frankfurter wrote a book about the case, critiquing the prosecution's contention and the presiding judge's handling of the trial. That case is still being "argued" in law schools today due to the belief of some legal experts the convicted killers were framed and/or victims of racial prejudice.

A year later, Frankfurter was asked by fellow Harvard graduate and then New York Governor Franklin D. Roosevelt for help concerning the regulation of public utilities. After Roosevelt became president in 1933, he often sought Frankfurter's advice in establishing his New Deal programs. Although he privately disagreed with President Roosevelt's 1937 court-packing plan, Frankfurter nonetheless provided the president with verbal and written arguments which were used in criticizing the Supreme Court's rejection of some New Deal legislation.

Roosevelt was captivated by Frankfurter [and] arranged for the Harvard professor to live in the White House for much of the summer of 1935; he told an acquaintance, "Felix has more ideas per minute than any man of my acquaintance. He has a brilliant mind but it clicks so fast, it makes my head spin. I find him tremendously interesting and stimulating." By the middle of the 1930s, Frankfurter was "perhaps the most important non-elected official in the national government." [236]

Frankfurter had been one of the country's leading judicial consultants for many years, and if he was a pedantic courtier "upon whom (Roosevelt) could always depend for instant laudatory assurance," he was excessively intelligent, versatile, loyal to Roosevelt, and ultimately an outstanding Supreme Court justice.[237] [In FDR's continuing masquerade of reluctance toward seeking an unprecedented third term in office, Frankfurter was instrumental in encouraging him, according to one writer. A mere five months after joining the Supreme Court on January 30, 1939,] Roosevelt dutifully asked Frankfurter in late June for a paper on whether he should seek a third term…. Frankfurter returned a learned treatise on the President's "unavoidable duty to continue."[238] (It wasn't until years later that the prohibition against Supreme Court justices advising presidents on policy, which dozens of justices in the past had engaged in, was passed.)

Following the death of Associate Justice Benjamin Cardozo in July of 1938, Roosevelt again turned to Frankfurter and asked him to provide him with a list of potential candidates for that vacant seat. The President rejected all the suggestions and instead, nominated the suggestion-maker. On January 5, 1939, Frankfurter – obviously a Roosevelt favorite, confidant and an influential voice since FDR's days as governor – was nominated as Cardozo's successor. Twelve days later, he was confirmed by the U. S. Senate as an Associate Justice of the United States Supreme Court. The Court, now with Justices Hugo Black, Stanley Reed, William O. Douglas and the addition of Felix Frankfurter, was giving Roosevelt the Court he wanted without the "packing."

It didn't take long for FDR to have second thoughts about this nomination. Despite his previous liberal political leanings, Frankfurter soon became the Court's most outspoken advocate of judicial restraint – the view that courts should not interpret the Constitution, and impose sharp limits upon the authority of the Executive and Legislative branches of government. His viewpoints quickly brought about clashes with some of his Court brethren who advocated a more activist role for the Judicial Branch. Obviously and with much chagrin for President Roosevelt, "…Felix Frankfurter shed [his] liberal politics and veered to the right on the bench."[239] According to a later member of the Court, Tom C. Clark, "Mr. Roosevelt thought that Judge Felix Frankfurter was going to be a flaming liberal, but he turned out in many areas to be a rank conservative."[240]

In *Nine Men Against America*, author Rosalie M. Gordon highlights some of Frankfurter's judicial inconsistencies. "Justice Frankfurter's philosophy is not an easy one to classify, perhaps because he really hasn't any, but suits his views to the exigencies of the moment. That, of course, is any man's right, but the Supreme Court of the United States is hardly a forum for opportunistic 'thinking'. Justice Frankfurter," Ms. Gordon continues, "has been called everything from a communist or socialist to a rank reactionary – not without reason. It would be possible to cite quotations from Frankfurter on every side of every question at one time or another. So slight is his concern with constitutionality and law that he has not only reversed decisions of innumerable preceding courts but has even reversed himself."[241]

Likewise, Frankfurter turned out to almost singlehandedly ruin Roosevelt's Supreme Court because of the divisiveness he brought to it. One could say that President Roosevelt had *Second Thoughts* in general about the Supreme Court for which he was almost totally responsible.

* * *

Second Thoughts — William T. Harper

The contentiousness among the Court's members was palpable. According to one observer, the justices often found themselves at odds with one another. "Felix Frankfurter and Robert Jackson detested Hugo Black, and William O. Douglas detested Frankfurter and found common cause with Black. Frank Murphy's abilities were derided by Frankfurter, and Black and Douglas had little respect for Owen Roberts [a Hoover appointee]."[242] On the other hand, it very well could be that the President was actually pleased with this contentiousness because he had a reputation of pitting his friends, appointees, and confidants against each other in an effort to get all points of view and to dig deeply into those opposing opinions.

According to yet another story relayed by one more of his Court brethren, Frank Murphy, "Frankfurter was a great divisive influence in any group that he joined and...that no group would be a happy group that Frankfurter joined. His tactics would be to try to split the group, to get one against the other...."[243] Those tactics would later repel Justice William Brennan who early on usually voted with Frankfurter but then opposed him. For many years Frankfurter feuded with liberals like Justices Black, Douglas, Frank Murphy and Wiley Rutledge. Michael E. Parrish, professor at the University of California at San Diego, said "...there is now almost a universal consensus that Frankfurter the justice was a failure, a judge who... became 'uncoupled from the locomotive of history' during the Second World War, and who thereafter left little in the way of an enduring jurisprudential legacy."[244]

Nonetheless, on January 30, 1939, as his latest nominee, Felix Frankfurter, was sworn in as a member of the Supreme Court, Franklin Roosevelt had high hopes. If ever there was a newly-appointed justice who was seen as possessing the traits necessary to lead the Court, it was Felix Frankfurter. The political liberals rejoiced at the choice. Harold Ikes, a highly-placed advisor to the President, told FDR, "If you appoint Frankfurter, his ability and learning are such that he will dominate the Supreme Court for fifteen or twenty years to come. The result will probably be after you are dead, it will still be known as your Court."[245] Roosevelt was a political and a judicial activist and the last thing he would have wanted in making a Supreme Court nomination was a practitioner of judicial restraint – which is exactly what Mr. Justice Frankfurter turned out to be. With his philosophical and judicial swing to the right, and with the "bar-room brawls" he brought to the inner workings of the Court, one might guess President Franklin Delano Roosevelt had *Second Thoughts* about Felix Frankfurter and whether or not, in Harold Ikes' words, he wanted it to be known as his Court for the next fifteen or twenty years.

* * *

Second Thoughts   William T. Harper

It would be hard, if not impossible, to say President Franklin D. Roosevelt had any initial second thoughts about his appointment of William O. Douglas to the Supreme Court on March 20, 1939 where he served until November 12, 1975 – thirty-six-plus years, the longest tenure in the Court's history. In the first place, Douglas was a personal friend, a guest aboard the presidential yacht *Sequoia* on the Potomac River, and a poker-playing partner of the 32nd President of the United States. FDR could and would see no wrong in the man he formerly had appointed as the third Chairman of the Securities and Exchange Commission (Joseph P. Kennedy, father of the 39th President, was Roosevelt's appointment as the first Chairman). It is doubtful that Roosevelt ever had any second thoughts about his appointment of William Orville Douglas to the highest court in the land. Maybe he would have if he had read the Justice's comments about others in the President's poker-playing circle; comments such as these from Douglas' autobiography:

> ..."On those weekends I got a new insight into Washington, D.C., life and politics. Men hungry for power, position, and publicity ate out their hearts to get a blessing, an approval, an assignment from FDR. Their happiness turned on his smile, his nod, his handshake. I came to realize...how immune my life had been to such influences, how lonely had been the trail I walked. I wanted nothing from any man. I had my own dreams; and they were dependent solely on me, not on the whim or caprice of another."[246]

But, many others were wary about the President's personal poker-playing pal who, whether or not by "whim or caprice," was appointed by Roosevelt to the United States Supreme Court at the age of forty – the second youngest Associate Justice in the history of that august body.[†]

Roosevelt's boating buddy couldn't even keep his prevarications straight, it seems. On the one hand, he wrote in his autobiography that he "had not the slightest idea I would ever be on the Court," that he "*never even dreamed of being there*" [emphasis added], that he "came to the Court without personal ambition ever playing a part." Douglas then contradicted himself "by his own diary entry for March 19, 1939, the date of Roosevelt's offer of the Court seat: 'I was quite overcome-dazed, to be more accurate. *That had always been my ambition* [emphasis added], as I suppose it is with most lawyers'."[247]

[†] Joseph Story was appointed in 1823 at age thirty-two.

Second Thoughts
William T. Harper

One of those subsequently alarmed was author and historian Bruce Allen Murphy who wrote a 2003 biography of the Supreme Court justice entitled, *Wild Bill: The Legend and Life of William O. Douglas*. Richard A. Posner, Judge, United States Seventh Circuit Court of Appeals and a Senior Lecturer at the University of Chicago Law School, wrote a review of the book that appears on the Arlington National Cemetery website. An extract thereof follows – pointing out just a few of some *Second Thoughts* others had about Franklin's friend, "Wild Bill":

> I met Justice William Douglas, the longest-serving member of the Supreme Court, when I was clerking for Justice William Brennan. Douglas struck me as cold and brusque but charismatic – the most charismatic judge (well, the only charismatic judge) on the Court. Little did I know that this elderly gentleman (he was sixty-four when I was a law clerk) was having sex with his soon-to-be third wife in his Supreme Court office, that he was being stalked by his justifiably suspicious soon-to-be ex-wife, and that on one occasion he had to hide the wife-to-be in his closet in order to prevent the current wife from discovering her.
>
> This is just one of the gamy bits in Bruce Allen Murphy's riveting biography of one of the most unwholesome figures in modern American political history, a field with many contenders. Murphy explains that he had expected the biography to take six years to complete but that it actually took almost fifteen. For Douglas turned out to be a liar to rival Baron Munchausen, and a great deal of patient digging was required to reconstruct his true life story. One of his typical lies, not only repeated in a judicial opinion but inscribed on his tombstone in Arlington National Cemetery, was that he had been a soldier in World War I. Douglas was never in the Armed Forces. The lie metastasized: a book about Arlington National Cemetery, published in 1986, reports: "Refusing to allow his polio to keep him from fighting for his nation during World War I, Douglas enlisted in the United States Army and fought in Europe." He never had polio, either.
>
> Apart from being a flagrant liar, Douglas was a compulsive womanizer, a heavy drinker, a terrible husband to each of his four wives, a terrible father to his two children, and a bored, distracted, uncollegial, irresponsible, and at times unethical Supreme Court justice who regularly left the Court for his summer vacation weeks before the term ended. Rude, ice-cold, hot-tempered, ungrateful, foul-mouthed, self-absorbed, and devoured by ambition, he was also financially reckless – at

once a big spender, a tightwad, and a sponge – who, while he was serving as a justice, received a substantial salary from a foundation established and controlled by a shady Las Vegas businessman.

For at least a decade before he was felled in 1974 by the massive stroke that forced his retirement from the Court a year later, Douglas (perhaps as a consequence of his heavy drinking) had been deteriorating morally and psychologically from an already low level. The deterioration manifested itself in paranoid delusions, senile rages and sulks, sadistic treatment of his staff to the point where his law clerks – whom he described as "the lowest form of human life" – took to calling him "shithead" behind his back, and increasingly bizarre behavior toward women, which included an assault in his office on an airline stewardess who had unsuspectingly accepted an invitation from this seemingly kind old man to visit him there. His third marriage, to a woman in her early twenties (the woman in the closet), lasted only two years, and began to disintegrate within weeks of the wedding. After that divorce Douglas speedily took up with two more women in their twenties, marrying one on an impulse but later resuming romantic relations with the other. This fourth marriage might well have dissolved had his stroke held off. As Murphy puts it, Douglas had "buyer's remorse" in the marriage market.

Does any of this matter? It would not – had not Douglas in his autobiographical writings and elsewhere presented his life to the public as exemplary of American individualism and achievement. I cannot begin to imagine his thinking in publishing lies that were readily refutable by documents certain one day to be discovered.[248]

Wild Bill author Bruce Allen Murphy finally concluded that all of Douglas' memoirs are generally inherently "suspect."[249] Likewise, Douglas was sometimes criticized for various ethical lapses in his personal life, and the heroic image that emerges in his autobiographical works has been tarnished by discoveries that he had bent the truth on a number of details, e.g., his youthful health and social status, his military service, and his academic record.[250]

In another controversy involving Douglas, still other historians take issue with the Justice's truthfulness. As a matter of fact, "He lied," is the flat-out claim in their book about FDR and the Supreme Court, said the three authors of a book about Roosevelt and the Court.[251] This opinion was centered on the 1944 Democratic Party's convention in Chicago and the battle amid a crowded field of potential FDR running mates, one of which was William O. Douglas. The authors go on to say that Douglas was "being less than truthful" about his involvement in the political jockeying for the Number Two slot on the ticket (that eventually went to Harry S. Truman).

Sixty-seven-year-old William O. Douglas takes twenty-three-year-old Cathleen Heffernan as his fourth wife.

Even then House Minority Leader (and future President of the United States) Gerald Ford denounced Douglas in April of 1970 when he called for Douglas' impeachment as a member of the Supreme Court. Ford questioned the Justice's association with a charitable foundation, his association with the "leftish" Center for the Study of Democratic Institutions, and blasted some of Douglas' writings, in particular *Points of Revolution* which said that unless the U. S. accepted the pressures for non-violent revolutionary change, it would be overthrown by violence.

Lying, philandering, facing possible impeachment, questionable associations? If these things are not enough to give a president *Second Thoughts* about a person he nominated to sit in judgment – longer than any Supreme Court justice in the Nation's history – on that Nation's court of last resort, they should be.

Second Thoughts   William T. Harper

* * *

Regarding another of President Roosevelt's nine Supreme Court nominations, author Geoffrey Stone has written, "It was never entirely clear why President Roosevelt nominated Attorney General Frank Murphy to replace Justice Pierce Butler. Murphy did not have the background or the intellectual depth ordinarily associated with a Supreme Court justice. Even Murphy doubted his capacity to handle the position. Robert Jackson, then Murphy's subordinate as Solicitor General of the United States, strongly advised the president against the appointment. Francis Biddle, [later Jackson's successor as Solicitor General], was certain Murphy was the wrong man for the job. Nonetheless, suggesting that Murphy could grow into an 'acceptable justice,' and that his colleagues on the Court would 'keep him straight,' Roosevelt nominated Murphy to the court on January 4, 1940. Roosevelt's motives included…his confidence that Murphy would support the New Deal; and his desire to move Murphy, who was not a particularly deft administrator, out of the Department of Justice…."[252]

Things apparently went along pretty much as Roosevelt expected. In Murphy, he had an "acceptable justice" and Murphy's other FDR-appointed colleagues on the Court kept "him straight." He so much supported the New Deal with his liberal opinions that he even earned the sobriquet, "Justice tempered with Murphy." But the *Korematsu* case, a Supreme Court landmark ruling five years after Murphy joined the Court, surely must have given the President second thoughts – perhaps for much of the less than four months Roosevelt had left to live.

Korematsu v. United States, concerned the constitutionality of Executive Order 9066 issued by President Roosevelt on February 19, 1942, shortly after war was declared against Japan on December 8, 1941. The presidential fiat required 110,000 Japanese-American citizens to report to West Coast internment camps because of their perceived threat to the United States should Japanese military forces invade Alaska, and California or other western states. Perhaps that Executive Order is less surprising when it was signed by the same man who once said:

> "Anyone who has traveled to the Far East knows that the mingling of Asiatic blood with European or American blood produces, in nine cases out of ten, the most unfortunate results. … The argument works both ways. I know a great many cultivated, highly educated and delightful Japanese. They have all told me that they would feel the same repugnance and objection to have thousands of Americans settle in Japan and intermarry with the Japanese as I would feel in having large

numbers of Japanese coming over here and intermarry with the American population. In this question, then, of Japanese exclusion from the United States it is necessary only to advance the true reason – the undesirability of mixing the blood of the two peoples. . . . The Japanese people and the American people are both opposed to intermarriage of the two races – there can be no quarrel there."[253]

In a 6-3 decision handed down on December 18, 1944, the Court sided against Fred Korematsu (one of those detainees who refused to report to the internment camps). In its ruling for the President, the Court declared Roosevelt's order was constitutional. The opinion, written by Supreme Court Justice Hugo Black, held that the need to protect against espionage outweighed Korematsu's individual rights, and the rights of Americans of Japanese descent.

Justice Murphy, in his dissenting opinion in *Korematsu*, charged, "This exclusion of 'all persons of Japanese ancestry, both alien and non-alien,' from the Pacific Coast area on a plea of military necessity in the absence of martial law ought not to be approved. Such exclusion goes over 'the very brink of constitutional power,' and falls into the ugly abyss of racism."[254] He continued his virulent dissent against Roosevelt's Executive Order by comparing its rationale to "the abhorrent and despicable treatment of minority groups by the dictatorial tyrannies which this nation is now pledged to destroy."[255]

Comparing Franklin Roosevelt as a racist with "dictatorial tyrannies" such as Adolph Hitler's, one has to wonder how "acceptable" were these comments to the man who appointed Frank Murphy as an Associate Justice of the United States Supreme Court? But in the long run and as Judge Richard A. Posner asked of Justice William O. Douglas in the preceding segment herein, "does any of this matter" when your political opposition labels you "King Frank the First"? According to the *St. Petersburg Times*, "Mr. Roosevelt has not only refashioned the Supreme Court, he has appointed 165 of the 275 principle Federal judges, and in that number somehow found only two Republicans qualified."[256]

* * *

As with many of FDR's appointments to high government office and considered by historians as his "cronies," James F. Byrnes, a friend and member of Roosevelt's famous "Brain Trust" of friendly advisors, was later described publicly by the President as his "Assistant President on the home front." Byrnes was another leading contender for the 1944 vice-presidential nomination when Roosevelt decided his 1940 running mate, Vice-President Henry Wallace would be a detriment to re-election.

Second Thoughts William T. Harper

Coming from an impoverished South Carolina family (his father died within weeks after he was born in 1879 which later forced him to drop out of school to financially help his dressmaker-mother by working as a messenger in a local law office), "Jimmy" Byrnes capitalized on his early surroundings and rose up the political ladder quickly. He was elected to the U. S. House of Representatives (1911) and ultimately the U. S. Senate (1930) where he soon became known as President Roosevelt's "legislative ball carrier." However, as FDR's legislative efforts moved left, Byrnes moved right in his second Senate term as he joined the opposition to pro-union New Deal legislation and also voted against the minimum wage law of 1938.

When Justice James C. McReynolds retired from the Court on January 31, 1941, the President felt comfortable enough – with five of his liberal acolytes already on the Supreme Court – to get Byrnes out of the Senate and on to the Court Bench with a nomination on June 10, 1941. No matter how far Byrnes was drifting to the right, he'd still be far to the left of McReynolds, one of the Court's conservative "Four Horsemen." Whether or not the Senate was just as anxious as the President to get rid of Byrnes or if that body was simply offering Senatorial Courtesy to one of its own is not for speculation here. However, Byrnes' nomination was approved by the Senate via a voice vote on the very same day.

Historians agree, it was not unusual for Roosevelt to favor his friends and followers and keep them guessing regarding his true intentions. Like Byrnes, William O. Douglas was another FDR appointee to the Court who thought the President wanted him as a V/P running mate because, among other attributes, the President thought the candidate "played an interesting game of poker." Roosevelt, it seems, liked running "beauty pageants" among his confidants but the trouble there is – as in all beauty pageants – there is only one winner and many losers. Since Byrnes was once a Catholic (though later an Episcopalian), divorced, and perceived as anti-labor (i.e., voting against the minimum wage bill), Roosevelt subsequently felt that Byrnes too would be rejected by large elements of the Democratic Party coalition. The nomination – and ultimately the presidency following Roosevelt's death in 1945 – went instead to Harry S. Truman from the old-line Kansas City "Boss" Tom Prendergast machine.

Whether he was bitter at being dumped by Roosevelt[257] – as were some other FDR pageant losers – or for additional reasons, Byrnes turned increasingly away from FDR's policies, especially on issues of race. Having once proclaimed, as a member of the U. S. House of Representatives, that "this is a white man's country, and will always remain a white man's country"[258] and publicly favoring school segregation, he re-affirmed the political conservatism of his South Carolina roots. Byrnes served only sixteen months on the Supreme Court, the shortest term in the history of the Court, when Roosevelt asked him in October 1942 to leave that position and take on new responsibilities in his wartime administration. At one point, Jimmy Byrnes called his Supreme Court sponsor's court-packing effort a "dramatic and historic attack by the Executive on the Judiciary."[259] James Francis Byrnes ultimately reached the point where he supported Republican presidential candidates Dwight D. Eisenhower in 1952, Barry Goldwater in 1964 and Richard M. Nixon in 1968. If he cared at all, what *Second Thoughts* would Franklin Delano Roosevelt have about that?

* * *

Chapter XXX
"Give 'em Hell, Harry" Really Did
(Term in Office: April 12, 1945-January 20, 1953)

Harry S. Truman, the nation's thirty-third President, sent four names to the United States Senate for confirmation as Supreme Court justices during his seven-plus years in the White House.

President Harry Truman's Nominees (in reverse order)				
Name	Replacing	Nominated	Vote	Result/Date
Sherman Minton	Rutledge	Sep 15, 1949	48-16	C 10/04/49
Tom Clark	Murphy	Aug 2, 1949	73-8	C 08/18/49
Fred Vinson[6]	Stone	Jun 6, 1946	V	C 06/20/46
Harold Burton	Roberts	Sep 19, 1945	V	C 09/19/45
6 Chief Justice C = Confirmed V = Voice Vote This chart lists only nominations officially submitted to the Senate, and does not include nominations announced but never officially submitted. Source: www.senate.gov/pagelayout/reference/nominations/Nominations.htm				

All four, as the chart shows, were confirmed. And all four must also have caused "the man from Missouri" to have *Second Thoughts*. Two of his nominees must have infuriated him when they voted against him in a landmark, very public Supreme Court decision. One of them was later described by the President as "a dumb son of a bitch." One was judged as "less than impressive" on the Bench, gave the bulk of his opinion-writing to his clerks, and "showed no great philosophic appreciation of Constitutional law." His even greater sin as a Truman appointee was that "he generally voted conservatively." The fourth, as viewed by his voting record on the Court, was said to have transformed from a New Deal senator into an almost reactionary judge.

The entire group was cited by one noted legal advisor, Lawrence H. Tribe, as "perhaps the least distinguished group of appointments made by any president in this century."[260] Even Justice Sherman Minton agreed with that assessment when he commented on his pending retirement, "There will be more interest in who will succeed me than in my passing. I am an echo." Yet another report slammed Truman-appointed Chief Justice Fred Vinson in a 1970 poll of "experts" that rated the entire conglomeration of Supreme Court justices and included Vinson as one of eight "failures," the only Chief Justice to be so categorized in that poll.

In any case, rousing President Truman's anger was not good a good idea. General Douglas MacArthur infuriated the President with his military conduct of the Korean War after "Mac" threatened to use nuclear weapons against the Chinese Red Army and chase it north of the Yalu River back into mainland China. The General was, in effect, cashiered (meaning "canned" in non-military speak). The President even ordered a press conference at one o'clock in the morning on April 11, 1951 to get out the word of Mac's firing just so the general couldn't beat the president to the publicity punch by resigning.

Another who faced Truman's wrath – though in a somewhat less of an Armageddon-lie nature – was a *Washington Post* newspaper music critic who judged the President's only child, his daughter Margaret, to be something less than a diva after her operatic performance on December 6, 1950. The critic, Paul Hume, wrote that although she was "extremely attractive on the stage...[she] cannot sing very well. She is flat a good deal of the time." The boiling mad President wrote the following letter to Hume on White House stationary:

Dec. 6, 1950

Mr. Hume:
    I've just read your lousy review of Margaret's concert. I've come to the conclusion that you are an "eight ulcer man on four ulcer pay."

It seems to me that you are a frustrated old man who wishes he could have been successful. When you write such poppy-cock as was in the back section of the paper you work for it shows conclusively that you're off the beam and at least four of your ulcers are at work.

Some day I hope to meet you. When that happens you'll need a new nose, a lot of beefsteak for black eyes, and perhaps a supporter below!

[Westbrook] Pegler [a Hearst newspaper writer and anti-New Dealer], a gutter snipe, is a gentleman alongside you. I hope you'll accept that statement as a worse insult than a reflection on your ancestry.

H.S.T.

Then there was the government's take-over of the steel industry in 1952. The United Steel Workers of America labor union voted to strike against the major steel manufacturing companies after the producers rejected a government-proposed wage increase that lacked a concurrent price hike. The Truman administration believed that a strike of any length would disrupt the then-raging Korean War effort, cause severe dislocations for defense contractors, and for the domestic economy as a whole. The President was most intolerant about union strikers who endangered a national emergency. Six years earlier, both coal miners and railroad workers staged nationwide strikes. President Truman decided that the unions had gone too far, and he seized control of the railroads. Undaunted, the railroad workers continued with their strike plans. On May 24, 1946, Truman called the strikers' bluff and issued an ultimatum: the government would operate the railroads, use the army as strikebreakers, and – with Congress' permission – draft strikers into the armed forces. When someone questioned him about the constitutionality of such a move, the President brushed him aside saying, "We'll draft 'em first and think about the law later."[261] At that point, the union decided to settle the strike on the President's terms.

The issue arose again when Truman, with the concurrence of his Attorney General, seized the steel companies on April 8, 1952, and the government began to run them using the then-current operating management. Things did not go quite as well as the President thought they would based on the 1946 railroad workers' cave-in. In the first place, he ran into fierce opposition from some members of Congress who feared if the President could seize the steel mills, he could do the same with such as the Nation's cattle industry, its farming industry, or any private entity. This, they felt, could ultimately lead to a national dictatorship.

Truman looked for legal guidance and the man he had appointed as Chief Justice of the Supreme Court after the death of Harlan Fiske Stone on April 22, 1946 – Fred M. Vinson – led the President astray. Vinson reportedly advised Truman (perhaps during one of their regular poker sessions) that if he did seize the mills, he shouldn't worry; a majority of the Court would support his decision. (The propriety of a Supreme Court Chief Justice personally advising a President of the Constitutionality of a potential Supreme Court ruling is questioned here. But under government-by-crony, it obviously happens.) The President's then Attorney General, Tom Campbell Clark whom he later appointed to the Supreme Court, supported Vinson's assessment of the legality of the takeover. The matter, commonly known as the Steel Seizure Case, came before the Court as *Youngstown Sheet & Tube Co. v. Sawyer* in 1952.

Facts of the Case:
In April of 1952, during the Korean War, President Truman issued an executive order directing Secretary of Commerce Charles Sawyer to seize and operate most of the nation's steel mills. This was done in order to avert the expected effects of a strike by the United Steel-workers of America.

Question:
Did the President have the constitutional authority to seize and operate the steel mills?

Conclusion:
In a 6-to-3 decision, the Court held that the President did not have the authority to issue such an order. The Court found that there was no congressional statute that authorized the President to take possession of private property. The Court also held that the President's military power as Commander in Chief of the Armed Forces did not extend to labor disputes. The Court argued that "the President's power to see that the laws are faithfully executed refutes the idea that he is to be a lawmaker."[262]

Vinson's and Clark's prognostications were proven wrong two years later by the Court's vote declaring the President's action unconstitutional. The Chief Justice voted in the President's favor but former Attorney General Clark, by then a member of the Supreme Court, joined the majority in proclaiming Truman's action unconstitutional – in effect, voting against himself and his earlier advice to the President.

Harry S. Truman was not, to say the least, pleased with the Court's action in general and with Clark's in particular – who declared the President violated the Constitution by usurping the legislative powers reserved to Congress. Later, in expressing his regret at his choice of Clark for a seat on the Bench, the President – in his best Missouri Mule-Skinner language – said, "It isn't so much that [Clark's] a bad man. It's just that he's such a dumb son of a bitch. He's about the dumbest man I've ever run across....I never will know what got into me when I made that appointment, and I'm sorry as I can be for making it."[263] Talk about *Second Thoughts*.

Another version of the President's opinion of his Attorney General/Supreme Court nominee was that Clark "was no damn good as Attorney General, and on the Supreme Court ... it doesn't seem possible, but he's been even worse. He hasn't made one right decision that I can think of. And so when you ask me what was my biggest mistake, that's it. Putting Tom Clark on the Supreme Court of the United States."[264] Historian, author and Rice University Professor Douglas Brinkley noted the end of the friendship between President Truman and Justice Clark brought about by the steel strike controversy: "Tom really had to sock it to Harry. It really strained their friendship."[265] One would say so. Obviously, President Harry S. Truman had more than one second thought about Associate Justice Tom C. Clark.

Associate Justice Tom C. Clark (standing left with the Vinson Court) was the target of a presidential tirade when Harry S. Truman reportedly called him "a dumb son of a bitch."

* * *

The fourth and last of Truman's Supreme Court appointees was Sherman Minton. Born on October 20, 1890 in rural southern Indiana, impoverished during his youth after his father was disabled and his mother died of breast cancer, he worked his way through high school and went on to Indiana and Yale Universities. At the latter, he came under the influence of former President and later Chief Justice of the Supreme Court, William Howard Taft. He served as a captain in World War I where he fought in the horrific Battle of Verdun, after which he embarked on his legal and political career. He won election to the United States Senate in 1934 where he championed President Roosevelt's unsuccessful court packing plans. He also became one of Roosevelt's top allies in the Senate through his investigations of Republican-controlled media conglomerates. He also became a close friend of a fellow senator from Missouri – Harry S. Truman.

In a devastating coincidence, two of President Roosevelt's most liberal Supreme Court Justices died within less than two months of each other – Frank Murphy on July .19, 1949 and Wiley B. Rutledge on September 9. Truman, still basking in the glow of his "Give-'em-Hell, Harry" upset victory in the presidential election campaign of the previous

Second Thoughts   William T. Harper

November, jabbed again with a one-two punch of Texan Tom Campbell Clark taking Murphy's place and his Indiana Senator friend, Sherman Minton, filling Rutledge's, with Minton being the last member of the Upper House to become a Supreme Court justice.

The news of the appointment five days after Rutledge's death was not generally lauded in the press. According to the *New York Times*, in naming Minton, Truman had allowed personal and political friendship to influence his choice. The *New Republic* said "the President is again reverting to his deplorable habit of choosing men for high post because they happen to be his friends...." Despite the assessments in the press, the thirty-third President of the United States would ruefully say later after these two friends of his (Clark and Minton), both former political sidekicks, went against him on big cases, "Whenever you put a man on the Supreme Court, he ceases to be your friend." The former County Judge from Independence, Missouri, put a lot of stock in friendships – such as those in the "Boss "Prendergast Missouri political machine where one hand washed the other.

As a friend, Minton's unsuccessful dissent supported President Truman in the *Youngtown Sheet & Tube Co. v. Sawyer* decision in 1952 which ruled unconstitutional the President's wartime seizure of the steel mills. But the friendships were slipping downhill faster than a two-man Olympic luge. Minton transformed from a New Deal senator into an almost reactionary judge under the influence of Justice Felix Frankfurter. According to some reports, his unwavering support of governmental policies made him one of the most conservative justices on the Court for the duration of his career.

According to author Linda C. Gugin, "Although there are exceptions, scholars generally consider Minton to have been an ineffective Justice who was put on the bench only because he was a crony of President Harry Truman. Indeed, the scholars who periodically provide a list of the 'greatest' and 'worst' Justices inevitably relegate Minton to the 'worst' category." Continuing Gugin wrote, "For example, Bernard Schwartz, who classified Minton as one of the ten worst Justices, said Minton 'was below mediocrity as a Justice. His opinions, relatively few for his tenure, are less than third-rate, characterized by their cavalier approach to complicated issues'."[266]

Voting with Clark in *Youngstown* was another Truman-appointee, Harold Burton. The man from Missouri again expressed his anger in the last paragraph of the unsent letter (shown below) to Supreme Court Associate Justice Associate Justice William O. Douglas expressing some of HST's rage at the votes cast against him by Justices Burton and Clark. Six months after writing this letter, President Truman did, indeed as he prognosticated therein, "quit" that office via Dwight Eisenhower's election to the presidency, but without – as far as is recorded – finding out the why to the questions asked in the letter. It may have been because that "Court made up of so-called 'Liberals'" was not exactly that. What "Give 'em Hell, Harry" may have missed was that a majority in his

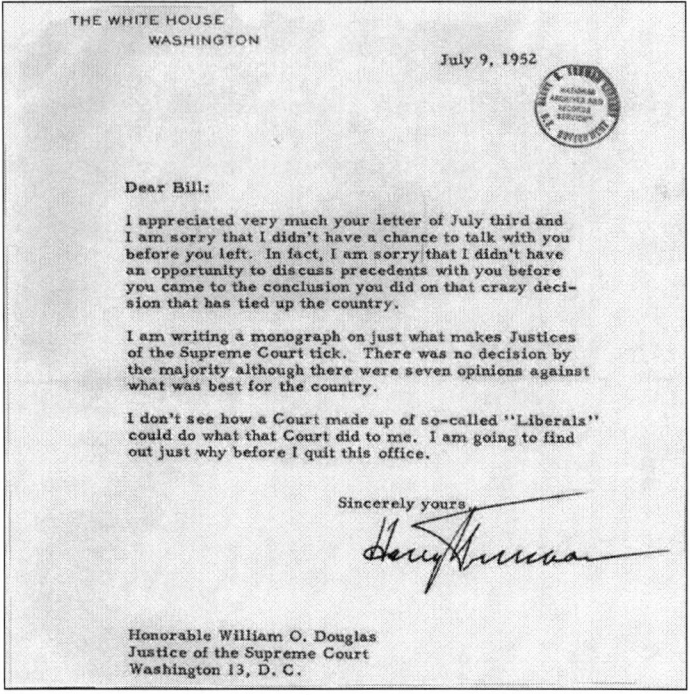

Courtesy: Harry S. Truman Library

Supreme Court had flip-flopped tendencies. Chief Justice Vinson was in that camp. The record shows that ideologically, Vinson usually voted with the conservative justices (Jackson, Frankfurter, Burton and Reed) and against the liberals (Douglas, Rutledge, Murphy, and Black). The conservative wing began to dominate the Court even further when Truman-appointees Tom Clark and Sherman Minton replaced Justices Murphy and Rutledge in 1949.

All four of Truman's Supreme Court appointees were personal friends or acquaintances of the President, with political backgrounds rather than judicial. Burton and Minton had served with Truman in the Senate; Vinson and Clark had served in Truman's Cabinet as Treasury Secretary and as Attorney General, respectively. Vinson was a favorite poker-playing companion of the President. Further clouding the issues, even the Vinson Court holdovers from President Roosevelt continued their philosophical and personal animosities on the Court, most notably between Justices Black and Jackson. Each of these two threatened President Truman with resignation should he appoint the other to the Chief Justice slot eventually awarded to Vinson as a consolation prize in a peace-making effort. President Truman had to have had *Second Thoughts* over Vinson's totally unexpected inability to bring these warring factions into a harmonious relationship and the political, philosophical and judicial U-turns made by the four men he elevated to the Supreme Court of the United States. And far as anyone knows, he did not – as he wrote to Justice Douglas – ever "find out just what makes Justices of the Supreme Court tick."

* * *

Chapter XXXI
"The Biggest Damn Fool Thing" Ike Ever Did
(Term in Office: 1953-1961)

It has been reported, often erroneously, five-star General Dwight David Eisenhower owed his 1952 presidential nomination at the national Republican convention to Earl Warren, then three-term Governor of California, and the party's Vice Presidential candidate in the losing "Give 'em Hell, Harry" national race in 1948. Some have said it was Warren's leap onto the Eisenhower convention bandwagon in 1952 that put Ike over the top as he took himself out of the balloting and cast his votes for the General. Not so. Actually, the vote of Minnesota Governor Harold Stassen cleared the way for Eisenhower. The confusion and misunderstanding was quickly glossed over in the wake of the November election, which Eisenhower won in a landslide over Adlai E. Stevenson.

Part of that huge victory did come from California voters who, with the hugely popular Warren's enthusiastic urging, cast their votes for the Republican candidate, thereby overcoming Vice Presidential candidate Richard M. Nixon's pre-election stumble regarding a so-called "secret slush fund." Was the General therefore indebted to the Governor? Again, confusion. There are those who say it was definitely so – that Ike admitted as much. Not so, say others. According to one historian, Michal Belknap, Eisenhower insisted, "I owed Governor Warren nothing."[267]

Whether or not he did – and some reports at the time convey the impression the General's convention handlers offered to reward Governor Warren for his convention support with almost any Cabinet job he wanted in the future administration – the new President (again according to Belknap and others) told the Governor, "I intend to offer you the first vacancy on the Supreme Court."[268] Much to Eisenhower's surprise – and everyone else's – that vacancy sprang up eight months into Ike's presidency, on September 8, 1953. Chief Justice Fred M. Vinson suffered a massive early morning heart attack and died. Whether or not Eisenhower had meant that "first vacancy" offer to be the Chief Justice's position is another matter for speculation. But true to his word, three weeks later, Eisenhower nominated Earl Warren as Chief Justice of the United States Supreme Court.

The son of Scandinavian immigrant parents, Warren became an immensely popular politician in his home state of California. Elected state Attorney General with the backing of both the Republican and Democratic parties in 1938 and elected governor of the Golden State in 1942, he gained re-election four years later – again with the backing of both major political parties. Following the Thomas E. Dewey-Warren loss to Truman-Alben Barkley in the 1948 presidential race, he won a third stay in the California governor's mansion in 1950 when he trounced Franklin D. Roosevelt's son James. To date, he is the only three-term governor of California.

President Dwight Eisenhower's Nominees (in reverse order)				
Name	Replacing	Nominated	Vote	Result & Date
Potter Stewart	Burton	Jan 17, 1959	70-17	C 05/05/59
Charles Whittaker	Reed	Mar 2, 1957	V	C 03/19/57
Wm. Brennan, Jr.	Minton	Jan 14, 1957	V	C 03/19/57
John Harlan	Jackson	Jan 10, 1955	71-11	C 03/16/55
John Harlan	Jackson	Nov 9, 1954	N	
Earl Warren[5]	Vinson	Jan 11, 1954	V	C 03/01/54
[5]-for Chief Justice C=Confirmed N=No Action V=Voice Vote This chart lists only nominations officially submitted to the Senate, and does not include nominations announced but never officially submitted. Source: www.senate.gov/pagelayout/reference/nominations/Nominations.htm				

Warren had a reputation as a tough-on-crime official and, as his state's Attorney General, he is most remembered for his support of President Roosevelt's policy of placing West Coast Japanese-Americans in internment camps during World War II. Testifying before Congress prior to FDR's fiat being enacted, Warren said, "The only reason that there has been no sabotage or espionage on the part of Japanese-Americans is that they are waiting for the right moment to strike." (He later recanted his stance in this matter.) During his governorship, he laid the infrastructure that led to twenty years of boom times in California. He was also instrumental in building his state's large public university system. In 1947, he signed a law repealing school segregation in California long before it became national law. All of this and more made him shine brightly in President Eisenhower's eyes when Ike – the Chief Executive who ordered Federal troops into Little Rock, Arkansas in support of the 1957 school desegregation struggle there – wrote to his brother Milton ten days after nominating Warren as Chief Justice:

> "I believe that we need *statesmanship* on the Supreme Court. Statesmanship is developed in the hard knocks of a general experience, private and public. Naturally, a man occupying the post must be competent in the law – and Warren has had seventeen years of practice in *public* law, during which his record was one of remarkable accomplishment and success, to say nothing of dedication. He has been very definitely a liberal-

conservative; he represents the kind of political, economic, and social thinking that I believe we need on the Supreme Court. Finally, he has a national name for integrity, uprightness, and courage that, again, I believe we need on the Court."[269]

In believing Warren was "a liberal-conservative," Eisenhower was hoping the new Chief Justice would be a middle-of-the-roader in philosophy as well as "statesmanship" in an effort to restore some harmony among the warring factions plaguing the Supreme Court justices throughout much of the two previous decades. But, it did not take long for the world's most famous soldier since Julius Caesar to realize he had made a tactical mistake on the battlefield of jurisprudence. When Eisenhower alluded to Warren's "political, economic, and social thinking that I believe we need on the Supreme Court," the planner of D-Day's tremendous ultimate victory in Europe saw his latest strategy for judicial and personal restraint go down to – what was in his mind – a defeat rivaling Napoleon's at Waterloo. Hoping he had nominated "a moderate conservative, Warren proved to be an unabashed liberal."[270] The Warren Court launched a program of liberal judicial activism never, in his wildest dreams, expected by the man who appointed him. Its rulings included, among others:

> *Brown v. Board of Education of Topeka* – ruling that state laws establishing separate public schools for black and white students denied black children equal educational opportunities; that "separate educational facilities are inherently unequal."
> *Loving v. Virginia*, ending all race-based legal restrictions on marriage.
> *Engel v. Vitale* made it unconstitutional for state officials to compose an official school prayer and require its recitation in public schools.
> *Miranda v. Arizona* ruled that statements made by those in police custody would not be admissible at trial if the defendant therein was not informed of the right to have an attorney present before and during questioning, that the defendant not only understood these rights, but voluntarily waived them. In other words, all persons questioned by police have to be read their "Miranda rights."

Many of the rulings coming from the Warren Court were based on what has been termed "evolving standards of decency," which according to many legal scholars, was in direct conflict with the Framers' intent in writing the U. S. Constitution. Under Chief Justice Warren's leadership, the Court was widely accused of "judicial activism, rejecting the tendency of more conservative Courts to make decisions based on precedent, following the reasoning and authority of earlier, similar decisions. The Warren Court frequently overruled earlier decisions…even when there was no precedent for such rulings."[271] These actions by the Warren Court led to billboards springing up across the country demanding: "Impeach Earl Warren!"

Along with the social activism of the Warren Court of the 1950s came what many historians view as the epitome of second thoughts, the origins of the politicization of the Supreme Court's confirmation process. Earl Warren's arrival as chief justice in 1954 coincided with the Court's decision in the famous desegregation case *Brown v. Board of Education*. In July 2005, University of New Hampshire history professor Ellen Fitzpatrick said the Supreme Court had traditionally been a fairly conservative institution, rarely leading in advance of Congress or the president himself. That changed with the Warren court. "[In *Brown v. Board of Education*], the court actually took a step far beyond where either the president or the Congress was ready to go," she said. [272]

The politicization of the confirmation process stemmed directly from the court taking on these hot-button issues, according to Dennis Hutchinson, professor at University of Chicago Law School and editor of the school's Supreme Court Review. "It has more to do with the sort of issues that the Supreme Court is willing to decide on and the stakes the various groups see in that jurisdiction," he said. Organizations with interests in issues such as abortion, the death penalty and homosexuality started to turn their attention toward the court.[273]

For those with conservative inclinations, like President Eisenhower, "the Warren Court converted constitutional law into ordinary politics."[274] For these and some other reasons, the nomination of Earl Warren as Chief Justice of the Supreme Court of the United States led President Dwight D. Eisenhower to declare publically that it was "the biggest damn fool thing I ever did."[275]

Thus, the epitome of *Second Thoughts*.

* * *

If Earl Warren's nomination was the "biggest damn fool thing" Dwight Eisenhower ever did, then also by his own admission, the nomination of William J. Brennan, Jr. as an Associate Justice of the United States Supreme Court on January 14, 1957, was his second biggest mistake.[276] Eisenhower lumped Justice Brennan right in there with Warren, though in somewhat milder tones, when he told Supreme Court Justice Tom C. Clark he "was very much disturbed over Chief Justice Warren and Justice Brennan." He went on to say he was "disappointed" with the latter.[277]

However, the "mistake" with Justice Brennan may have been of the General's own making. After forty-two years in the military, like any good officer, he had learned to trust and depend on his subordinates – as Robert E. Lee did with T. J. "Stonewall" Jackson and as U. S. Grant did with William Tecumseh Sherman in the War Between the States, and as Eisenhower did in World War II with Omar Bradley and others. In this case, Ike's political lieutenants may have let him down.

Brennan first crossed Eisenhower's radar screen in the months leading up to the 1956 presidential election. In the vetting process, much attention was paid to a May 22, 1956 speech Brennan delivered for his mentor on the New Jersey State Supreme Court, Arthur Vanderbilt, in which reformation of the judicial system was Topic A. Based on that speech (in which some historians say Brennan was only mouthing Vanderbilt's views while others say he totally subscribed to them), and on Vanderbilt's generous recommendation to the Eisenhower high command, Brennan got the nod to replace the retiring Sherman Minton on the Bench.

The fact that the Garden-Stater fit some of the other perceived needs seen by Ike's aides – he was young (50), he was Catholic, he was Irish, he was a Democrat – are said by some to indicate the Republican team operating from the White House wanted to appeal to those same constituencies. The aim was to head off a looming political threat posed by another young, Catholic, Irish, Democrat emerging on the national scene in 1956; a man named John F. Kennedy. (Not that it mattered a great deal as Dwight Eisenhower beat Adlai Stevenson in 1956 by an even wider margin than he did in 1952 – 57%-42% vs. 55-44.) However, the President's vetting team was said to have been caught up in the politics of the Court nominating process. It felt the need to counter the "activism" on the Bench as personified by Chief Justice Earl Warren (which they thought the Vanderbilt speech implied). Instead, they completely missed the thrust of Brennan's judicial record on the State's Supreme Court. As it turned out, Brennan proved to be the most liberal and influential justice on the modern Supreme Court.[278]

Had the vetters looked more closely at Brennan's judicial philosophy, there they would have found an almost total record of liberal leanings in his rulings over the years. According to Brennan's "official" biographer, Stephen J. Wermiel, "Brennan's friends in New Jersey at the time and other local legal observers knew he was unmistakably liberal, and his record of decisions affirmed that view."[279] Nonetheless, reported Wermiel, Eisenhower's Attorney General, Herbert Brownell, told the President he had "read all his opinions on the New Jersey Court and he seemed to be qualified…. There were no opinions of his that really grappled with the constitutional problems the Supreme Court constantly faces but we felt…there's no doubt about his character, and his legal and judicial experience were not only adequate but really outstanding."[280] If, in 1944, the Supreme Commander of the European Theater of Operations had received information on the eve of D-Day as faulty as that, we might all now be speaking German.

Because Congress was in recess at the time (the members were home campaigning for the November elections), Brennan joined the Court on an interim basis on October 16, 1956. It was one of the three times during the 1950s in which President Eisenhower resorted to recess appointments when Justices died or announced their retirement after Congress had already adjourned for the year. In each case, President Eisenhower formally submitted the nomination on the following January 14th, after the Senate convened. Of the five persons whom he nominated to the Court, three first received recess appointments and served as Justices before being confirmed — Earl Warren (as Chief Justice) in 1953, William Brennan in 1956, and Potter Stewart in 1958.[281]

According to Professor Melvin I. Urofsky, Professor of History and Director of Doctoral Program in Public Policy & Administration at Virginia Commonwealth University, "Although the state court had little occasion to deal with federal constitutional questions, Brennan touched on a number of issues that later became hallmarks of his decisions on the Supreme Court. He took a broad view of the privileges against self-discrimination…. He took a strong position against prior restraint of free expression [and] in his most famous state court dissent…he excoriated the majority for refusing to allow an accused murderer to inspect his own confession."[282] That Brownell saw no liberal leanings in these cases and recommended Brennan as a moderate was puzzling in some quarters.

Brennan was formally nominated by President Eisenhower on January 14, 1957 and the Senate's consent came on the following March 19. Senator Joseph R. McCarthy (R-WI) provided the single dissenting vote because of two speeches Brennan gave in 1954 criticizing "congressional investigations that threaten the rights of individuals."[283] It was just these kinds of investigations that were dear to the heart of the man who launched "the McCarthy Era."

President Eisenhower, who had sent him to the Court, was only slightly less irked by and disenchanted with Brennan's evolving record than with Chief Justice Earl Warren's (whose opinions Brennan joined in most instances). When Eisenhower was asked later if he had made any mistakes while he had been president, he replied: "Yes, two and they are both sitting on the Supreme Court." The "both" referred to Warren and Brennan.[284] Some historians, such as Melvin I. Urofsky, have said there is no evidence to prove Eisenhower ever said this.

Together with Justice Thurgood Marshall, Brennan thus evolved into the leading liberal activist on the (Warren) Burger court after 1969.[285] For instance, in the long-simmering Constitutional argument of "evolving standards" versus "original intent," Brennan opted for the former. In 1961 he said: "What 'due process' under the 14th Amendment meant to the wisdom of other days cannot be its measure of the vision of our time."[286] Similarly, his liberal leanings were likewise expressed in *Goldberg v. Kelly*, regarding termination of welfare benefits and requiring notice and a hearing before benefits can be ended. In dissenting to Justice Brennan's opinion, Justice Hugo Black said, "Termination of aid pending a resolution of a controversy over eligibility may deprive an eligible recipient of the very means by which to live while he waits."[287] Continuing his dissent, Black said, "the court was making political judgments, acting like a legislature rather than a group of judges."[288]

True to form, Associate Justice William J. Brennan, Jr., rarely varied from his liberal judicial background. He:

- Opened the door to the "reapportionment revolution" (redistribution of representation in legislative bodies) of the 1960s and 1970s and the rule of "one person, one vote" in legislative districting,
- Led the Court in extending the protections of the First and Fourteenth Amendments to criticism of public officials,
- Authored eminent opinions that, for example, restricted loyalty oaths and government regulation of pornography,
- Recognized a broad freedom of association (the individual right to come together with other individuals and collectively express and defend common interests),
- Supported curbs on prayer in public schools, and
- Expanded the availability of *habeas corpus* and other federal judicial remedies for constitutional violations.

No opinion by Justice Brennan has received more widespread recognition, nor more practical effect, than *Baker v. Carr* (1962)…which led directly to the subsequent principle of one person, one vote. Chief Justice Warren remarked later that the ruling was the "most important" of his tenure.[289]

* * *

Eisenhower, born in Texas and raised in the Kansas cow-country, saw law-and-order as an everyday way of life. His entire career in the U. S. Army came under its Uniform Code of Military Justice. As Commanding officer of the entire European Theater of Operations during the closing phases of World War II, he had the responsibility as a court-of-last-resort. As such, he became the one who confirmed the sentence ordering the firing-squad execution of Private Eddie Slovik for desertion. Slovik thus became the only American soldier to die in that manner since the Civil War. Eisenhower was also the last *President* to approve a military execution – that of Army Private John Bennett, convicted of raping and attempting to kill an eleven-year-old girl. Likewise, Eisenhower refused to grant executive clemency to convicted spies Ethel and Julius Rosenberg. He felt certain of their guilt and acquiesced in their execution in the electric chair in 1953.

Dwight David Eisenhower obviously believed in "an eye for an eye." When one of his Supreme Court candidates, William Brennan, Jr., declared in a dissenting opinion the death sentence is in *all circumstances* cruel and unusual, it had to cause anyone with a record like Eisenhower's to have regrets over the nomination of Justice Brennan to the Supreme Court.

Eisenhower may have said the appointment of William J. Brennan to the highest court in the land was "his second greatest mistake." If he said it, he erred. His second greatest mistake came in deciding to present that nomination based on his White House G-2 (Intelligence) team. Brownell maintained, according to Wermiel, "that he read the opinions, knew what was in them, and made no mistake" in presenting his "intelligence."[290] If, as Wermiel wrote, all of Brennan's New Jersey legal associates and friends knew him as unmistakably liberal, why didn't Brownell? Could it have been an overpowering effort to counter John F. Kennedy's burgeoning popularity? Whatever the reason, the General/President should have had some *Second Thoughts*.

* * *

Chapter XXXII
LBJ Didn't Always Get His Way
(Term in Office: November 22, 1963-January 20, 1969)

Even though Robert Caro has not yet completed the "last" volume of his all-encompassing biography on Lyndon Baines Johnson, there's not much left for anyone else to say about "Landslide Lyndon" after the author's first three volumes. An exception may be LBJ's regrets (if any?) with his double-play choices of Abe Fortas for Chief Justice and Homer Thornberry for Associate Justice of the Supreme Court in 1968.

Warren E. Burger, who worked his way through college and law school in St. Paul, Minnesota and who graduated *magna cum laude*, eventually was nominated as Chief Justice of the United States Supreme Court by President Richard M. Nixon on May 21, 1969. The opening came for Nixon to make that appointment after LBJ, his White House predecessor, failed in his ploy to have then-Associate Justice Abe Fortas succeed the soon-to-be-retired Chief Justice Earl Warren. The plan between Johnson and Warren developed during the summer of 1968 when Warren went to Johnson's White House and handed the President a letter of resignation effective "at your convenience." It was an effort to allow Johnson to appoint a new Chief Justice of the same liberal stripe and thereby deny a possible incoming Republican president of that opportunity. With his term in office running out, this led to LBJ's hasty decision to nominate Associate Justice Fortas as Chief Justice on June 26, 1968.

The plan backfired during lengthy and contested confirmation hearings because some saw Fortas as "a man with great abilities and strong convictions, but few, if any, principles." Writing a book review in *Washington Monthly*, Allen J. Lichtman continued saying Fortas lacked "the internal gyroscope to harmonize his disparate beliefs or guide his personal conduct. Ends would always sanction means, and contradictions could be rationalized or simply ignored."[291] Although the Committee on the Judiciary reported the nomination favorably, several committee members strongly dissented. One Senator wrote that Fortas's "judicial philosophy disqualifies him for this high office." Another criticized Fortas as part of the majority on the Supreme Court led by Chief Justice Earl Warren (the Warren Court) making an "extremist effort ... to set itself up as a super-legislature." A third Senator also found Fortas lacking on the "broader question of the nominee's judicial philosophy which includes his willingness to subject himself to the restraint inherent in the judicial process." Yet another Senator objected to "positions taken by Justice Fortas since he went on the Supreme Court as Associate Justice [which had] reflected a view to the Constitution insufficiently rooted to the Constitution as it is written."[292]

Another stumbling block, seen as considerable, came from Fortas' influence on President Johnson. "Newsweek" magazine reported: "More mornings than not, Fortas wakes up to a phone call from the President.... And few important problems are settled without an opinion from Mister Justice Fortas. 'My guess,' says an insider well-placed to make one, 'is that the first person the President consults on anything is Abe Fortas'," the magazine article concluded. [293]

Likewise, Fortas had earned the nickname "Dishonest Abe." According to Laura Hellman, University of California-Santa Barbara professor, Fortas "perjured himself" in nomination hearings before the Senate Judiciary Committee by saying President Johnson had never discussed with him any matter that might come before the Court.[294] This fabrication is further confirmed by author-historian Michael Beschloss. President Johnson, wrote Beschloss in a recounting of secret White House tapes, "wanted to appoint Abe Fortas to the Court [because] Fortas would not only be a reliable pro-Great Society vote but, from Johnson's point of view, he could keep the President confidentially informed of what the justices were doing and warn him if there was trouble in the offing."[295]

In yet another example of "Dishonest Abe," in its May 9, 1969 edition, "Life" magazine revealed that Fortas, while a member of the Supreme Court, accepted a $20,000 fee from the family foundation of Wall Street financier Louis Wolfson in 1966. Fortas returned the money only after Wolfson was indicted for stock manipulation. Fortas conceded he had arranged to receive $20,000 annually for life, and for the life of his wife, for "consulting services" to the Wolfson family foundation. He disclosed that Wolfson had consulted him several times while he was on the Court, but maintained that he had never interceded or taken part in any matter affecting Wolfson.... Conversely, "Life" later reported Wolfson told federal agents he had discussed an SEC case against him with Fortas and Fortas had said the case against him was based on legal technicalities.[296]

Financial concerns plagued Memphis-born Abe Fortas for most of his life. At age thirteen in 1923 and the youngest of five children of recent Russian-Jewish immigrants, he was working nights in a shoe store to help out at home. But through guile, wit and attention to details for others, he made his mark in the Franklin D. Roosevelt administration where he became Undersecretary of the Interior Department in 1941 at age thirty-one. Another Southerner making his mark in Washington, D.C. at the same time was a young Texas Congressman named Lyndon Baines Johnson. Fortas and Johnson formed a political partnership/friendship –

congealed by their similar early backgrounds of living with financial difficulty – that would continue for the rest of their lives.

Their career similarities grew as Fortas started to make some big money in law and Congressman Johnson did likewise in the newly developing field of television station operations following World War II. And when LBJ needed legal help – in TV contracts or contested elections – Fortas was there to provide it. It was the lawyer who saved the future president's career when he staved off the outraged challenges of former Texas Governor Coke R. Stevenson in Johnson's notorious "Landslide Lyndon" campaign with its eighty-seven vote margin in the 1948 senatorial election. "That the election was stolen was obvious at the time, and only fast legal footwork (with the help of Johnson's crony Abe Fortas, later to be rewarded with a Supreme Court seat) prevented investigation."[297]

Following John F. Kennedy's assassination in 1963 and LBJ's ascendancy to the presidency, Johnson tried to reward his friend and confidant in 1965 by offering the post of Attorney General to the man who helped him survive personal and political crises because "LBJ wants to be sure that his Attorney General will walk through fire for the president.[298] It was even more than that. Speaking with Democratic Senator James Eastland, Chairman of the Senate Judiciary Committee about his pending appointment of Fortas as Attorney General on January 22, 1965, Johnson said, "I've got to have a man kind of like my priest – that I can confess to and I can say – 'Here are the problems. Now you tell me what the law is and tell me how to fix it'."[299]

Always financially cautious, "Mr. Fix-It" Fortas turned him down because the job's salary wasn't enough to allow him to continue the lifestyle to which he had grown accustomed. The President also got the same kind of refusal when he first approached the lawyer about becoming his eyes and ears on the Supreme Court. By this time, Johnson had had enough of Fortas' refusals and "after twisting Fortas' arm for days, Johnson has now concluded that the only way to get his friend onto the Supreme Court is to shove him into the swimming pool."

Under the pretext of having Fortas attend a planned press conference as a resource on July 28, 1965, LBJ told Fortas he was going to announce he was sending 50,000 men to Vietnam and – "that Fortas would join the Supreme Court. If those men could sacrifice for their country, so could Fortas," Johnson said to his stunned legal aide. Fortas said later he didn't remember saying yes.[300] For Johnson, it didn't matter either way. As usual, he got what he wanted.

(Not mattering "either way" was a Johnson trait for as long as he was in the political arena – if not longer. In his earliest days in the U. S. House of Representatives, the young Texas Congressman "came out swinging" for President Roosevelt's 1937 "Court-Packing" plan. "Now

Lyndon,' said his closest advisor" – according to author Jeff Shesol – "'of course [the plan is] a bunch of bullshit...but if you flow with it, Roosevelt's friends will support you.' Privately, Johnson expressed no opinion on the plan one way or the other. 'It didn't make a rats-ass [of difference] to him,' recalled a member of his circle. What mattered was winning."[301])

Fortas served on the Supreme Court from August 11, 1965 until May 14, 1969. During that time, the Associate Justice was a constant advisor to President Johnson – a direct (although not the only) violation of the separation of powers doctrine. In the book *Mutual Contempt* by author Jeff Shesol, one gets the feeling Fortas practically took up residence in the White House because he seemed always to be there, listening to Johnson rant about this "injustice" or that. The Justice was a particular sounding board in the aftermath of the 1967 publication of William Manchester's book, *The Death of a President*, especially on the Kennedy Administration in general, JFK's assassination in particular, and what happened on Air Force One at Love Field in Dallas in detail.

For much of the Kennedy brothers' political base, some of the conversations had to be particularly galling. In one case, the paranoid President told the compliant Justice, in light of the flap caused by Manchester's controversial description of the swearing-in ceremony on November 22, 1963, the press was out to get him and "that Bobby [Kennedy] is having his governors jump on me, and he's having his mayors, and he's having his nigras, and he's having his Catholics" come after him.[302] Should any justice of the Supreme Court of the United States engage in that kind of conversation with anyone? And particularly, should a justice of the Supreme Court serving thereon with Thurgood Marshall, the first African-American on the Bench, sit still for such talk?

With Kennedy "spies" perceived to be in every corner, Johnson asked Fortas, "Who is the perpetrator of the fraud on us – Kenny O'Donnell or General McHugh or who?" Satisfying the President's obsession, Fortas answered, "Both. Those two. It's pretty obviously those two fellas."[303] This sounds like the infamous "Hanging Judge" Roy Bean, "the law west of the Pecos" in Texas in the last half of the Nineteenth Century. He is reputed to have sentenced dozens to the gallows, saying "Hang 'em first, try 'em later." LBJ literally did consult with Supreme Court Justice Abe Fortas on just about everything – up to and including the conduct of the War in Vietnam.[304]

For those who may ask "what made Fortas so special to Johnson," the answer comes from the Justice's instrumental role in courthouse maneuvering that legitimized "Landslide Lyndon's" 87-vote, controversial victory in that 1948 election. To this day, some say the voting was more than "controversial." It was fraudulent. For instance, in Jim Wells County's precinct #13 in deep south Texas, all voters apparently voted in alphabetical order and many of them were legally dead at the time of that runoff election for a U. S. Senate seat. The Johnson-Fortas liaison continued to the point where in May of 1965, Johnson even "sent his confidant and friend on a secret mission to San Juan, where [Justice] Abe Fortas has been negotiating with [Dominican Republic President] Juan Bosch in an effort to form a Dominican coalition government."[305]

Johnson's moves to further his influence into the Judicial Branch of the federal government by putting his confidant on the Bench would have made Machiavelli himself proud of LBJ's cunningness. First he had to create a vacancy on the Court. To do that, he had to get JFK-appointee Justice Arthur Goldberg out of the way. That opportunity presented itself following United Nations Ambassador Adlai Stevenson's death on July 14, 1965. According to Beschloss' book, LBJ persuaded Arthur Goldberg to leave the Supreme Court to take Stevenson's post at the UN and help him bring peace to Vietnam. (Later an angry Goldberg said it was "the biggest mistake of my life."[306]) "LBJ told Goldberg that his next UN Ambassador had the chance to make peace in Vietnam. With that under his belt, Goldberg might be in line to become the first Jewish Vice President: 'You never know what can happen, Arthur….You can't get to the Vice Presidency from the Court'."[307] Then, in a conspiracy-theorist's dream and as noted above in the duplicitous press conference supposedly on Vietnam, Johnson – "having opened a vacancy [on the Court], forces his friend Abe Fortas against his will onto the Supreme Court."[308] As noted, Fortas didn't want to take a pay cut.

As usual, President Johnson wanted even more control. But by the time he had the opportunity to present a name to succeed Chief Justice Earl Warren, the President was a self-declared "lame-duck" who stunned the nation by saying in a nationally-televised address on March 31, 1968 that "I shall not seek, and I will not accept, the nomination of my party for another term as your president."[u] (There are those who even to this day insist it was Johnson who was stunned because he was seeking, but did not get, a "draft" for his continuation in office.)

In any case, LBJ had thereby removed himself from any ability to influence his decisions, especially within the U. S. Congress. Nineteen Senators issued a statement indicating that, on this basis, they would oppose any nomination from President Johnson. Because of all the negative publicity during the 1968 presidential election campaign about the Johnson/Fortas relationship and the threat of a judicial impeachment being talked about in the Senate, Fortas eventually resigned from the

---

[u] "Lame-duck" in this context is understood to be the nomination for the Supreme Court made by a President in the final year of his last term in office.

Court one week before new-President Nixon submitted Warren Burger's name on May 21, 1969.

* * *

Another one who was thereby removed from the consideration was Homer Thornberry, a federal judge, former U. S. House of Representatives member from Texas, and – not surprisingly – another Johnson crony. Early in Johnson's grand plan to elevate Fortas to Earl Warren's Chief Justice post, the President thought he had still one more opportunity to influence the makeup of the Court by naming Thornberry as Fortas' replacement as Associate Justice, thus getting a two-fer. LBJ, just like his hero, FDR, was in fact attempting to "pack the Court" with "cronies" who would not rule some of his Great Society programs unconstitutional. Although Thornberry was not implicated by concerns such as Fortas' liberal decisions and alleged ethical improprieties, he was viewed as a "decent and experienced public servant of moderate ability, but he was hardly of the caliber that would have prompted a basically hostile Senate to overlook political factors"[309]

In baseball parlance, fans remember "Tinker to Evers to Chance," the great Chicago Cubs' double-play combination in the era of the Taft and Wilson administrations. In the politics of Washington, it became "Johnson to Fortas to Thornberry" – only in this case, all three were "thrown out trying to steal home." Warren Earl Burger was eventually sworn in as the fifteenth Chief Justice (1969-1986). Not covered here are any second thoughts Lyndon Johnson might have had about his nominations of the disgraced Abe Fortas and the embarrassed Homer Thornberry because it is doubtful – at least in this writer's mind as well as that of some notable historians – that Lyndon Baines Johnson ever had a second thought about any action he took – other than, perhaps, his conduct of the War in Vietnam.

But consider what might have happened if Mr. Goldberg hadn't quit, as later on did a *New York Times* writer. According to David A. Kaplan's hypothesis therein, "There would have been no Court vacancy until 1968, when Chief Justice Warren retired. To replace Mr. Warren, President Johnson likely would have selected Abe Fortas, or maybe Justice Potter Stewart or even Justice Goldberg. The latter two would have sailed through the Senate. …Still, the Court in 1971 would have been very liberal, probably consisting of Justices [Hugo] Black, [William] Brennan, [William O.] Douglas, Fortas, Goldberg, [John M.] Harlan, [Thurgood] Marshall, [Potter] Stewart and [Byron] White. It would have had no Nixon appointees."[310] One has to wonder if not being able to post that batting lineup gave Lyndon Baines Johnson any *Second Thoughts* about

Second Thoughts   William T. Harper

the Abe Fortas nomination long before he went to the big Oval Office in the Sky on January 22, 1973?

* * *

Second Thoughts   William T. Harper

Chapter XXXIII
How Many More Reasons Did Nixon Need?
(Term in Office: January 20, 1969-August 9, 1974)

Without going into the lengthy litany of litigation in the "Watergate Scandal," let it be noted the final outcome thereof – President Richard M. Nixon's resignation from office – turned primarily on the *United States v. Nixon* case decision handed down by the Supreme Court of the United States under the Chief Justiceship of Warren Burger on July 24, 1974. As briefly as possible, the facts of the case were:

Hypotheses:
A grand jury returned indictments against seven of President Richard Nixon's closest aides in the Watergate affair – the attempted burglarizing of the Democratic National Committee offices at the Watergate Hotel's office complex in Washington D. C. on June 17, 1972. The special prosecutor, reluctantly appointed by Nixon, and the defendants sought audio tapes of conversations regarding the break-in recorded by Nixon in the Oval Office. Nixon asserted that he was immune from the subpoena claiming "executive privilege," which is the right to withhold information from other government branches to preserve confidential communications within the Executive Branch or to secure the national interest....
Question:
Is the President's right to safeguard certain information, using his "executive privilege" confidentiality power, entirely immune from judicial review?[v]
Conclusion:
No.

The Court held that neither the doctrine of separation of powers nor the generalized need for confidentiality of high-level communications, without more national interest, can sustain an absolute, unqualified, presidential privilege. The Court granted there was a limited executive privilege in areas of military or diplomatic affairs, but gave preference to

---

[v] a claim by the President or another high official of the executive branch that he/she need not answer a request (including a subpoena issued by a court or Congress) for confidential government or personal communications, on the ground that such revelations would hamper effective governmental operations and decision-making.

"the fundamental demands of due process of law in the fair administration of justice." Therefore, the president must obey the subpoena and produce the tapes and documents. Nixon resigned shortly after the release of the tapes.[311]

Chief Justice Warren E. Burger, Associate Justices Harry A. Blackmun and Lewis F. Powell, Jr. – all three appointed to the Supreme Court of the United States by President Richard M. Nixon – joined in the unanimous 8-0 vote that brought down the presidency of the man who nominated them to their lofty positions.[w] The opinion was presented by Chief Justice Burger who, like the other Nixon Supreme Court appointees, was chosen because of his judicial experience, his opposition to decisions of the Warren Court on criminal procedures, his criticism of judicial activism, and because his career was free of ethical blemishes (unlike the disgraced Fortas). The Nixon White House saw him as moderately conservative, as opposed to extending the rights of criminal defendants and modernizing the insanity defense, preferring instead to give considerable leeway to police, prosecution, and trial judges.

President Richard Nixon's Nominees (in reverse order)				
Name	Replacing	Nominated	Vote	Result/Date
William Rehnquist	Harlan	Oct 22, 1971	68-26	C 12/10/71
Lewis Powell, Jr.	Black	Oct 22, 1971	89-1	C 12/06/71
Harry Blackmun	Fortas	Apr 15, 1970	94-0	C 05/12/70
G. Harrold Carswell	Fortas	Jan 19, 1970	45-51	R 04/08/70
C. Haynsworth, Jr.	Fortas	Aug 21, 1969	45-55	R 11/21/69
Warren Burger[a]	Warren	May 23, 1969	74-3	C 06/09/69

[a]-for Chief Justice   C=Confirmed   R=Rejected
This chart lists only nominations officially submitted to the Senate, and does not include nominations announced but never officially submitted.
Source: www.senate.gov/pagelayout/reference/nominations/Nominations.htm

He (along with Justices Blackmun, Lewis Powell, and William Rehnquist) seemed to be just what "the law and order" President Nixon wanted after the activist Court of Earl Warren. But, as has been said before, "what you see is not always what you get." Richard Milhous Nixon (especially when considering his failed Associate Justice nominations of Clement Haynesworth, Jr. in 1969, and G. Harold Carswell in 1970 in a Roosevelt-like effort to "pack the Court" – this time with conservative judges), probably had more *Second Thoughts* and more personal presidential regrets about his Supreme Court nominees than

---

[w] Associate Justice (and later Chief Justice), William H. Rehnquist, another Nixon-appointee, recused himself from these deliberations.

anyone ever serving as the Nation's Chief Executive. Their actions forced Richard Milhous Nixon to retire – the only President in the history of the Republic to do so.

*   *   *

Harry Andrew Blackmun belongs to an exclusive membership club in Washington, D. C. It is a club that no President of the United States ever belonged to. It is not the Cosmos Club nor the Metropolitan Club nor any of those other snobbery hangouts frequented by the movers and shakers in the Nation's capitol. Harry Blackmun has an eternal membership in the good old "Number Three Club." However, it isn't much of an honor to be enrolled therein. Furthermore, the man who sponsored Blackmun's membership into that club ended up with serious *Second Thoughts* about putting him there.

What is this exclusive, almost secret society that few people have ever heard about? The Number Three Club's membership roster contains the names of those members of the Supreme Court of the United States who were their presidential sponsors' third choice for the nomination. Two members of the current Supreme Court – Arthur Kennedy and Samuel Alito – are among Blackmun's club members. Throughout the history of the Court and on some of these pages are other examples of those who were a president's third choice (Joseph Storey, Samuel Nelson, et al). At least two Chief Justices are members of the Club. A few other Justices are charter members of the even more exclusive "Number Four Club." But if you really are seeking total exclusivity, turn to Robert C. Grier. Over the span of two different administrations (Polk's and Tyler's), Grier became the one and only member of the Number Five Club on August 4, 1846.

Harry Blackmun was President Nixon's third choice to fill the vacated seat of Associate Justice Abe Fortas after President Johnson failed to get him nominated as Chief Justice in 1968 replacing Earl Warren and "Dishonest Abe's" subsequent retirement from the Bench. Nixon at first tried to get Clement Haynesworth and then G. Harold Carswell on the Court. Both nominations failed to get Senate approval. Haynesworth went down partly because as chief judge of the Fourth Circuit, he owned a one-seventh interest in Vend-a-Matic, which had contracts to sell food through machines located in plants of Deering Milliken & Co. He cast the deciding vote in favor of Deering Milliken in *Darlington Manufacturing Co. v. NLRB*, an unfair labor practices suit.[312] It seemed like not the ethical thing to do – and it was all an anti-Nixon Senate needed as a reason for withholding its "consent."

A little more than one month after President Nixon and all Americans were basking in the glory of the first-manned rocket launching for and the subsequent landing on the Lunar surface, Nixon – at what was probably the public peak of his political career – on August 18, 1969 named Clement Furman Haynesworth, Jr. as his choice as an Associate Justice of the Supreme Court. Unfortunately, that popularity was not present in the Democratic-dominated 90th Congress and especially in the advice and consenting Senate where the Republicans were in a 36-64 minority.

      The Democrats had a lot to be angry about vis-à-vis recent events setting the makeup of the Supreme Court. The fact that some Senators saw the Haynesworth nomination as a Nixon effort to slow down the implementation of school desegregation in the Court's *Brown v. Board of Education of Topeka* didn't help. The fact that House Minority Leader (and later President) Gerald R. Ford was rumored to be developing impeachment charges against Justice William O. Douglas – which he did eight months later – became an agitation. And the fact the Democrats' latest perceived affront stemmed from the wide-spread Republican efforts that scuttled Democratic "Mr. Fix-It" Abe Fortas' nomination as Chief Justice of the Supreme Court the previous October added to their pique. Joining with the opposition to Haynesworth in general and Nixon in particular – anything Nixonian – were the National Association for the Advancement of Colored People, the Leadership Conference on Civil Rights, and an alliance of 125 religious, labor, welfare and other civil rights groups.[313]

      Not only did the Democrats get their revenge in shooting down the Nixon/Haynesworth nomination, they also did it by one of the widest margin in Supreme Court history, 55-45. Born October 30, 1912, in Greenville, South Carolina, and raised in South Carolina, Clement Furman Haynesworth, Jr., graduated from Furman University in 1933 and from Harvard Law School in 1936. Thirty-three years later, on November 21, 1969, Clement Furman Haynesworth, Jr. was the first nominee for the Supreme Court to be rejected by the Senate since it defeated President Hoover's candidate, John J. Parker, in 1930. Some people have *Second Thoughts* and learn from them. Evidently, Richard Nixon did not.

* * *

Two months after the Haynesworth fiasco, it was G. Harrold Carswell's turn. Born on December 22, 1919 to a prominent family in Irwinton, Georgia, Carswell saw his bid for a seat on the Supreme Court fail, in part, because of a 1948 speech. According to an article published by the University of Pittsburgh's school of law, a story uncovered by journalist Edward Roeder in *The Irwinton Bulletin*, a weekly newspaper Carswell edited, Carswell said:

Second Thoughts William T. Harper

"I Am A Southerner By Ancestry, Birth, Training, Inclination, Belief And Practice. I Believe That Segregation Of The Races is Proper And The ONLY Practical And Correct Way Of Life In Our States."

(This inflammatory quote is also covered by Leon Friedman and William F. Levantrosser in their work, *Watergate and afterward: the legacy of Richard M. Nixon*, Hofstra University, 1992, p. 79).

Roeder noted the first letter of each word was capitalized, and the word ONLY in all caps. Two paragraphs later, Roeder reported a "white supremacy" quote from Carswell is just as strident:

"I Yield To NO MAN, As A Fellow Candidate, Or As A Fellow Citizen, In The Firm Vigorous Belief In The Principles Of White Supremacy, And I Shall Always Be So Governed."

Again, the first letter of each word is capitalized, and NO MAN is all caps.[314] Carswell was further criticized for his courtroom treatment of African-Americans, and for helping a municipal golf course evade desegregation while he was U.S. attorney. How could such as astute politician as Nixon was judged to have been be so politically incorrect as to think those remarks would go unchallenged? Was it hubris or another case of poor staff preparation?

Even further, some deemed Carswell "mediocre." Prominent lawyers and law professors criticized his judicial record, noting his reversal rate as district judge, a dismal 58 percent, was among the highest in the Fifth Circuit Court of Appeals. During Carswell's confirmation hearing, Democratic Senator Russell B. Long – in his typical Cajun back-country style, much the same as his father, Huey Pierce "Kingfish" Long – asked the graduate of the U.S. Naval Academy, the University of Georgia School of Law, Duke University, A.B., and Mercer University, LL.B., "Does it not seem that we have had enough of those upside-down, corkscrew thinkers? Would it not appear," the Louisiana State University law school graduate continued, "that it might be well to take a B-student or a C-student who was able to think straight, compared to one of those A-students who are capable of the kind of thinking that winds up getting a 100% increase in crime in this country?"[315]

These charges of mediocrity led to a famous and amusing "defense" by Carswell's fellow Republican and his chief sponsor in the Upper House hearings, Senator Roman Hruska from Nebraska. The arch-Conservative orated, "Even if [Carswell] were mediocre, there are a lot of mediocre judges and people and lawyers. They are entitled to a little representation, aren't they, and a little chance? We can't have all Brandeises, Frankfurters and Cardozos."

* * *

Six days after the Senate rejected the candidate for the "Mediocrity Seat," 51-45, Nixon chose Harry Blackmun on April 15, 1970 – thereby confirming the judge's membership in the "Number Three Club" – because the Minnesota jurist had a very conservative record on the Eighth Circuit Court of Appeals. Blackmun had been a Phi Beta Kappa at Harvard, served as general counsel to the famed Mayo Clinic in Rochester, Minnesota, and had been appointed to the Eighth Circuit Court by President Eisenhower. Nixon's Chief Justice Warren Burger thought highly of Blackmun, his fellow Minnesotan; that he was decent, consistent, wedded to routine, and he was "unlikely to venture far." All Nixon wanted to know, despite his own legal background but perhaps because of his then-current state of mind, was if any of the judge's three daughters were "hippies." It was "The Age of Aquarius." Blackmun assured him they weren't.[316] That seemed to be all Nixon wanted to know.

Following Senate confirmation less than a month later with its 94-0 consent, the White House put out a statement saying it was "highly pleased and gratified that the Senate has acted so expeditiously. The President believes that Judge Blackmun will have an outstanding record on the Supreme Court."[317] Blackmun was also a good friend of Chief Justice Burger, for whom he stood as his best man at his wedding. Initially, Nixon had to be pleased with Blackmun when he continued his conservative tendencies on the Supreme Court, voting that way almost ninety percent of the time. He dissented in the landmark court case that banned the death penalty in 1972, and he voted to reinstate it in another case four years later.

However, despite his vote in those two cases, Blackmun harbored serious reservations about the death penalty. Ultimately, he uttered what became the battle cry of the death penalty abolishment movement: "I no longer shall tinker with the machinery of death." As those reservations began to manifest themselves, the Judge's entire philosophical outlook swung over to the side of his liberal brethren, and his voting record flip-flopped in later years to the point where he voted with Burger, his boyhood friend from Minnesota, only thirteen percent of the time. Neither one of them carried that friendship to the grave.

In 1973, the Supreme Court handed down the *Roe v. Wade* decision legalizing a woman's right to have an abortion. The 7-2 decision was authored by none other than Nixon-appointee Harry Blackmun (who was, again, supported by the very same two Nixon Justices – Lewis Powell and Warren Burger – who would later cast votes that led to their mentor's

Second Thoughts — William T. Harper

resignation from the Highest Office in the Land). Many legal scholars and millions of other critics – including President Richard Milhous Nixon - cried foul. The Court, they argued, was again legislating from the Bench. It was one of the very things the thirty-seventh President of the United States had railed against in his campaign for the Oval Office as he stressed "law and order," the "silent majority," and caution on civil rights – all these things which he had promised to address during his term.

Nonetheless, Associate Justice Blackmun came up strong for anti-death penalty positions. And support for *Roe v. Wade*. All in all an extremely liberal voting record from the Bench. And the *coup d'état*: came in casting one of the votes in *United States v. Nixon*, 418 U.S. 683 (1974) that led to the President's resignation on August 9, 1974. How many more second thoughts could Richard Nixon have had about his nomination of Harry Andrew Blackmun to the Supreme Court of the United States? It's one thing to be embarrassed by a nominee. It's quite another to be thrown into infamy.

Two of President Nixon's Supreme Court nominees were rejected by the Senate – one of them by one of the widest margin in the history of the Court and the other almost matching that ignominious record. Four more of his appointees did make it through the process and three of the four voted against in him in the *United States v. Nixon* case which led to his resignation as President of the United States – the only President of the United States to leave the office in such abject disgrace. How many more *Second Thoughts* could Richard Nixon have had about his Supreme Court nominations?

* * *

Epilogue
We End This Journal Here

As former Supreme Court Chief Justice William H. Rehnquist said about his book, *The Supreme Court: How It Was, How It Is*, its intent was "designed to convey to the interested, informed layman as well as to the lawyers who do not specialize in constitutional law, a better understanding of the role of the Supreme Court in American government." It was presented as a history of the Supreme Court as an institution. As one of the book's reviewers commented, "all but the most informed scholars who read this book will increase their knowledge of the Supreme Court."[318] Just as the late Chief Justice Rehnquist said, so too it is the intent and the hopes here for *Second Thoughts: Presidential Regrets with their Supreme Court Nominations*."

As noted herein, "The pressures upon a president in considering Supreme Court appointments are now immense, and in most cases have been since the inception of the Court in 1789. Those pressures come from all directions, not the least of which are the candidates' qualifications for filling the post. Other considerations for a president come from personal friendships, from influential friends and family members of potential candidates leaning on a president, from political debts owed (or presumed to be owed) to a candidate by the president, from political parties and considerations, to name but a few."

Excluding the four U. S. Presidents who didn't get to put anyone on the Supreme Court bench (William Henry Harrison, Zachery Taylor, Andrew Johnson, and James Earl Carter) the thirty-three Chief Executives covered in these pages made their appointments to the highest court in the land for many of the reasons cited above. It should be noted in what seems like an anomaly, some of the nominations were actually based on the candidate's *judicial expertise*! What isn't covered completely in the paragraph above turns out to be the primary reason why those thirty-three Presidents had many more than thirty-three *Second Thoughts* about some of their candidates? The primary reason so many of the Justices and would-be Justices failed to live up to their mentors' expectations or otherwise disappointed them seems to be what is politely called "personal friendships" and what has since evolved into one word – "Cronyism."

Putting friends in high places isn't a recent phenomenon. As far as the Supreme Court is concerned, the practice goes back to President Number One, George Washington. Given the fact that the Father of His Country also "sired" the first Supreme Court and that he ultimately made more Supreme Court appointments than any of his successors, it made him susceptible for second-guessing. Nonetheless, it was his engagement in "cronyism" that brought him his biggest Supreme Court disappointment – the interim appointment of John Rutledge as Chief Justice, rejected out-of-hand by the reconvened and angry Senate.

With President Washington setting the precedent, cronyism reared its ugly head consistently throughout the next 185 years covered in these pages. Paraphrasing the poet Elizabeth Barrett Browning, "Let us count [some of] the ways" among the 143 names officially submitted for the Senate's advice and consent during those years.

George Washington – In addition to the aforementioned John Rutledge, his initial complement of six Supreme Court justices (John Jay, William Cushing, Robert Harrison, James Wilson, and John Blair) were men who served with and under him during the American Revolutionary War. Of that cadre – Jay, Cushing, Harrison, and Wilson – all gave the Squire of Mount Vernon cause to wonder. Capability against the Redcoats didn't necessarily translate into ability in black robes.

Ulysses S. Grant – Not that the 16 presidents between these two great wartime generals didn't promote their friends (literally and figuratively), too. However, none of them did to the degree "Sam" Grant did. Andrew Jackson nominated his friend Henry Baldwin. Millard Fillmore named Benjamin Curtis. And Abraham Lincoln had his regrets with David Davis. But Hiram Ulysses Grant's "pal-ship" with such as Morrison Waite and Caleb Cushing only added to his presidential woes. His cronyism with his Civil War boss, Secretary of War Edwin M. Stanton, brought him regret and grief as Stanton suddenly and unexpectedly died four days after he was confirmed for a seat on the Bench.

Franklin D. Roosevelt – There's a considerable jump in appointment-by-cronyism after Grant left office in 1877 and FDR's arrival at 1600 Pennsylvania Avenue in 1933. Not that it was non-existent. Rutherford B. Hayes named his friend Stanley Matthews but he never made it to the confirmation process. Grover Cleveland put his old pal Melville Fuller in the center seat on the Bench. William McKinley named Joseph McKenna who vis-à-vis Matthews, unfortunately, did make it. William Howard Taft named his friend Horace Lurton. Maybe Taft's successors – Woodrow Wilson, Warren G. Harding, Calvin Coolidge and Herbert Hoover – didn't have any friends or cronies to name. But the 32nd President of the United States surely did. A whole raft of them.

If you played poker with him, stayed up late drinking bourbon with the ex-Governor of New York, and flattered him enough, chances were pretty good you could get lifetime tenure as a member of the Supreme Court of the United States. William O. Douglas, James F. Byrnes, and Felix Frankfurter fit their crony clothes better than they did their black robes in their service to the President as members of the Court.

Harry S. Truman – When it comes to cronyism in the selection of Supreme Court candidates, poker-playing HST came up with a four-of-a-kind. All four of his appointments were FOPs (Friends of the President). Sherman Minton was rated as one of the worst justices to ever sit on the Bench. Another of Harry's poker-playing pals, Chief Justice Fred Vinson, got an "F" rating in one poll – the only Top Judge to do so in that poll. The Man from Missouri later saw his friendship with Justice Tom Clark (the "dumb SOB") strained, to put it mildly. Harold Burton, a Senate cloakroom buddy of the President's from their days together in the Upper House, sent "Give 'em Hell, Harry" on an unfulfilled quest to see why "so-called 'liberals' could do [this] to me."

Lyndon B. Johnson – When it came to handing out favors to his back-scratchers from his personal cracker barrel, he found a couple of really stale ones. The most notorious of the graham crackers had to be, of course, Associate Justice Abe Fortas. "Dishonest Abe" resigned from the Court in 1969 and barely beat a charge of corruption in office by Congressional investigators. Fortas saved Johnson's political career in the scandalous "Landslide Lyndon" Senate race in 1948. However, Fortas didn't have a Fortas to save his skin in 1969. With Fortas out, LBJ tried to get his old Texas crony, Federal Judge Homer Thornberry in. It was Thornberry who succeeded Johnson in the House of Representatives in a game of musical chairs following the 1948 elections. In the United States Senate, its members wouldn't even give the Lame-Duck President and former Senate Majority Leader the courtesy of a vote on a bosom-buddy candidate.

These are not the only examples of the failure of cronyism as criteria for nomination to the Supreme Court of the United States. But, nowhere in the thirty-three chapters of this opus does one find such a pattern of failure in Supreme Court nominations as is cronyism. Maybe it all boils down to another one of the Missouri Mule-Skinner's observations. "Whenever you put a man on the Supreme Court," said the former County Judge from Independence, Missouri, "he ceases to be your friend."

For you future Presidents of the United States, let that be a lesson to you.

* * *

On that ominous note, we end this journal here. Chronologically speaking, the next Justice we could possibly cite would be John Paul Stevens, sworn in on December 19, 1975. The record shows his conservative nominator, President Gerald R. Ford, had nothing but high praise for the judge – despite his subsequently attained label as the Court's most liberal jurist. Ford even went so far as to say if he (the President) accomplished anything during his brief term in office, it would be that Justice Stevens be known as his legacy. Justice Stevens retired on June 29, 2010. May his retirement be as bright as his service.

On February 18, 1988, Anthony M. Kennedy took his seat as an Associate Justice after being nominated by President Ronald W. Reagan. Within a year, President Reagan would be out of the White House and on the downward slope of the devastating Alzheimer's disease – leaving him with few current thoughts, let alone second thoughts about Justice Kennedy – who still sits on the Supreme Court of the United States.

William O. Douglas served the longest term on the Court, just four days short of thirty-six years and seven months. If – as they say – "the good Lord's willin' and the creek don't rise," it would take Justice Kennedy to the year 2025 before he could do it (at age 89). If the newest member of the current Court, Elena Kagen, is to break the record, it will be sometime in the year 2047!

With the history of the present members of the Supreme Court of the United States still to be written, we'll leave it to future writers to recall if any of the subsequent presidents had second thoughts about any of the successors to Antonin Scalia, et al.

We have found it hard in these pages to make some judgments and form opinions when writing about semi-ancient history. Here is just one reason why: In reading up on Supreme Court Chief Justice Melville W. Fuller who served in that capacity from 1888-1910, one is led to believe that "he quickly *distinguished himself as one of its most able and important holders* [emphasis added]." [319] His election to that office came via a substantial 41-20 Senate approval vote. And then, in practically the very next source, this evaluation of Justice Fuller appears: "By and large, however, history has not been kind to Fuller and his associates. Historians have been all too prone to echo the views of the Progressives, who pictured the Fuller Court as a handmaiden of big business. Thus, Owen M. Fiss in his recent book expressed the conventional wisdom: 'By all accounts, the Court over which Melville Weston Fuller presided, ...*ranks among the worst* [emphasis added]'."[320]

Another critic says, "With its focus on a limited national government and support of legally enforced racial segregation, the twenty-two-year period of the Fuller Court has, in the words of legal historian Richard A. Epstein, 'often been regarded as a black hole of American Constitutional law'."[321] One more naysayer put it this way: "At the time [of Fuller's appointment] the press described Fuller as 'the most obscure man ever appointed Chief Justice' (Baker 1991, 360). Others were even more unkind, dubbing him 'the fifth best lawyer from the City of Chicago'."[322] Countering those negative opinions was distinguished jurist Oliver Wendell Holmes, Jr., who defended Fuller, saying he was "the best chief justice under whom he had served."[323]

Second Thoughts — William T. Harper

Although President Grover Cleveland may not have had any *Second Thoughts* about his choice of Melville W. Fuller as Chief Justice of the United States Supreme Court, many critics obviously have. As they say in gambling halls and also in book publishing offices around the world, "You pays your money and you takes your choice."

Meanwhile, *Second Thoughts* simply tries to answer, in part, President Truman's question: "…what make Justices of the Supreme Court tick?"

* * *

About the Author

William T. (Bill) Harper completed a career as a newspaper and magazine reporter, writer, editor, and natural gas industry executive before "running away from home" on his sailboat. *Second Thoughts* is his fifth book, one of which is the award-winning *Eleven Days in Hell: The 1974 Carrasco Prison Siege in Huntsville, Texas* – honored by the Writers League of Texas as "the best in Texas non-fiction for 2005".

He teaches *Memoir Writing* in College Station, Texas and was a Guest Lecturer at University of Houston and Sam Houston State University in Huntsville. Twice-elected President of the Brazos Writers group, he is also the creator, writer, and co-host of the PBS radio program, "The Classics and Their Times," broadcast weekly on Texas A&M University's KAMU-FM station. He lives in Bryan, Texas with his wife, Joyce (Juntune, PhD, professor at Texas A&M University). Bill's e-mail address is harpersferry_2000@yahoo.com

* * *

The publication of this book would have been more difficult – if not impossible – without the help of fellow writers Barbara Althaus (*Kyle Tough*), Dr. William R. Klemm (*Thank You Brain*), and Bridgeman H. Carney (*PT-157*). It is difficult for an author to "see the forest but for the trees." This "forest" was a new one to this trio of authors and therefore, they could help me "clear out the ground cover" so everyone could see "the trees" in these stories.

Index

1600 Pennsylvania Avenue, 132, 221
1840 census, 70
1866 Judicial Courts Act, 98
1948 presidential race, 199
1st U.S. Volunteer Cavalry Regiment, 143
51st Congress, 137
a pro-slavery Democrat, 115
a total on-bench failure, 153
Abolition Party, 94
abolitionist movement, 62
Abraham, Henry Julian, 169
Adams, Abigail, 46
Adams, John Quincy, 36, 44, 46-7, 54-5, 58, 67
Adams, John, 5, 19, 22-4, 26, 28-9, 33-4, 36, 38-9, 41, 45-6, 57, 64, 70, 99
advice and consent, 5, 8-9, 12,15, 18, 20, 53, 79, 102, 106, 131, 140, 151, 158, 161, 165, 216, 221
African-American seat, 209
African-Americans, 91, 105, 118, 217
Agricultural Adjustment Act (AAA), 173
Alabama legislature, 68
Alabama, State of, 63, 67-8, 87, 118, 172-3
Albany *Law Journal,* 111
Albany, New York, 122, 132
Aliens and Seditions Acts, 21, 24
Alito, Samuel A. Jr., 215
Allen, Robert, 166
Aluminum Company of America, 161
Alzheimer's, 223
American Cincinnatus, 17
American Civil Liberties Union (ACLU), 179
American Civil War, 27, 34, 72, 80, 83, 84, 86, 87, 89, 92, 93, 99, 101, 103, 104, 106, 114, 115, 117, 119, 122, 127, 129, 130, 135, 137, 143, 144, 174, 205, 221
American Federation of Labor (AFL), 169, 170, 226
Americans of Japanese descent, 186, 187, 199
Amherst College, 161, 162
Amistad, 57, 67, 68
Anthony, Susan B., 107, 108, 109, 110, 111, 112, 113
anti-Jackson Democrats, 60
anti-labor, 168, 170, 188
Anti-Masons, 55, 60
Anti-Semitism, 154
Appomattox, Virginia, 103, 113
Arlington National Cemetery, 183
Arthur, Chester A., 122, 123, 1224, 127, 128,160
Assistant President on the home front, 187
Baker, Lafayette C., 103
Baldwin, Henry, 59, 64, 65, 66, 73, 74, 77, 78, 221
Bank of the United States, 66
Barkley, Alben, 199
Bastogne, Belgium, 122
Bates, Edward, 92, 93
Battle of the Bulge, The, 122
beauty pageants, 188
"beings of an inferior order," 81
Belknap, Michael, 198
belonged [sic] to the Ages, 102
Benton, Thomas Hart, 77,78

Biddle, Francis, 186
big business, 146, 167, 168, 223
bitter disappointment to the president, 148
Black Hills, South Dakota, 144
Black, Hugo Lafayette, 172, 176, 177, 178, 181, 196, 204
Black, Jeremiah, 83, 84
black-ball,
Blackmun, Harry Andrew, 6, 214, 218
Blackstone, Sir William, 49
Blaine, James Gillespie, 123
Blair, John, 11, 14, 18, 20
Blair, Montgomery, 92, 95, 221
Blatchford, Samuel, 41, 131, 133
Bly, Nellie, 141
Bollmann, Erich, 39
Bonaparte, Napoleon, 200
"boorish and bigoted," 154
Booth, John Wilkes, 91, 103
Bork, Robert, 6, 9, 171
Boston Columbian Centinel, 48
Bradley, Joseph P., 101, 104, 106
Bradley, Omar, 202
Brain Trust, 187
Brandeis, Louis, 154, 161, 168, 172, 177, 217
Brennan, William, 181, 183, 199, 201, 211
Britton, Nan, 60, 157
Brown v. Board of Education, 200, 216
Brown, Henry B., 126, 128
Brown, John, 81
Brownell, Herbert, 202, 205
Browning, Elizabeth Barrett, 221
Bryan, William Jennings, 141, 149
Buchanan, James, 73, 76, 83, 87
Bully! 145

Burger, Warren, 6, 203, 206, 211, 213, 219
Burnside, Ambrose, 106
Burr, Aaron, 22, 39
Burton, Harold H., 161, 190, 195, 199, 222
Butler, Pierce, 20, 172, 177, 186
Butler, William, 80
Byrnes, James F., 176, 187, 221
Calhoun, Floride, 61
Calhoun, John C., 41, 61
California's third district, 137
Callender, James, 22
Caminetti v. United States, 156
Campbell, John A., 87, 89
Canandaigua, New York, 108
Cardozo, Benjamin Nathan, 41, 154, 164, 168, 172, 177, 180, 217
Caro, Robert, 206
Carpenter, Matthew, 112
Carpetbagger, 117
Carswell, G. Harold, 9, 47, 171, 214, 217
Carter, James Earl, 12, 220
Cass, Lewis, 78, 80
Castle, William, R., 166
Catholic seat, 140
Catron, John, 59, 68, 70, 89, 98
Catton, Bruce, 92
Cave Hill Cemetery, 68
Center for the Study of Democratic Institutions, 185
Central Pacific Railroad, 137
Chapman, Carrie, 110
Chase, Salmon P., 92, 101, 107, 113, 123
Chase, Samuel, 14, 21, 27, 36, 40, 44, 52, 69
Chase, Thomas, 22
Chinese immigrants, 138
Chinese Red Army, 191
Christianity, 50
church v. state, 52

Cinqué, Joseph, 67
Circuit Court of Appeals Act of 1891, 70
Circuit Judges Act, 99
Circuit-riding, 8, 68, 105
Civil Rights Act of 1875, 118
Clark, Tom C., 6, 12, 180, 190, 192, 201, 222
Clarke, John, 154
Clay, Darrell A., 113
Clay, Henry, 56, 67, 73
"clear and present danger," 143
Coke, Sir Edward, 49
College of the City of New York, 178
Colonel Sanders, 68
Columbia University, 41, 132, 139, 162
Compromise of 1850, The, 80
Compromise of 1877, The, 116, 120
Comstock Silver Lode, 90
Congressional Research Service, 137
Conkling, Roscoe, 101, 107, 110, 122
Constitutional Convention, 7, 16, 19, 49
Connecticut Yankee, 89
Conspiracy Theory, 103
Constitution, Article I, Section 9, 86
Constitution, Article II, Section 2, 15
Constitution, Article III, Section 1, 7
constitutional authority, 193
Continental Congress, 132
Coolidge, Calvin, 155, 160, 172, 176, 221
Cooper, Thomas, 50
Copeland, John, 81
Cosmos Club, 215
Court of St. James, 76

Court-Packing Plan, 175, 179
cowboy image, 143
Credit Mobilier, 114
Crony, 114, 193, 195, 208, 211, 221
Cronyism, 115, 220
Crowley, Richard, 108
Curley, James Michael, 122
Currie, David P., 52, 67, 107
Curtis, Benjamin R., 79, 81, 89, 125, 221
Curtis, Charles, 170
Cushing, William, 11, 14, 18, 27, 30, 39, 44, 49, 221
Cushing, Caleb, 101, 114
Czolgosz, Leon, 142, 144
Daley, Richard J. Sr., 122
Daniel, Peter Vivian, 83, 87, 89
Daugherty, Harry M., 161
Davis, David, 87, 89, 95, 221
Davis, Jefferson, 102, 114
death penalty, 201, 218
Declaration of Independence, 20, 22, 41
Democratic Party, 58, 67, 72, 95, 114, 132, 135, 167, 174, 184, 188
Democrat-Republican, 22, 34, 39, 42, 45, 47, 51, 55, 57, 64, 99
Department of Justice, 186
Dewey-Warren ticket, 199
Dickerson, Donna Lee, 110
Diggs, Mary, 154
Discrimination, 118, 126, 203
Donelson, Emily, 61
Douglas, Stephen A., 84, 88
Douglas, William O., 177, 180, 187, 193, 195, 211, 216, 221, 223
Dred Scott v. Sandford, 81, 88, 91, 125
due process clause, 90
Duvall, Gabriel, 36, 44, 52, 54, 59

Eaton, John Henry, 61
Eaton, Peggy, 60
Eighth Circuit Court of Appeals, 218
Eisenhower, Dwight D., 5, 12, 147, 189, 195, 198, 218
Eisenhower, Milton, 199
Eisenschiml, Otto, 103
Electoral College, 45, 58, 63, 98, 116, 153, 158, 172
Electoral Commission, 116
Ellsworth, Oliver, 14, 27, 33, 70
Emancipation Proclamation, 105, 116
Embargo Act, 40
Emoluments, 24
Engel v. Vitale, 200
Era of Good Feeling, 45
European Theater of Operations, 203
"evolving standards of decency," 200
Executive Mansion, 27, 45, 74, 79, 123, 128, 131
Executive Order 9066, 186
executive privilege, 6, 213
Father of the Constitution, 53
Federal Judicial Center, 112
Federalist Congress, 23
Federalist Party, 15
Ferguson, John H., 126
Field, Stephen Johnson, 88
Fifteenth Amendment, 115
Fifth Circuit Court of Appeals, 217
Fillmore, Millard, 79, 108, 125, 221
Finley v. Lynn, 37
First Amendment, 24
Fish, Hamilton, 102
Fitzpatrick, Ellen, 201
Ford, Gerald R., 185, 216, 222
Ford's Theater, 90, 103
Fort Stevens, 143

Fort Sumter, 51, 62, 83, 89, 92
Fortas, Abe, 171, 206, 214, 222
Four Horsemen, 157, 172, 188
Fourteenth Amendment, 90, 106, 110, 116, 125, 204
Fourth Circuit Court of Appeals, 215
Frankfurter, Felix, 177, 195, 217, 221
Franklin House, 60
free enterprise, 89
Free Soil, Free Labor, Free Men, 80
Free Soilers, 60
Free State vs. Slave State controversy, 80
Fremont, John C., 93
Fries, John, 22
Fuller, J. F. C., 101
Fuller, Melville W., 128, 131, 150, 152, 221, 223
"future relations with darkies," 154
Garfield, James A., 121, 123, 157
Garrow, David, 90
Gilded Age, 90, 113, 122
Ginsburg, Ruth Bader, 42
gold fever, 89
Goodwin, Doris Kearns, 93
government by senility, 175
Grand Wizard, 178
Grant, Ulysses S., 27, 51, 56, 58, 94, 97, 99, 101, 110, 118, 122, 202, 221
Gray, Horace, 128, 145
Great Depression, The, 168, 170, 173
"great dissenter, the," 39, 106, 146, 148
Great Lakes, 16
Great Northern Railway, 146
Great War, The, 166

"greatest general of his age," 101
Greeley, Horace, 95
Green, William, 168
Greensboro (N.C.) *Daily News,* 169
Grier, Robert C., 78, 89, 99, 101, 104, 215
Guiteau, Charles Julius, 123
Habeas Corpus, 84, 86, 97, 204
Hague, Frank, 122
Hamilton, Alexander, 8, 22, 102
Hanna, Mark, 144
Harding, Warren G., 60, 150, 155, 157, 165, 168, 221
Harlan, John M., 106, 128, 150
Harlan, John M. II, 199, 211, 214
Harper, Ida Husted, 109
Harper's Ferry, Virginia, 81
Harper's Weekly, 84
Harriman, Edward H., 146
Harrison, Benjamin, 127, 150, 221
Harrison, William Henry, 12 72, 125, 157, 220
Hart, Gary, 60
Harvard College, 46, 49
Harvard Law School, 154, 216
Harvard University, 114, 132, 145, 178
Hayes, Rutherford B. Presidential Center, 117
Hayes, Rutherford B., 116, 120, 123, 150, 221
Hayes-Tilden, 116, 120
Haynesworth, Clement, Jr., 9, 214
Hearst newspapers, 177, 191
Hemenway, Alfred, 145
Henry, Patrick, 8, 23
Hill, David B., 132
Hill, James J., 146
hippies, 218
His Accidency, 72

Hitler, Adolph, 187
Hoar, Ebenezer R., 101, 104, 106
Minister to Holland, 46
Holmes, Oliver Wendell, 4. 91, 143, 151, 161, 164, 223
Hoover, Herbert Clark, 155, 158, 160, 164, 172, 176, 178, 181, 216, 221
Hoover, J. Edgar, 6
Hornblower, William B., 104, 131
Hornblower-Hill feud, 131
Hornblower-Hill-Cleveland feud, 131
Horniblow's Tavern, 20
horse and buggy definition of interstate commerce, 176
Howe, Timothy, 102
Hruska, Roman, 217
Hughes, Charles Evans, 41, 150, 164, 172, 177
Hughes, Charles Evans, Jr., 166
Hume, Paul, 191
Hunt, Ward, 88, 101, 106, 112, 122
Huntington, Collis P., 119, 121, 137, 141
Hutchinson, Dennis, 201
Ikes, Harold, 181
"Impeach Earl Warren!" 201
Impeachment, 4, 6, 12, 21, 23, 27, 40, 99, 113, 185, 210, 216
Independence Hall, 7
international relations, 131
internment camps, 186, 199
Jackson, Andrew, 36, 55, 58, 70, 72, 86, 221
Jackson, Howell E., 131, 134
Jackson, Rachel, 61
Jackson, Robert, 177, 181, 186, 196, 199
Jackson, T. J. "Stonewall," 202
Japanese military forces, 186

Jay, John, 8, 11, 14, 23, 26, 28, 41, 70, 221
Jay's Treaty, 16
Jeffersonian Republicans, 35
Johnson, Andrew, 12, 34, 98, 113, 220
Johnson, Lyndon B., 206, 215, 222
Johnson, Thomas, 14
Johnson, Timothy, 9
Johnson, William, 20, 36, 38, 45, 59
judicial activism, 200, 214
judicial restraint, 180
judicial review, 120, 213
Judiciary Act of 1789, 7, 25, 51, 69
Judiciary Act of 1801, 22
Judiciary Act of 1869, 70, 104
Judiciary Reorganization Bill of 1937, 173
Julian, George, 94
Caesar, Julius, 200
Justice tempered with Murphy, 186
Kennedy, Anthony M., 6, 215, 223
Kennedy, John F., 104, 157, 203, 205, 208
Kennedy, Joseph, 182
Kennedy, Robert F., 209
Kentucky Fried Chicken, 68
King, Edward, 73
King, Florence, 60
Know-Nothing, 94
Knox, John F., 154
Korean War, 191
Korematsu v. United States, 186
Korematsu, Fred, 187
Ku Klux Klan, 4, 7, 106, 118, 177
labor disputes, 193
lacking any legal significance, 67

laissez-faire attitude, 169
Lamar, Joseph, 52, 150
Lamar, Lucius Q. C., 52, 131, 135
Landon, Alfred M., 172
Last of the Whigs, The 79, 81
Legal Tender Acts, 94, 104, 123
lengthy though undistinguished, 88
"leprosy of the Bench," 40
Lewinsky, Monica, 60
liberal-conservative, 162, 200
like a madman, 90
Lincoln, Abraham, 12, 55, 84, 86, 102, 115, 127, 139, 143, 221
Lincoln, Levi, 44, 52, 54
Lincoln, Mary Todd, 103
Livingston, Henry Brockholst, 41, 45, 52, 55
Lodge, Henry Cabot, 145
log-cabin, 79
London, England, 16
Long, Huey, 122, 217
loose cannon, 39
Loving v. Virginia, 200
loyalty oaths, 204
Lurton, Horace H., 150, 153, 221
MacArthur, Douglas, 191
mad messiah, 144
Madison, James, 19, 21, 21, 33, 36, 40, 44
Mann Act, 155
Marbury v. Madison, 33, 35, 37
Marbury, William, 34
March to the Sea, Sherman's, 118
Marshall, John, 5, 212, 28, 33, 42, 45, 49, 51, 53, 56, 59, 65, 90, 134, 203
Marshall, Thurgood, 203, 209, 211

Massachusetts House of Representatives, 49, 114
Massachusetts Supreme Court, 145
Master of Monticello, 38
Maynard, Isaac H., 132
Mayo Clinic, 218
McClellan, George B., 98
McKenna, Joseph, 137, 151, 160, 221
McKinley, John, 52, 67
McKinley, William B., 137, 139, 144, 157, 221
McLean, John, 59, 62, 68, 86, 89
McMenamin, Michael, 113
McReynolds, James C., 153, 172, 177, 188
mediocre legal talent, 48
Mellon, Andrew, 161
mental illness, 65
Metropolitan Club, 215
Mexican War, 79
Miller Center for Current Affairs, 56
Miller, Samuel F., 84, 87, 89, 96, 101
minimum wage bill, 188
Minton, Sherman, 190, 194, 199, 202, 222
Miranda rights, 200
Miranda v. Arizona, 200
Missouri Mule-Skinner, 193, 222
Monkey Business, 60
Monroe Doctrine, 47
Moore, Alfred, 38
Morgan, Jay Pierpont, 146
Morton, Oliver, 102
Most Exclusive Club in the World, 176
most important non-elected official, 179
most insignificant U.S. Supreme Court justice, 37, 52
Mount Vernon, 15, 21, 42, 221

Mr. Bigs, 153
"Mr. I dissent," 53
Mr. Lincoln's War, 92
Mt. Rushmore, 144
mulligan, 12
Munchausen, Baron, 183
Murphy, Bruce Allen, 184
Murphy, Frank, 177, 181, 186, 190, 194
NAACP Legal Advisory Committee, 179
National Association for the Advancement of Colored People (NAACP), 169, 216
National Industrial Recovery Act (NIRA), 172
National Labor Relations Act, 173
National Republicans, 55
nattering nabobs of negativism, 104
Naturalization Act, 23
Navy Yard Bridge, 103
Nazi SS troops, 122
Neagle, David, 90
Nelson, Samuel, 73, 89, 101, 106, 215
New Deal, 161, 168, 173, 176, 1179, 186, 188, 190, 195
New Jersey State Supreme Court, 202
New York Court of Appeals, 132
New York Gazette Advertiser, 48
New York Herald-Tribune, 115, 174
New York seat, the, 134
New York Times, 68, 115, 119, 124, 126, 149, 195, 211
New York Tribune, 84
New York World, 141
Newark (New Jersey) *News,* 174
"nine scorpions in a bottle," 4

Ninth Circuit Court of Appeals, 68, 139
Nixon, Richard M., 6, 9, 12, 48, 189, 198, 206, 211, 213, 219
Northern Pacific Railroads, 146
Northern Securities Co. v. United States, 147
Northwest Territories ("54.40 or Fight"), 76
nuclear weapons, 131, 191
Number Five Club, 215
Number Four Club, 215
Number Three Club, 215, 218
O'Neale, Peggy, 60
Ohio Judicial Center, 101
Ohio Supreme Court, 59
Old #22-24, 134
one person, one vote, 204
opposition "leaked" to the press, 170
Oregon congressional delegation, 89
Oswald, Lee Harvey, 104
Otis v. Parker, 143
Our American Cousin, 103
out of context, 169
Pacific Legal Foundation, 90
Pacific Railway robbers, 141
Parker, Harry, 164, 168, 216
Parker, John J., 154
Parrish, Michael E., 181
partially deranged, 4, 65
Paterson, William, 14, 24, 30, 39
Pearson, Drew, 166
Pease, Lute, 174
Peckham, Rufus W., 128, 131, 134
Peckham, Wheeler, 131, 134, 150
pedantic courtier, 179
Pegler, Westbrook, 191
Pennsylvania Supreme Court, 74, 83
Petticoat Affair, 4, 60, 62

Phi Beta Kappa, 218
Philadelphia Bar Association, 20
Philadelphia lawyer, 20, 73
Pierce, Franklin, 79, 82, 87, 114
Pittsburgh Post-Gazette, 177
Plessy v. Ferguson, 9, 91, 125, 128, 145
Plessy, Homer, 125
Points of Revolution, 185
poker-playing companion, 196
polio, 178, 183
political debts, 91, 220
Politician on the Supreme Court, 60
Polk, James K., 74, 76, 80, 83, 215
Pomeroy circular, 94
popular vote, 80, 116, 153, 172
populist's views, 59
Porcellian social club, 145
Pork-barrel legislation, 137
Pornography, 155, 204
Portland (Oregon) bar, 140
Posner, Richard A., 183, 187
Powell, Lewis F. Jr., 6, 214, 219
prayer in public schools, 204
President's House, 58, 63, 77, 80, 127
Princeton University, 38, 51, 132, 153, 156
Progressive "Bull Moose" ticket, 153
Prohibition, 126, 151, 113
Puerto Rico, Territory of, 145
Pulitzer, Joseph, 141
Quaker, 87
Radical Republican, 93, 95, 122
Read, John M., 74
Reagan, Ronald W., 6, 9, 223
reapportionment revolution, 204
Reconstructionists, 98
Red Jacket defense, 170

Reed, Stanley, 41, 74, 177, 180
Rehnquist, William, 6, 28, 43, 94, 101, 214, 220
Republican Party, 27, 55, 58, 86, 93, 104, 107, 116, 118, 121, 123, 129, 153, 167, 169
Resignation, 15, 83, 86, 93, 154, 164, 176, 196, 206, 213, 218
Revolutionary War, 7, 16, 22, 29, 38, 48, 103, 221
riding the circuit, 29, 38, 68, 70, 107
Roane, Archibald, 115
Roberts, Jason M., 9
Roberts, Owen J., 164, 172, 181, 190
Rochester Democrat and Chronicle, 111
Rodney, Caesar, 40
Roe v. Wade, 218
Roosevelt, Franklin D., 7, 12, 34, 58, 82, 86, 143, 151, 157, 161, 168, 172, 184, 186, 196, 199, 207, 214, 221
Roosevelt, James, 199
Roosevelt, Theodore, 7, 16, 82, 143, 153, 158
Rough Riders, 143
Ruby, Jack, 104
Russia, ambassador to, 46, 76
Rutledge, John, 14, 17, 27, 33, 47, 221
Rutledge, Wiley, 177, 181, 190, 194
Sacco, Ferdinando, 179
San Juan Hill, Cuba, 143
Sandefer, Timothy, 90
Sanford, Edward T., 164, 168
Sawyer, Charles, 192
Schenck v. United States, 143
Schlesinger, Arthur, 160
Secession, 62, 80, 83
Second Circuit Court of Appeals, 55

secret slush fund, 198
Securities and Exchange Commission, 182
Selden, Henry, 109
"selfish to the last degree," 155
Senate Judiciary Committee, 9, 120, 163, 207
senatorial courtesy, 5, 131, 178, 188
separate but equal, 9, 91, 125, 128, 130, 145
separation of church and state, 49
separation of powers, 31, 39, 209, 213
Seventh Circuit Court of Appeals, 37, 183
Sharon, William, 90
Sherman, John, 87
Sherman, William Tecumseh, 47, 202
Shields, James, 77, 158
Shiras, George Jr., 128
Shuler, Nettie Rogers, 110
silent majority, 219
Sixth Amendment, 113
Skidmore, Max J., 169
Slavery, 40, 45, 51, 75, 79, 87, 94, 96, 98, 115, 118, 136, 169
"slow and incompetent," 140
Smith, Caleb, 92
Smith, William, 58, 63
Snow White and the Seven Dwarfs, 33
Social Security Act, 173
Solomon, 35, 134, 166
South Carolina Court of Common Pleas, 17
South Carolina House of Representatives, 38
Southern aristocracy, 79
Southern Pacific Railroad, 137
Spanish-American War, 143, 145

Spencer, John, C., 72
St. John, Gerald J., 20
Stanbery, Henry, 98
Stanford, Leland, 119, 137, 141
Stanton, Edwin, 92, 101, 106, 221
Stassen, Harold, 198
Stevens, John Paul, 222
Stevenson, Adlai E., 199, 202, 210
Stevenson, Coke, 208
Stewart, Potter, 199, 203, 211
Stone, Geoffrey, 186
Stone, Harlan Fiske, 32, 41, 160, 164, 166, 168, 172, 176, 190, 192
Storey, Joseph, 215
Strauder (no first name) 91
Strauder v. West Virginia, 91
Strong, William, 88, 101, 104, 106, 117
Supreme Court Historical Society, 31, 137, 147
Sutherland, George, 172, 177
Swain, H.V.S., 90
Swartwout, Samuel, 39
Swayne, Noah H., 86, 96, 99, 102, 107, 119
Taft, William Howard, 31, 149, 155, 158, 160, 164, 167, 172, 194, 211, 221
Taney Court, 81, 87
Taney, Roger Brooke, 36, 67, 88, 91, 140
Taylor, Zachary, 12, 79, 157, 220
Taylor/Fillmore ticket, 79
Team of Rivals, 93
Teapot Dome, 158, 161
Temple of Karnak, 32
Terry, David S., 90
"that crippled son-of-a-bitch," 155
"that damned cowboy," 144

the business of America is business, 172
The Canandaigua Times, 111
The Framers, 7, 200
"the law is the law," 84
The Legal News, 111
the will of the people, 82
third term, 179
third-party candidate, 80
Thirteenth Amendment, 118
"this is a white man's country," 188
Thomas, Cal, 160
Thompson, Seymour, 133
Thompson, Smith, 44, 55, 57, 68, 72, 86, 94
Thornberry, Homer, 171, 206, 211, 222
Tiger tank commander, 122
Tilden, Samuel, 87, 116, 119, 123
Timberlake, John, 61
Tinker to Evers to Chance, 211
to the victor belonged the spoils, 122
Todd, Thomas, 29, 37, 45, 52, 67, 70
took the bullet, 92
Treaty of Paris, 16
Tribe, Lawrence H., 190
Trimble, Robert, 59
Truman, Harry S, 4, 6, 12, 107, 185, 188, 190, 199, 222, 224
Truman, Margaret, 107, 191
Truman-Barkley ticket, 199
trust-buster, 146
"turkey-gobbler strut," 123
Turner, Nat Rebellion, 62
Tweed, William H. ("Boss"), 122, 134
Tyler Whig, 115
Tyler, John, 72, 106, 114
U. S. federal currency, 95
U. S. Postmaster General, 59, 92

U. S. Secret Service, 103
U. S. Senate Art and History Office, 47
"unavoidable duty to continue," 179
Union Armies, 92
United Mine Workers Union, 168
United Mine Workers v. Red Jacket Coal & Coke Co., 169
United States v. Nixon, **6, 213, 219**
United States v. Susan B. Anthony, 108
United Steel Workers of America, 191
Universal suffrage, 106
University of Alabama Law School, 176
University of California at San Diego, 181
University of Chicago Law Review, 37, 52
University of Chicago Law School, 52, 183, 201
University of New Hampshire, 201
University of Pennsylvania, 19
Usher, John, 95
Utica Observer, 111
Van Buren, Martin, 67, 70, 72, 80, 83, 86
Van Devanter, Willis, 150, 172, 176
Vanderbilt, Arthur, 202
Vanderbilt, Cornelius, 119
Vanzetti, Bartolomeo, 179
Vienna, Austria, 178
Vinson, Fred M., 190, 192, 196, 198, 222
Virginia dynasty, 45
Wade, Benjamin, 87
Waite, Morrison, 101, 115, 131, 221

"Walk softly and carry a big stick," 143
Wallace, Henry, 187
Walworth, Reuben H., 73
War Between the States, 95, 101, 202
War in Vietnam, 208, 211
War of Yankee Aggression, 83
Warren, Earl, 5, 198, 201, 206, 210, 214
Washington Post, 43, 191
Washington, Bushrod, 36, 45, 64
Washington, George, 7, 11, 14, 16, 19, 23, 27, 29, 42, 58, 74, 102, 133, 151, 220
Watergate, 6, 158, 213
Wayne, James, 59, 68, 89
Webster, Daniel, 56, 71
Wermiel, Stephen J., 202, 205
Wheeler, Burton K., 161
Whigs, 60, 72, 79, 81
White, Byron, 211
White, Edward D., 128, 131, 134, 140, 149
White, Walter, 169
Williams, George H., 101, 113, 140
Williams, Mrs. George H., 114
Wilson, James, 11, 14, 18, 20, 27, 30, 65, 221
Wilson, Woodrow, 150, 153, 158, 165, 167, 211, 221
Wolcott, Alexander, 44, 47, 51, 54
woman's suffrage, 107, 110, 156
Woods, William, 105, 116, 131, 135
World War I, 176, 183, 194
World War II, 122, 158, 174, 199, 202, 205, 208
Yale College, 48
Yale University Law School, 64, 96, 194

Yalu River, 191
"yelled fire in a crowded theater," 143

yellow fever, 68, 199
yellow-dog contracts, 155

Notes

1 Hogue, Henry, "Supreme Court nominations not confirmed, 1789-2007," Congressional Research Service, 2008

2 "Nixon, Hoover Bashed Justices in '71 Phone Call," Walter Pincus, *Washington Post*, September 28, 2007

3 Novak, Robert, *The Prince of Darkness*, Crown Forum, New York, 2007, 487

4 http://www.supremecourthistory.org/myweb/81journal/pusey81.htm - accessed February 28, 2009

5 Johnson, Timothy R. and Jason M. Roberts, "Presidential Capital and the Supreme Court Confirmation Process," The Journal of Politics, Vol. 66, No. 3, Cambridge University Press, 2004, 663

6 Http://Etext.Virginia.Edu/Etcbin/Ot2www-Washington?Specfile=/Texts/English/Washington/Fitzpatrick/Search/Gw.O2w&Act=Surround&Offset=38208436&Tag=Writings+Of+Washington,+Vol.+30:+To+The+Associate+Justices+Of+The+Supreme+Court&Query=Judges&Id=Gw300384 – Accessed On 10-21-2008

7 http://www.senate.gov/pagelayout/reference/nominations/Nominations.htm - accessed 07-20-11

8 Marcus, Maeva and James Russell Perry, *The Documentary History of the Supreme Court of the United States*, 1789-1800, Columbia University Press, 1985, 780

9 http://www.senate.gov/artandhistory/history/minute/A_Chief_Justice_Rejected.htm - accessed October 27, 2008

10 Ryter, Jon Christian, "Cronyism On The High Court," NewsWithViews.com, October 15, 2005

11 Marcus, Maeva (editor), *The Documentary History of the Supreme Court of the United States, Volume 8*, Columbia University Press, February 2007, 94

12 Ibid, 96

13 Ibid, 98

14 www.lifeissues.net/writers/tay/tay_03foundingfather.html - accessed October 19, 2008

15 Ibid

16 www.philadelphiabar.org/page/TPLWinter04JamesWilson?appNum=2&wosid=3Q8gsKZUITqS9nssgNH7Mw – accessed October 18, 2008

17 Ibid

18 Ibid

19 http://www.let.rug.nl/~usa/B/jwilson/wil.htm - -accessed 11-19-09]]

20 http://images.google.com/imgres?imgurl=http://www.supremecourthistory.org/history/images_history/04_d.jpg&imgrefurl=http://www.supremecourthistory.org/history/supremecourthistory_history_history_marshall.htm&usg=__SmDxSZefMIuBmjecmAdtp0VHoUg=&h=275&w=425&sz=95&hl=en&start=30&um=1&tbnid=Iuzc36AX-6akgM:&tbnh=82&tbnw=126&prev=/images%3Fq%3D%2522Thomas%2BTodd%2522%2B%252B%2B%2522S

upreme%2BCourt%2522%26ndsp%3D20%26hl%3Den%26rlz%3D1T4ADRA_enUS352US352%26sa%3DN%26s tart%3D20%26um%3D1 – accessed November 23, 2009

21 www.answers.com/topic/samuel-chase – accessed February 15, 2009

22 Rhodehamel, John H., Editor, George Washington: Writings, Library of America, 1997, 490

23 Baumann, Mary, U.S. Senate Historical Office, correspondence with author, October 28, 2008

24 Ibid

25 Ibid

26 Abraham, Henry Julian, *Justices, Presidents, and Senators: A History of the U.S. Supreme Court Appointments from Washington to Clinton*, Rowman & Littlefield, 1999, 62

27 www.oyez.org/justices/john_jay/ - accessed November 26, 2008

28 Rehnquist, William, "Remarks of The Chief Justice," My Life in the Law Series, Duke University School of Law, April 13, 2002

29 http://www.supremecourtus.gov/publicinfo/speeches/sp_04-14-03.html - accessed April 27, 2009

30 Ibid

31 White, G. Edward, "Neglected Justices: Discounting for History," Vanderbilt Law Review, Vol. 62:2:319

32 Warren, Charles, *Supreme Court in United States History, The*, rev. edition, 2 vols., Boston: Little Brown, 1926, vol. 1, 178

33 Ibid, Ryter

34 "Sheer, Raw Politics the Only Reason," *Register-Guard*, Eugene, Oregon, July 8, 1968

35 http://www.landmarkcases.org/marbury/jefferson.html – accessed November 23, 2009

36 http://www.supremecourthistory.org/history-of-the-court/history-of-the-court/the-marshall-court-1801-1835/ - accessed July 19, 2011

37 http://usgovinfo.about.com/blcthistory.htm, accessed October 27, 2008

38 Easterbrook, Frank H., "The Most Insignificant Justice: Further Evidence, " 50 University of Chicago Law Review, 481 (1983)

39 Hall, Kermit L., ed., *Oxford Companion to the Supreme Court of the United States, The*, Oxford University Press, New York & Oxford, 1992

40 Diary Entry of John Quincy Adams (Mar. 27, 1820), in 5 ADAMS, MEMOIRS (Mar. 27, 1820), supra note 33, at 39, 43

41 Biographies, Answers Corporation, 2006, http://www.answers.com/topic/william-johnson-1771-1834 - accessed November 4, 2008

42 http://web.princeton.edu/sites/pucra/FunFacts.htm

43 Ibid, Abraham, 70

44 Ibid, 71

45 http://books.google.com/books?id=ZTIoAAAAYAAJ&pg=PA846&lpg=PA846&dq=%22The+death+of+Cushing%22&source=web&ots=v9iioVbbW1&sig=GePV-oUD-LPXjMhHRjU7oU9fYYU&hl=en&sa=X&oi=book_result&resnum=2&ct=result – accessed December 3, 2008

46 http://www.answers.com/topic/levi-lincoln - accessed November 22, 2009

47 www.pbs.org/newshour/bb/law/supreme_court/alito/timeline.html - accessed November 4, 2008

48 Ideas & Trends; Battlefield: Supreme Court, *New York Times*, July 3, 2005

49 Wills, Gary, James Madison, Time Books, The American Presidents series, 2003, 71-2 – access November 21, 2209

50 Adams, Henry, *History of the United States During the Administrations of Madison (1809–1817)*, Library of America, 1986, 249

51 http://www.supremecourthistory.org/04_library/subs_volumes/04_c03_h.html - accessed November 5, 2008

52 <a href="http://law.jrank.org/pages/10540/Story-Joseph.html">Joseph Story</a>

53 http://candst.tripod.com/joestor2.htm - accessed December 8, 2008

54 Ibid

55 Ibid

56 http://amistad.mysticseaport.org/discovery/people/bio.story.joseph.html - accessed November 28, 2009

57 http://lawreview.wustl.edu/inprint/77-1/771-137.pdf

58 Ibid Currie, 468

59 Ibid, 479

60 www.law.umkc.edu/faculty/projects/ftrials/amistad/AMI_BTHO.HTM - accessed December 4, 2008

61 *Ogden v. Saunders* 25 U. S. 213 (1827)

62 www.cqpress.com/incontext/SupremeCourt/politics_and_the_court.htm - accessed November 7, 2008

63 Rosenbaum, David E., "Presidents May Disagree, but Justices Are Generally Loyal to Them," *New York Times*, April 7, 1994

64 Carney, Thomas E., "The Political Judge: Justice John McLean's Pursuit of the Presidency," Ohio History – the Scholarly Journal of the Ohio Historical Society, Summer-Autumn 2002, 121-144

65 Ibid

66 www.encyclopedia.com/doc/1O184-JacksonAndrew.html - accessed November 6, 2008

67 King, Florence, "The Petticoat Affair: Manners, Mutiny, and Sex in Andrew Jackson's White House," National Review, Feb 23, 1998

68 Ibid

69 www.jstor.org/pss/20093015 - accessed June 8, 2009

70 Ilisevich, Robert D., "Henry Baldwin and Andrew Jackson: A Political Relationship in Trust," The Pennsylvania Magazine of History and Biography, Vol. CXX, Nos. 1/2 January/April 1996

71 http://www.pbs.org/wnet/supremecourt/personality/robes_baldwin.html - accessed November 8, 2008

72 Ibid

73 http://www.oyez.org/justices/henry_baldwin/ - accessed November 8, 2008

74 http://law.jrank.org/pages/4638/Baldwin-Henry.html">Henry Baldwin</a> - accessed November 8, 2008

75 Ibid, Ilisevich

76 Ibid

77 http://www.answers.com/topic/john-mckinley - accessed November 29, 2009

78 Oxford Companion to the Supreme Court of the United States, The, Oxford University Press, 1992, 2005. http://www.answers.com/topic/john-mckinley - accessed November 21, 2008

79 Currie, David, P., "The Most Insignificant Justice: A Preliminary Inquiry," University of Chicago Law Review, Vol. 50, No. 2, 1983, 472

80 http://www.law.louisville.edu/node/1656 – accessed November 21, 2008

81 http://www.leftjustified.com/leftjust/lib/sc/ht/fed/jbio.html – accessed November 25, 2008

82 Ibid, Oxford Companion to the Supreme Court of the United States

83 Stras, David R., "Why Supreme Court Justices Should Ride Circuit Again," Minnesota Law Review, 2007; Minnesota Legal Studies Research Paper No. 06-67. Available at SSRN: http://ssrn.com/abstract=951219 – accessed December 1, 2008

84 Baker, Jean H., *James Buchanan*, McMillan, 2004, 40

85 Bergeron, Paul H., *The Presidency of James K. Polk* (American Presidency Series), University Press of Kansas, 1987, 34

86 Ibid, Baker, 42

87 Ibid, Bergeron, 164

88 Ibid, 166

89 http://www.booknotes.org/Transcript/?ProgramID=1763 – accessed December 15, 2008

90 www.pbs.org/wgbh/al\ia/part4/4h2933.html - accessed December 16, 2008

91 *Scott v. Sandford*, 60 U.S. 19 How. 393 393 (1856)

92 http://www.enotes.com/supreme-court-drama/Plessy-v-fergusonn - accessed January 20, 2009

93 Lee, Rex E., "Lawyering in the Supreme Court: The Role of the Solicitor General, Supreme Court Historical Society," 1985 Yearbook

94 West's Encyclopedia of American Law. The Gale Group, Inc, 1998. http://www.answers.com/topic/jeremiah-s-black - accessed February 6, 2009

95 Ross, Michael Anthony, *Justice of Shattered Dreams: Samuel Freeman Miller and the Supreme Court During the Civil War Era*, LSU Press, 2003, 124

96 Huebner, Timothy and Peter Renstrom, *The Taney Court: Justices, Rulings, and Legacy*, ABC-CLIO; 2003, 28

97 Ibid, 105

98 Urofsky, Melvin I., *The Supreme Court Justices: A Biographical Dictionary*, Taylor & Francis, 1994, 493

99 Ibid, Ross

100 Ibid, Huebner, 105

101 Ibid, 106

102 www.pbs.org/wnet/supremecourt/capitalism/robes_field.html – accessed March 15, 2009

103 Ibid

104 Ibid

105 http://irreference.com/?p=8495 accessed March 15, 2009

106 http://www.usmarshals.gov/history/neagle/neagle4.htm - accessed March 16, 2009

107 http://www.callawyer.com/story.cfm?eid=898041&evid=1 – accessed March 16, 2009

108 http://www.mrlincolnswhitehouse.org/inside.asp?ID=83&subjectID=2- accessed December 23, 2008

109 Ibid, http://www.supremecourtus.gov/

110 Ibid, www.mrlincolnswhitehouse.org

111 Ibid

112 Ibid, http://www.supremecourtus.gov/

113 http://www.windsofchange.net/archives/of_miers_and_men.php - accessed on December 20, 2008]]

114 Ibid

115 Ibid, http://www.supremecourtus.gov/

116 Ibid

117 Ibid, Ryter

118 http://www.mrlincolnandfriends.org/inside.asp?pageID=40&subjectID=3 –accessed 12-21-08

119 Ibid

120 Ibid

121 Ibid

122 Ibid

123 http://www.oyez.org/justices/david_davis – accessed January 22, 2010

124 Ibid, http://www.supremecourtus.gov/

125 Ibid, Ryter

126 Eisenschiml, Otto, *Why Was Lincoln Murdered?*, Read Books, 2007, 140

127 RCBAonline, Richmond County Bar Association, Staten Island, New York, The Day Freedom Died - The Colfax Massacre, The Supreme Court, and the Betrayal of Reconstruction, by Charles Lane, Book Review by: Hon. Matthew Sciarrino, Jr., Published: March 2008

128 <a href="http://law.jrank.org/pages/4840/Bradley-Joseph-P.html">Joseph P. Bradley - Further Readings</a>

129 Ibid

130 "Joseph P. Bradley: An Aspect of a Judicial Personality," Anthony Champagne and Dennis Pope, "Political Psychology," Vol. 6, No. 3, 1985, International Society of Political Psychology, 491

131 www.u-s-history.com/pages/h706.html – accessed January 7, 2009

132 Harper, Ida Husted, *The Life and Work of Susan B. Anthony*, Bowen-Merrill Co., Indianapolis and Kansas City, 1899, 441

133 http://www.oyez.org/justices/ward_hunt/ - accessed December 29, 2008

134 Currie, David P., The Constitution in the Supreme Court, University of Chicago Press, 1994, 362

135 Ibid, Abraham, 97

136 Truman, Margaret, *Women of Courage*, Morrow, 1976

137 Ibid, Harper, 437-9

138 Ibid, 441

139 Dickerson, Donna Lee, The Reconstruction Era: Primary Documents on Events from 1865 to 1877, Greenwood Publishing Group, 2003, 348

140 Catt, Chapman, and Nettie Rogers Shuler, Woman Suffrage and Politics: The Inner Story of the Suffrage Movement, Wm. S. Hein Publishing, 2005, 103

141 Ibid, 104

142 Ibid, Harper, 443-4

143 http://www.law.umkc.edu/faculty/projects/ftrials/anthony/sbaaccount.html - accessed December 29, 2009

144 "The Trial of Susan B. Anthony," Papers of Elizabeth Cady Stanton and Susan B. Anthony, Ann D. Gordon, Editor, Rutgers University, for the Federal Judicial Center, 2005

145 McMenamin, Michael, Walter & Haverfield, LLP, Cleveland, Ohio, correspondence with author, January 20, 2009

146 Ibid

147 Belohlavek, John M., *Broken Glass: Caleb Cushing & the Shattering of the Union*, Kent State University Press, 2005, 357

148 "Williams, George H.," Answers.com. West's Encyclopedia of American Law, The Gale Group, Inc., 1998

149 Ibid, Belohlavek

150 Ibid, Rehnquist

151 Ibid,

152 http://www.rbhayes.org/hayes/scholarworks/display.asp?id=506 – accessed on January 9, 2009

153 Ibid

154 Ibid

155 "Woods, William Burnham." West's Encyclopedia of American Law. The Gale Group, Inc. 2005. Encyclopedia.com. 14 Dec. 2009

156 Ibid, Urofsky, 539

157 Ibid, Abraham, 100

158 "National Grange Influence on the Supreme Court Confirmation of Stanley Matthews," Scott H. Ainsworth and John Anthony Maltese, Duke University Press on behalf of the Social Science History Association, 1996, 41

159 Ibid

160 Ibid

161 http://www.rbhayes.org/hayes/mssfind/487/MatthewsStanleywebpage.htm – accessed January 6, 2010

162 Maltese, John Anthony, *The Selling of Supreme Court Nominees*, John Hopkins University Press, 1998, 41

163 Ibid

164 Ibid, 44

165 http://www.mrlincolnandnewyork.org/inside.asp?ID=53&subjectID=3 – accessed January 7, 2010

166 http://74.125.93.132/search?q=cache:C8TpQv16ZZ0J:etd.lib.ttu.edu/theses/available/etd-04282009-31295015501249/unrestricted/31295015501249.pdf+%22Matthew+Breen%22+%2B+Conkling&cd=9&hl=en&ct=clnk&gl=us – accessed January 7, 2010

167 Conkling, Alfred R., *The Life And Letters Of Roscoe Conkling: Orator, Statesman and Advocate*, D. C. F. Class, 1889, 676-7

168 Ibid

169 http://www.enotes.com/supreme-court-drama/plessy-v-ferguson - accessed December 16, 2009

170 http://www.supremecourthistory.org/myweb/81journal/morris81.htm – accessed January 21, 2009

171 http://www.bsos.umd.edu/gvpt/lpbr/subpages/reviews/elyjr95.htm – accessed December 30, 2009

172 http://baic.house.gov/historical-essays/essay.html?intID=5&intSectionID=24#foot66 - accessed December 16, 2009

173 http://elections.harpweek.com/1892/Overview-1892-1.htm - accessed December 16, 2009

174 http://www.answers.com/topic/samuel-blatcford - accessed January 18, 2009

175 http://www.senate.gov/artandhistory/history/minute/The_Senate_Irritates_President_George_Washington.htm - accessed December 21, 2009

176 Frank, John P. Judicial "Appointments: Controversy and Accomplishment," Address to May 1976 annual banquet of The Supreme Court Historical Society

177 Congressional Record, Forty-ninth Congress, Second Session, Vol. 18, Part I: pp. 857 and 881.

178 http://www.archive.org/stream/collectionofsixa00russrich/collectionofsixa00russrich_djvu.txt - accessed 11-20-09

179 Myers, Gustavus, *History of the Supreme Court of the United States*, C.H. Kerr, Chicago, 1912, 439-48

180 http://www.oyez.org/justices/joseph_mckenna – accessed December 21, 2009

181 Ibid, Myers

182 Ibid, Abraham, 143

183 Ibid, Myers

184 Ibid

185 Ibid

186 Morris, Edmund, *Theodore Rex*, Modern Library-a Division of Random House, 2002, 313

187 Rosen, Jeffrey, *The Supreme Court, The Personalities and Rivalries that Defined America*, Macmillan, 2007, 115

188 Ibid, Abraham, 118

189 Ibid, Maltese, 46

190 http://www3.interscience.wiley.com/journal/118929821/abstract - accessed December 26, 2009

191 McHargue, Daniel S., *President Taft's Appointments to the Supreme Court*, Cambridge University Press, 1950, 480

192 Department of Health and Human Services, National Center for Health Statistics, National Vital Statistics Report, vol. 54, no. 19, June 28, 2006

193 http://www.answers.com/topic/edward-douglass-white - accessed December 29, 2009

194 Ibid, McHargue, 491

195 Ibid, Abraham, 139

196 Ibid, 138

197 Ibid, Maltese, 49

198 http://www.michaelariens.com/ConLaw/justices/mcreynolds.htm – accessed March 4, 2009

199 Knox, John, *The Forgotten Memoir of John Knox: A Year in the Life of a Supreme Court Clerk in FDR's Washington*, edited and with a Foreword and Afterword by Dennis J. Hutchinson and David J. Garrow, University of Chicago Press, 2002

200 Schughart II, William F., "Bending Before the Storm: The U. S. Supreme Court in Economic Crisis, 1935-1937", "The Independent Review," v. ix, n. 1, Summer 2004, 80

201 Ibid, Abraham, 134

202 http://www.pbs.org/wnet/supremecourt/capitalism/robes_mcreynolds.html – accessed March 15, 2009

203 Ibid

204 Ibid, pbs.org/wnet/supremecourt/capitalism/robes_mcreynolds.html

205 Ibid, www.supremecourthistory.org

206 Shesol, Jeff, *Supreme Power*, W. W. Norton & Company, 2010, 102

207 "Warren Harding," A Dictionary of Political Biography. Oxford University Press, 1998, 2003. Answers.com 25 Dec. 2009. http://www.answers.com/topic/warren-harding

208 http://www.whitehouse.gov/about/presidents/warrenharding

209 Whitaker, Robert, *On the Lap of Gods: The Red Summer of 1919 and the Struggle for Justice,* Crown, a division of Random House, 2008, 276

210 Thomas, Cal, at the Heritage Foundation, October 31, 1996

211 http://www.presidentprofiles.com/Grant-Eisenhower/Calvin-Coolidge-Relations-with-congress.html

212 Ibid, Thomas

213 Time magazine, May 6, 1929

214 Ibid, Shesol, 191

215 http://www.pbs.org/wnet/supremecourt/capitalism/robes_stone.html – accessed December 30, 2009

216 Tomlins, Christopher L., *The United States Supreme Court: The Pursuit of Justice*, Houghton-Mifflin, 2005, 224-5

217 Fink, Carole, et al, *Genoa, Rapallo, and European Reconstruction in 1922*, Cambridge University Press, 2002, 109

218 Ibid,

219 Rauh Jr., Joseph, "An Unabashed Liberal Looks at a Half-Century of the Supreme Court," North Carolina Law Review, Volume 69, 1990, 213-49

220 Wittes, Benjamin, *Confirmation Wars: Preserving Independent Courts in Angry Times*, Rowman & Littlefield, 2006, 50

221 Ibid, Maltese, 58

222 Ibid, 59

223 Skidmore, Max J., *Presidential Performance: A Comprehensive Review*, McFarland & Company, 2004, 225

224 Ibid, Abraham, 189

225 Ibid, Shesol, 239

226 http://modern-us-history.suite101.com/article.cfm/franklin_roosevelts_court_packing_scheme - accessed March 20, 2009

227 www.nisk.k12.ny.us/fdr/1937/37_scgifs/large/37010714.gif – accessed March 30, 2009

228 http://newdeal.feri.org/texts/666.htm – accessed March 30, 2009

229 Ibid, Shesol, 272

230 Ferren, John M., *Salt of the Earth, Conscience of the Court: The Story of Justice Wiley Rutledge*, University of North Carolina Press, 2004, 122-3

231 http://www.answers.com/topic/james-f-byrnes – accessed May 14, 2009

232 http://www.opinionjournal.com/extra/?id=110011033 – accessed May 14, 2009

233 Klarman, Michael J., *From Jim Crow to Civil Rights: The Supreme Court and the Struggle for Racial Equality*, Oxford University Press, 2003, 195

234 Ibid, Shesol, 514

235 http://law.jrank.org/pages/8014/Ku-Klux-Klan-Hugo-L-Black-KKK.html - accessed July 15, 2010

236 Wrightsman, Lawrence S., *The Psychology of the Supreme Court*, Oxford University Press, 2006, 182-3

237 Black, Conrad, *Franklin Delano Roosevelt: Champion of Freedom*, Perseus Publishing, 2005, 318

238 Ibid, 566

239 Ibid, Urofsky, 331

240 http://www.trumanlibrary.org/oralhist/clarktc.htm – accessed May 29, 2009

241 Gordon, Rosalie M., *Nine Men Against America: The Supreme Court and its Attack on American Liberties*, Western Islands, 1966, 22

242 http://www.michaelariens.com/ConLaw/justices/stone.htm – accessed March 15, 2009

243 http://www.princeton.edu/~mudd/finding_aids/douglas/douglas5.html – accessed May 14, 2009

244 Ball, Howard, *Hugo L. Black: Cold Steel Warrior*, Oxford University Press, 2006, 137

245 Ibid, Wrightsman, 182

246 Ibid, Klarman

247 Ibid, http://www.answers.com/topic/james-f-byrnes

248 Published with Judge Posner's permission, granted March 30, 2009

249 Ibid, http://works.bepress.com – p. 75

250 http://www.encyclopedia.com/topic/William_Orville_Douglas.aspx – accessed April 28, 2009

251 Shaw, Stephen K., William D. Pederson, Frank J. Williams, *Franklin D. Roosevelt and the transformation of the Supreme Court*, M.E. Sharpe, 2003, 155

252 Stone, Geoffrey R., *Perilous times: free speech in wartime from the Sedition Act of 1798 to the war on terrorism*, W. W. Norton & Company, 2004, 307-8

253 Ibid, http://www.opinionjournal.com

254 *Korematsu V. United States*, 323 U. S. 214 (1944), Page 323, U. S. 233

255 Ibid, Page 323, U. S. 240

256 *St. Petersburg Times*, November 6, 1944

257 Donovan, Robert J., *Conflict and Crisis: The Presidency of Harry S. Truman, 1945-1948*, University of Missouri Press, 1996, 155

258 http://www.opinionjournal.com/extra/?id=110011033 – accessed May 14, 2009

259 http://www.ca6.uscourts.gov/lib_hist/Courts/supreme/judges/mcreynolds/jcm-bio.html – accessed May 15, 2009

260 http://www.allacademic.com/meta/p_mla_apa_research_citation/0/8/3/4/4/p83446_index.html – accessed May 16, 2009

261 Hess, Jerry N., Oral History Interview with Tom C. Clark, Washington, D.C., 1972-73, 95

262 http://www.scribd.com/doc/15247110/Constitutional-Law-Outline – accessed June 3, 2009

263 Bowles, Nigel, *The Government and Politics of the United States: Second Edition*, Palgrave Macmillan, 1993, 191

264 Miecek, William and Stantly N. Katz, *History of the Supreme Court of the United States: The Birth of the Modern Constitution*, 1941-1953, Vol. 12, Cambridge University Press, 2006, 433

265 C-Span TV panel program, The FDR Library, Hyde Park, NY, November 11, 2007

266 http://docs.google.com/viewer?a=v&q=cache:EtZwVgDuMksJ:law.vanderbilt.edu/publications/vanderbilt-law-review/archive/volume-62-number-2-march-2009/download.aspx%3Fid%3D3834+sherman+minton&hl=en&gl=us&sig=AHIEtbRpvbWn0SwRsvvYTZ5OG14l6XzWAw – accessed January 16, 2010

267 Belknap, Michal R., *The Supreme Court under Earl Warren, 1953-1969*, University of South Carolina Press, 2005, 5]

268 Ibid

269 http://www.eisenhowermemorial.org/presidential-papers/first-term/documents/460.cfm – accessed May 31, 2009

270 http://www.oyez.org/justices/earl_warren/ - accessed October 8, 2008

271 www.encyclopedia.com/doc/1G2-3468301950.html – accessed October 7, 2008

272 www.pbs.org/newshour/bb/law/supreme_court/alito/politicization.html - accessed 12-07-08

273 Ibid

274 Tushnet, Mark, "Constitutional Interpretation, Character and Experience," 72 Boston University Law Review, 1992, 747, 759

275 Hall, Kermit L., *The Justices, Judging, and Judicial Reputation*, Taylor and Francis, Inc., 2000, 71

276 www.law.com/jsp/article.jsp?id=1120640710962 – accessed May 31, 2009

277 Ibid, Hess, 213

278 http://www.oyez.org/justices/william_j_brennan_jr – accessed January 18, 2010

279 http://findarticles.com/p/articles/mi_hb3086/is_n3_11/ai_n28650227/ - accessed June 1, 2009

280 Ibid

281 http://www.fas.org/sgp/crs/misc/RL33118.pdf

282 Urofsky, Melvin I., *The Supreme Court Justices: A Biographical Dictionary*, Garland Publishing 1994, 50

283 Ibid

284 http://www.encyclopedia.com/doc/1G2-3404700872.html – accessed January 18, 2010

285 ibid

286 Ibid, Urofsky, 50

287 Ibid, 52

288 Ibid

289 Ibid, 57

290 Ibid, www.encyclopedia

291 http://findarticles.com/p/articles/mi_m1316/is_n11_v22/ai_9218004/?tag=content;col1 – accessed April 2, 2009

292 CRS Report for Congress, "Supreme Court Nominations Not Confirmed, 1789-2007," Henry B. Hogue, Updated January 9, 2008, page 11

293 Bell, Peter Alan, "Extrajudicial Activity of Supreme Court Justices," Stanford Law Review, 1970, 591

294 Ibid, C-Span

295 Beschloss, Michael R., *Reaching for Glory: Lyndon Johnson's Secret White House Tapes 1964-1965* (Paperback), 395

296 Ibid, Bell

297 http://findarticles.com/p/articles/mi_m1282/is_n6_v42/ai_8878223/ - accessed January 19, 2010]

298 Ibid, Beschloss, 166

299 Ibid, 167

300 Ibid, 414

301 Ibid, Shesol, 440

302 Shesol, Jeff, *Mutual Contempt*, W. W. Norton Co., N. Y., 1997, 361

303 Ibid, Shesol, 360

304 Ibid, 433

305 Ibid, Beschloss, 324

306 Ibid, 266

307 Ibid, 395

308 Ibid, 266

309 Ibid, Abraham, 286

310 *New York Times*, "The Reagan Court - Child of Lyndon Johnson?" David A. Kaplan, September 4, 1989

311 The Oyez Project, *United States v. Nixon*, 418 U.S. 683 (1974) available at: http://oyez.org/cases/1970-1979/1974/1974_73_1766 – accessed June 2, 2009

312 Ibid, Bell

313 *New York Times*, "Clement Haynesworth Dies at 77, Lost Struggle for High Court Seat," Alfonso A. Narvaez, November 23, 1989

314 http://jurist.law.pitt.edu/thisday/ – accessed January 21, 2010

315 http://www.time.com/time/magazine/article/0,9171,942208,00.html#ixzz0dHqiYO3u – accessed January 21, 2010

316 Woodward, Bob and Scott Armstrong, *The Brethren: Inside the Supreme Court*, Simon and Shuster, 2005

317 *New York Times*, May 13, 1970, 1

318 Larisa, Jr., Joseph S., "Review: A Supreme Court Primer for the Public," Duke Law Journal, Vol. 1988, No. 1, 1988, 203

319 http://www.mackinac.org/article.aspx?ID=7642 – accessed January 19, 2009

320 http://www.greenbag.org/What's%2520New/Fuller%25202/ely.pdf+%22Melville+W.+Fuller%22+%2B+%22Cleveland%22+%2B+%22Supreme+Court%22&hl=en&ct=clnk&cd=4&gl=us – accessed January 19, 2009

321 http://www.answers.com/topic/melville-fuller

322 Ibid

323 Ibid

Second Thoughts   William T. Harper

Made in the USA
Charleston, SC
18 September 2011